Illustrations Of The Life Of Shakespeare: In A Discursive Series Of Essays On A Variety Of Subjects Connected With The Personal And Literary History Of The Great Dramatist...

James Orchard Halliwell-Phillipps

Nabu Public Domain Reprints:

You are holding a reproduction of an original work published before 1923 that is in the public domain in the United States of America, and possibly other countries. You may freely copy and distribute this work as no entity (individual or corporate) has a copyright on the body of the work. This book may contain prior copyright references, and library stamps (as most of these works were scanned from library copies). These have been scanned and retained as part of the historical artifact.

This book may have occasional imperfections such as missing or blurred pages, poor pictures, errant marks, etc. that were either part of the original artifact, or were introduced by the scanning process. We believe this work is culturally important, and despite the imperfections, have elected to bring it back into print as part of our continuing commitment to the preservation of printed works worldwide. We appreciate your understanding of the imperfections in the preservation process, and hope you enjoy this valuable book.

Presented to the Lenox Library,
New York. U.S.
by the Author
J. O. Halliwell-Phillipps

No. 11. Tregunter Road
West Brompton
London
England
Dec. 1876.

*Lenox Library,
New York. U.S.*

ILLUSTRATIONS

OF THE

LIFE OF SHAKESPEARE.

THE SAND HEAPED BY ONE FLOOD IS SCATTERED BY ANOTHER, BUT THE ROCK ALWAYS CONTINUES IN ITS PLACE. THE STREAM OF TIME, WHICH IS CONTINUALLY WASHING THE DISSOLUBLE FABRICS OF OTHER POETS, PASSES WITHOUT INJURY BY THE ADAMANT OF SHAKESPEARE.—*Dr. Johnson.*

ILLUSTRATIONS

OF THE

LIFE OF SHAKESPEARE

IN A DISCURSIVE SERIES OF ESSAYS

ON A

VARIETY OF SUBJECTS CONNECTED WITH THE PERSONAL AND LITERARY HISTORY OF
THE GREAT DRAMATIST.

PART THE FIRST.

by
James Orchard Halliwell-Phillipps

LONDON:
PUBLISHED BY MESSRS. LONGMANS, GREEN & CO.
1874.

Lenox Library,
New York. U.S.

PREFACE.

THE remains of New Place, a sketch of which is engraved on the title-page, are typical of the fragments of the personal history of Shakespeare which have hitherto been discovered. In this respect the great dramatist participates in the fate of most of his literary contemporaries, for if a collection of the known facts relating to all of them were tabularly arranged, it would be found that the number of the ascertained particulars of his life reached at least the average. At the present day, with biography carried to a wasteful and ridiculous excess and Shakespeare the idol not merely of a nation but of the educated world, it is difficult to realize a period when no interest was taken in the events of the lives of authors, and when the great poet himself, notwithstanding the immense popularity of some of his works, was held in no general reverence. It must be borne in mind that actors then occupied an inferior position in society, and even the vocation of a dramatic writer was scarcely considered respectable. The intelligent appreciation of genius by individuals was not sufficient to neutralize in these matters the effect of public opinion and the animosity of the religious world; all circumstances thus uniting to banish general interest in the history of persons connected in any way with the stage. This biographical indifference continued for many years, and long before the season arrived for a real curiosity to be taken in the subject, the records from which alone a satisfactory memoir could have been constructed had disappeared. At the time of Shakespeare's decease, non-political correspondence was rarely preserved, elaborate diaries were not the fashion, and no one, excepting in semi-apocryphal collections of jests, thought it worth while to record many of the sayings and doings, or to delineate at any length the characters of actors and dramatists, so that it is generally by the merest accident that any particulars of interest respecting them have been recovered.

In the absence of some very important discovery the general and intense desire to penetrate the mystery which surrounds the personal history of Shakespeare cannot be wholly gratified. Something, however, may be accomplished in that direction by a diligent and critical study of the materials now accessible, especially if care be taken to avoid the temptation of endeavouring to decipher his inner life and character through the media of his works. The genius which so rapidly converted the dull pages of a novel or history into an imperishable drama was transmuted into other forces in actual life, as may be gathered even from the scanty records of his biography which still remain. Let these latter be studied in that truest spirit of criticism which deals with facts in preference to conjecture and sentiment, regard being ever watchfully paid to the circumstances by which he was surrounded. A minute examination of those circumstances is essential to the effective study not merely of the personal but of the literary history of the great poet. It will dissipate many an illusion, amongst others the propriety of criticism being grounded upon a reverential belief in the unvarying perfection of Shakespeare's dramatic art. He indeed unquestionably obtained a complete mastery over that art at an early period of his literary career, but his control over it was continually liable to be governed by the customs and exigencies of the ancient stage, so much so that in not a few instances the action of a scene was diverted for the express purpose of complying with those necessities. Hence amongst other reasons the importance of a study of the history of the contemporary stage, which constitutes so prominent a feature in the following pages, and without which it is impossible to understand the conditions under which Shakespeare acted and wrote. It should be remembered that his dramas were not written for posterity, but as a matter of business, never for his own speculation but always for that of the managers of his own day, the choice of subject being occasionally dictated by them or by patrons of the stage. Those works in which the perfection of art was attained may have been the fruits of express or cherished literary design, but all his writings were the products of an intellect which was applied to authorship as the readiest path to material advancement; his task having been to construct out of certain given or selected materials successful dramas for the audiences of the day, some for the polished few, others for the multitude. It is not pretended that he did not invariably take an earnest interest in his work, his intense sympathy with each character forbidding such an assumption; but simply that his tastes were subordinated when necessary to his duty to his employers. If a play were required at a short notice, it was hurriedly written. If the managers considered that the popular feeling was likely to encourage, or if an influential patron or the Court desired, the production of a drama on some special theme, it was composed to order on that subject no matter how repulsive the character of the plot or how intrinsically it was unfitted for dramatic purposes; and, again, it is not improbable that some of Shakespeare's works, perfect in their art when represented before a select audience, might have been deteriorated by their adaptation to the public stage, and that in some instances the later copies only have been preserved. From some of these causes may have arisen inequalities in taste and art which otherwise appear to be inexplicable, and which would doubtlessly have been removed had Shakespeare lived to have given the public an edition of his works during his retirement at Stratford-on-Avon. The Burbages had no conception of his intellectual supremacy, and, if they had, it is certain that they would not have deviated on that account from the course they were in the habit of pursuing. In their estimation, however, he was merely, to use their own words, a "deserving man," an effective actor and a popular writer, one who would not have been considered so valuable a member of their staff had he not also worked as a practical man of business, knowing that the success of the theatre was identified with his own, and that within certain limits it was necessary that his art should be regulated by expediency. Neither does it appear at all probable that he could have had time, under the conditions in which he worked, for the studied application of those subtle devices underlying his art which are attributed to his sagacity by the philosophical critics, and some of which, it is amusing to notice, may be equally observed, if they exist at all, in the original plot-sources of his dramas. Entertaining these views, no space in the present work will be devoted to the examination of conjectural generic ethical designs, imaginary moral unities and such like. It is one thing to admit that Shakespeare's art was frequently influenced by the emergencies of the stage,—another that he would have gratuitously permitted it to have been controlled by the necessity of blending a variety of actions in subjection to one leading moral idea or by other similar limitations. The phenomenon of a moral unity is not to be found either in nature or in the works of nature's poet, whose truthful and impartial genius could never have voluntarily endured a submission to a preconception which involved violent deviations from the course prescribed by his sovereign knowledge of human nature and the human mind.

The literary history of Shakespeare cannot of course be perfected until the order in which he composed his works has been ascertained, but unless the books of the theatrical managers or licensers of the time are discovered it is not likely that the exact chronological arrangement will be determined. The dates of some of his productions rest on positive testimony or distinct allusions, and these are stand-points of great value. In respect, however, to the majority of them the period of composition has unfortunately been merely the subject of refined and useless conjecture. Internal evidences of construction and style, obscure contemporary references, and metrical or grammatical tests can very rarely in themselves be relied upon to establish the year of authorship. Specific phases of style or metre necessarily had periods of commencement in Shakespeare's work, but so long as those epochs are merely conjectural no real progress is made in the enquiry. Nor as a rule are the results obtained from æsthetic criticism, which depend to some extent upon the individual sentiment of the critic, of much greater certainty. No sufficient allowances appear to be made for the high probability of the intermittent use of various styles during the long interval which elapsed after the era of comparative immaturity had passed away, and in which, so far as constructive and delineative power was concerned, there was neither progress nor retrogression. Shakespeare's genius arrived at maturity with such celerity it is perilous to assert from any kind of internal evidence alone what he could not have written at any particular subsequent period, and style frequently varies not only with the subject but with the purpose of authorship. It may be presumed for instance that the diction and construction of a drama written for performance at the Court might be essentially dissimilar from those of a play of the same date composed for the ordinary stage, where the audiences were of a more promiscuous character and the usages and appliances of the actors in many respects of a different nature. Bearing these probabilities in mind, conjecture will generally be avoided in discussing the chronological order, but several new evidences of importance will be produced in this as well as in most of the other cognate branches of criticism.

Further occasional discoveries of isolated facts respecting the poet and his writings may still be reasonably expected. If no more are made, it will not be for lack of opportunity, for unusual facilities have been and are being given to me in the collection of materials. Private and other libraries, family archives, municipal records and official collections have been made accessible with a kind and ready liberality for which I cannot feel too grateful.

The main design of the present work is a critical investigation into the truth or purport of every recorded incident in the personal and literary history of Shakespeare; but it is proposed to add notices of his surroundings, that is to say, amongst others, of the members of his family, the persons with whom he associated, the books he used, the stage on which he acted, the estates he purchased, the houses and towns in which he resided and the country through which he travelled. The consideration of these and similar topics will not be without its biographical value. It will bring us nearer to a knowledge of Shakespeare's personality if we can form even an approximate idea of the condition of England and its people in his own day, the sort of places in which he lived, how he made his fortune, the occupations and social positions of his relatives and friends, the nature of the ancient stage and the usages of contemporary domestic life.

It only remains to add that no chronological or other specific order has been attempted in the following pages. The arrangement of the various essays is the fortuitous result of my own convenience or humour, the compilation of this work being in fact merely one of the amusements of the declining years of life. It is followed, as all recreations should be, earnestly and lovingly, but in complete subjection to the vicissitudes of one's own temperament and inclination.

J. O. HALLIWELL.

No. 11, Tregunter Road, London;
September, 1874.

SYMBOLS AND RULES IN COPIES AND EXTRACTS.

1. When ⊛ is attached to a word, it denotes that the original text has been followed, but that an error is suspected either in that word or in the omission of a previous one. It is sometimes added when there has been a misreading by a predecessor.

2. The division between lines of poetry which are quoted in the text is indicated by the parallel marks =.

3. In extracts from printed books or manuscripts written in the English language, the original mode of spelling is retained excepting in the cases of the ancient forms of the consonants *j* and *v* and the vowels *i* and *u*, but they are modernized in other respects, such as in the punctuation, use of capitals, &c. It may be well to observe that, in documents of the Shakespearean period, the letters *ff* at the commencement of a word merely stand for a capital *F*, and that it is not always possible to decide whether a transcriber of that time intended *o*ʳ to be a contraction for *our* or whether he merely used it for *or*. There is often also a difficulty in ascertaining if a final stroke of a word is an *e* or simply a flourish.

4. In special instances, denoted by the letters V. L., the original texts are followed in every particular with minute accuracy.

5. The orthography of old Latin documents is generally followed, e. g., *e* for *æ*, *capud* for *caput*, *set* for *sed*, *nichil* for *nihil*, &c. In the Latin as well as in the English extracts errors which are obviously merely clerical ones are occasionally corrected.

ILLUSTRATIONS

OF THE

LIFE OF SHAKESPEARE.

THE FIRST PART.

The precise time at which Shakespeare commenced his professional career in London is not known, but it must be assigned to some period after May, 1583, and before the year 1592. He left Stratford-on-Avon after the birth of his eldest child, Rowe distinctly stating that, when he fled to the metropolis, "he was oblig'd to leave his business and family in Warwickshire," Life, ed. 1709, p. 5. In 1592, as we learn from the indisputable testimony of Greene, he was one of the actors and was also engaged in remodelling some of the dramas of the time. According to the most reliable authorities, Shakespeare held at first a subordinate position in the theatre. A person named Dowdall, who visited the Church of the Holy Trinity at Stratford-on-Avon early in the year 1693, gives the following interesting notice of the traditional belief, then current in the poet's native county, respecting this incident in his life,—"the clarke that shew'd me this church is above eighty years old; he says that this Shakespear was formerly in this towne bound apprentie to a butcher, but that he run from his master to London, and there was received into the play-house as a serviture, and by this meanes had an oppertunity to be what he afterwards prov'd." Although the parish clerk, alluded to by Dowdall, was not so old as is here represented, William Castle, who was then clerk and sexton (Stratford Vestry-book), having been born in the year 1628 (Stratford Register), there can be no hesitation in receiving his narrative as the truthful report of a tradition accepted in the neighbourhood at the time at which it was recorded. Rowe, in his Account of the Life of Shakespear, published in 1709, assigns a special reason for the poet's departure from Stratford, but agrees with the clerk in the point now under consideration,—"he was receiv'd into the company then in being, at first in a very mean rank; but his admirable wit, and the natural turn of it to the stage, soon distinguish'd him, if not as an extraordinary actor, yet as an excellent writer," p. 6. A similar account appears in a later biographical essay of less authority and smaller value, published in a newspaper called the London Chronicle in 1769,—"his first admission into the playhouse was suitable to his appearance; a stranger, and ignorant of the art, he was glad to be taken into the company in a very mean rank; nor did his performance recommend him to any distinguished notice." The tradition current amongst the actors of the last century is somewhat more in detail, but it is not inconsistent with the statements of the three writers above quoted. Malone, in his Supplement to Shakspeare's Plays, 1780, i. 67, observes that "there is a stage tradition that his first office in the theatre was that of prompter's attendant, whose employment it is to give the performers notice to be ready to enter as often as the business of the play requires their appearance on the stage." This functionary is termed the call-boy, each actor being summoned by him a few minutes before the prompter is ready to give the cue for entrance on the stage; nor can the future eminence of Shakespeare be considered to be opposed to the reception of the tradition recorded by Malone. "I have known men within my remembrance," observes Downes, "arrive to the highest dignities of the theatre, who made their entrance in the quality of mutes, joint-stools, flower-pots and tapestry-hangings;" Letter in the Tatler, No. 193, July, 1710. The office of prompter's attendant was at least as respectable as any of the occupations which are here enumerated.

At the period of Shakespeare's arrival in London, any reputable kind of employment was obtained with considerable difficulty. There is an evidence of this in the history of the early life of John Sadler, a native of Stratford-on-Avon and one of the poet's contemporaries, who tried his fortunes in the metropolis under similar though less discouraging circumstances. This youth, upon quitting Stratford, "join'd himself to the carrier, and came to London, where he had never been before, and sold his horse in Smithfield; and, having no acquaintance in London to recommend him or assist him, he went from street to street, and house to house, asking if they wanted an apprentice, and, though he met with many discouraging scorns and a thousand denials, he went on till he light on Mr. Brokesbank, a grocer in Bucklersbury, who, though he long denied him for want of sureties for his fidelity, and because the money he had (but ten pounds) was so disproportionable to what he used to receive with apprentices, yet, upon his discreet account he gave of himself and the motives which put him upon that course, and promise to compensate with diligent and faithfull service whatever else was short of his expectation, he ventured to receive him upon trial, in which he so well approved himself that he accepted him into his service, to which he bound him for eight years." This narrative is or was preserved in a manuscript written by Sadler's daughter, but it is here taken from extracts from the original which were published in the Holy Life of Mrs. Elizabeth Walker, 8vo. Lond. 1690, pp. 10, 11. It is to be gathered, from the accounts given by Castle and Rowe, that Shakespeare, a fugitive, leaving his native town unexpectedly, must have reached London more unfavourably situated than Sadler, although the latter experienced so much trouble in finding suitable occupation. At all events, there would have been greater difficulty in Shakespeare's case in accounting satisfactorily to employers for his sudden departure from home. That he was also nearly, if not quite, moneyless, is to be inferred from tradition, the latter supported by the ascertained fact of the adverse circumstances of his father at the time rendering it impossible for him to have received effectual assistance from his parents; nor is there any reason for believing that he was likely to have obtained substantial aid from the relatives of his wife. Johnson no doubt accurately reported the tradition of his day, when, in 1765, he stated that Shakespeare "came to London a needy adventurer, and lived for a time by very mean employments," Preface to his Edition of Shakespear's

Plays, 1765, separate edition, p. 41. To the same effect is the earlier testimony given by the author of Ratseis Ghost or the Second Part of his Madde Prankes and Robberies, 1606, where the strolling player, in a passage reasonably believed to refer to Shakespeare, says, speaking of actors, "I have heard, indeede, of some that have gone to London *very meanly*, and have come in time to be exceeding wealthy." The author of the last named tract was evidently well acquainted with the theatrical gossip of his day, and the chapter in which this passage occurs is so extremely curious, including other covert allusions, some possibly to Shakespeare himself, it is given at length in the Appendix, pp. 84-86.

The stage was in those days one of the few professions which required no capital and little preparation; but it does not follow that an inexperienced youth, fresh from the provinces, would easily have gained employment at once on the metropolitan boards even as a supernumerary. The quotations above given from Johnson's Preface and Ratseis Ghost seem to indicate that his earlier occupation was something of a meaner character. A traditional story was current about the middle of the last century, according to which it would appear that Shakespeare, if connected in any sort of manner with the theatre immediately upon his arrival in London, could only have been engaged in a servile capacity, and that there was, in the career of the great poet, an interval which some may consider one of degradation, to be regarded with either incredulity or sorrow. Others may, with more reason and without reluctance, receive the tradition as a testimony to Shakespeare's practical wisdom in accepting any kind of honest occupation in preference to starvation or mendicancy, and cheerfully making the best of the circumstances by which he was surrounded. The earliest record of the anecdote which is known to be extant is a manuscript note preserved in the University Library, Edinburgh, written about the year 1748, in which the tale is narrated in the following terms,—" Sir William Davenant, who has been call'd a natural son of our author, us'd to tell the following whimsical story of him;—Shakespear, when he first came from the country to the play-house, was not admitted to act; but as it was then the custom for all the people of fashion to come on horseback to entertainments of all kinds, it was Shakespear's employment for a time, with several other poor boys belonging to the company, to hold the horses and take care of them during the representation;—by his dexterity and care he soon got a great deal of business in this way, and was personally known to most of the quality that frequented the house, insomuch that, being obliged, before he was taken into a higher and more honorable employment within doors, to train up boys to assist him, it became long afterwards a usual way among them to recommend themselves by saying that they were Shakespear's boys." Shakespeare is here mentioned as one of "several poor boys belonging to the company," a statement which agrees with the earliest traditions that have been recorded, although he could not have been strictly considered a boy at the time. The inference seems to be that he was engaged in an occupation usually assigned to mere youths. The writer assumes it as an established fact that, on his arrival in London, he proceeded at once to the theatre in search of employment. "This William," grotesquely observes Aubrey, was "naturally inclined to poetry and acting." A taste for the drama had probably been imbibed in his early youth at Stratford-on-Avon, where, at that time, various companies of itinerant players at least occasionally, and perhaps frequently, exhibited their performances. The few recorded notices of the latter are restricted to those which took place at the

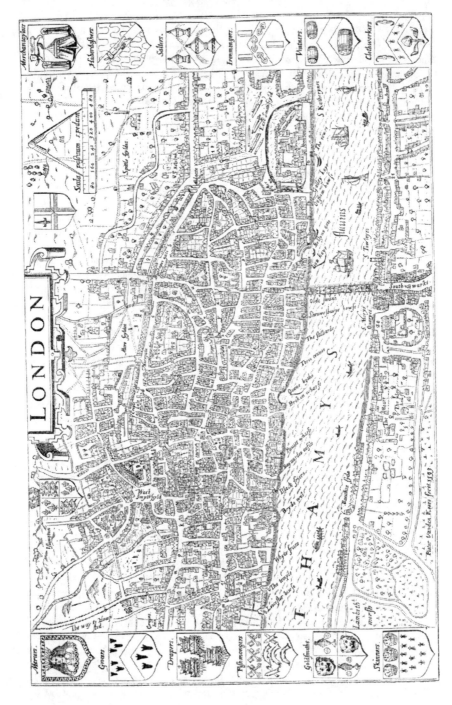

There are numerous engravings which are stated to be plans of the metropolis as it existed in the latter part of the reign of Queen Elizabeth, but the only one of undoubted accuracy is that which was engraved by Pieter Vanden Keere in 1593 from a drawing made by John Norden, the ablest surveyor of the day. It appears that Norden's survey was executed, or at least completed, in the same year, the following memorandum,—*Joannes Norden Anglus descripsit anno* 1593,—being inserted after the list of references. The copy of this plan here given has been carefully taken from a fine example of the original engraving of 1593. There are several imitations of it, and one so-called facsimile, all of which are inaccurate and worthless. Annexed to Norden's plan is the following list of streets and buildings, —*a*. Bushops gate streete; *b*. Papie; *c*. Alhallowes in the wall; *d*. S. Taphyns; *e*. Sylver streete; *f*. Aldermanburye; *g*. Barbican; *h*. Aldersgate streete; *i*. Charterhowse; *k*. Holborne Conduct; *l*. Chauncery lane; *m*. Temple barr; *n*. Holbourn; *o*. Grayes Inn lane; *p*. S. Androwes; *q*. Newgate; *r*. S. Jones; *s*. S. Nic. shambels; *t*. Cheap syde; *u*. Bucklers burye; *w*. Brodestreete; *x*. The stockes; *y*. The Exchannge; *z*. Cornehill; 2.⦿ Colmanstreete; 3. Bassings hall; 4. Honnsditche; 5. Leaden hall; 6. Gratious streete; 7. Heneage house; 8. Fancshurche; 9. Marke lane; 10. Minchyn lane; 11. Paules; 12. Eastcheape; 13. Fleetstreete; 14. Fetter lane; 15. S. Dunshous; 16. Themes streete; 17. London stone; 18. Olde Baylye; 19. Clerkenwell; 20. Winchester house; 21. Battle bridge; 22. Bermodsoy⦿ streete.

This extremely curious and valuable plan enables us to form a correct notion of the extent, and a tolerably effective idea of the general aspect, of London as it appeared in the early years of Shakespeare's residence in the metropolis. The circular building in Southwark, noted as "the play-howse," is the Rose Theatre. It is the earliest representation of an English theatre known to exist. The Theatre and the Curtain stood in the fields to the left of the road which leads upwards from Bishopsgate, but most unfortunately the limit of the plan in that direction just suffices for the exclusion of those interesting structures.

There are but two other surveys of London belonging to the reigns of Elizabeth and James which can be considered to be of any authority. One of these is a very large one of uncertain date, executed on wood, and generally attributed to Aggas. It was first issued in the time of Queen Elizabeth and reproduced in the reign of her successor. The other plan is an engraving on a much smaller scale, published by Braun at Cologne in 1572 from a survey evidently made before 1561, the steeple of St. Paul's, destroyed in that year, being introduced. Neither of these maps appear to be copies of absolutely original surveys taken for the object of publication, there being indications which lead to the conclusion either that they are alterations of a plan which was executed some years previously, or that the latter was used in their formation. The larger map is the only one of the time which represents the City with minuteness of detail, and it is unfortunate that its value should be impaired by this uncertainty. That there is much, however, in it on the fidelity of which reliance can be placed is unquestionable. The survey of the locality in which the Theatre and Curtain were situated must have been taken before 1576, the year in which the former was erected, for the artist engaged in a plan on such a large scale could not have failed to have introduced so conspicuous a building, had it then been in existence.

Guildhall under the immediate patronage of the Corporation, and to which the inhabitants were admitted without payment; but there were no doubt numerous other representations given in the town.

The same tradition is related by the writer of the Life of Shakespear, published in Cibber's Lives of the Poets of Great Britain and Ireland, 1753, i. 130-131, a collection only partially the work of Theophilus Cibber, and professedly "compiled from ample materials scattered in a variety of books, and especially from the manuscript notes of the late ingenious Mr. Coxeter and others collected for this design." The author of this biographical account of Shakespeare has been generally assumed, but without direct evidence, to be Robert Shiels, a person who was certainly associated with Cibber in the preparation of some other parts of the work. He introduces the tradition now under consideration in the following manner,—"I cannot forbear relating a story which Sir William Davenant told Mr. Betterton, who communicated it to Mr. Rowe; Rowe told it Mr. Pope, and Mr. Pope told it to Dr. Newton, the late editor of Milton, and from a gentleman who heard it from him, 'tis here related. Concerning Shakespear's first appearance in the playhouse;—When he came to London, he was without money and friends, and being a stranger he knew not to whom to apply, nor by what means to support himself. At that time, coaches not being in use, and as gentlemen were accustomed to ride to the playhouse, Shakespear, driven to the last necessity, went to the playhouse door, and pick'd up a little money by taking care of the gentlemen's horses who came to the play. He became eminent even in that profession, and was taken notice of for his diligence and skill in it; he had soon more business than he himself could manage, and at last hired boys under him, who were known by the name of Shakespear's boys. Some of the players, accidentally conversing with him, found him so acute, and master of so fine a conversation that, struck therewith, they and[*] recommended him to the house, in which he was first admitted in a very low station, but he did not long remain so, for he soon distinguished himself, if not as an extraordinary actor at least as a fine writer."

The gentleman who heard the story from Dr. Newton was Dr. Johnson, one of his schoolfellows, and it is told as follows by the latter, apparently as an independent version, in the edition of Shakespeare which appeared in the year 1765,—"To the foregoing accounts of Shakespear's life I have only one passage to add, which Mr. Pope related as communicated to him by Mr. Rowe.—In the time of Elizabeth, coaches being yet uncommon and hired coaches not at all in use, those who were too proud, too tender or too idle to walk, went on horseback to any distant business or diversion. Many came on horseback to the play, and when Shakespear fled to London from the terrour of a criminal prosecution, his first expedient was to wait at the door of the play-house, and hold the horses of those that had no servants that they might be ready again after the performance. In this office he became so conspicuous for his care and readiness, that in a short time every man as he alighted called for Will Shakespear, and scarcely any other waiter was trusted with a horse while Will Shakespear could be had. This was the first dawn of better fortune. Shakespear, finding more horses put into his hand than he could hold, hired boys to wait under his inspection, who, when Will Shakespear was summoned, were immediately to present themselves, 'I am Shakespear's boy, sir.' In time Shakespear found higher employment, but as long as the practice of riding to the play-house continued the waiters that held the horses retained the appellation of Shakespear's Boys."

The anecdote is told somewhat differently by Jordan, a native of Stratford-on-Avon, in a manuscript written about the year 1783,—"Some relate that he had the care of gentlemen's horses, for carriages at that time were very little used; his business, therefore, say they, was to take the horses to the inn and order them to be fed until the play was over, and then see that they were returned to their owners, and that he had several boys under him constantly in employ, from which they were called Shakespear's boys." It may be doubted if this be a correct version of any tradition current at the time it was written, Jordan having been in the habit of recording the Shakespearean tales with fanciful additions of his own. Gentlemen's horses in Shakespeare's days were more hardy than those of modern times, so that stables or sheds for them, during the two hours the performance then lasted, were not absolute necessities. At the same time it is worth recording that there were taverns, with accommodation for horses, in the neighbourhood of the theatres at Shoreditch. A witness, whose deposition respecting some land in the immediate locality was taken in 1602, states that he recollected, in years previously, "a greate ponde wherein the servauntes of the said Earle, and diverse his neighbours inholders, did usually wasshe and water theire horses, which ponde was commonly called the Earles horsepond." The nobleman here mentioned was the Earl of Rutland.

There is another and much simpler version of the anecdote recorded in the Monthly Magazine, in 1818, on the authority of an inhabitant of Stratford-on-Avon, who was one of the descendants from the poet's sister. It is given in the following words,—"Mr. J. M. Smith said he had often heard his mother state that Shakspeare owed his rise in life, and his introduction to the theatre, to his accidentally holding the horse of a gentleman at the door of the theatre on his first arriving in London; his appearance led to enquiry and subsequent patronage;" Monthly Magazine, February, 1818, repeated in Moncrieff's Guide, ed. 1822, p. 227; ed. 1824, p. 25. The mother of J. M. Smith was, according to a pedigree compiled by Wheler, the son of Mary Hart, who had married one William Smith. This Mary was, on the same authority, the daughter of the George Hart who married Sarah Mumford in the year 1729. She was the fifth in descent from Joan Shakespeare, the sister of Shakespeare. Versions of any tradition, however, respecting the great dramatist which cannot be traced beyond the chief era of the commencement of Shakesperean deceptions, the Stratford Jubilee of 1769, should be received with the utmost caution, especially if emanating from Warwickshire. The narratives of Jordan and Smith must be regarded as evidences which are at least of a questionable character.

The precise interpretation to be given to the term *serviture*, in Dowdall's narrative, is a matter of uncertainty. It may mean simply an attendant or servant, in the modern acceptation of the latter word, or what was formerly called a hireling. Henslowe, in 1597, speaks of a hireling actor, who was engaged at ten shillings a week when in London and five shillings a week when in the country, as "a covenaunt servant." It seems all but certain that Shakespeare commenced his real theatrical career as one of the hirelings or supernumeraries. The question is whether there is sufficient evidence to enable us to conclude that he was previously connected with the theatre in a still lower position. There appears to be valid testimony in favour of this opinion, and, if this be conceded, there is no sufficient obstacle to prevent the reception of the belief, however greatly the notion may now disturb our sentimental views of the career of the great dramatist, that in the first instance he had some engagement which in one way or other was connected with the protection of the horses of visitors during the performances, a duty for which his previous country life must have rendered him well fitted.

It has been and is the fashion with most biographers to discredit the horse tradition entirely, but that it was originally related by Sir William Davenant, and belongs in some form to the earlier half of the seventeenth century, cannot reasonably be doubted. The circumstance of the anecdote being founded upon the daily practice of numerous gentlemen riding to the theatres, a custom obsolete after the Restoration, is sufficient to establish the antiquity of the story. In a little volume of epigrams by Sir John Davis, printed at Middleborough in or about the year 1599, a man of inferior position is ridiculed for being constantly on horseback, imitating in that respect persons of higher rank,—"*He rides into the fieldes playes to behold.*" Ben Jonson, in the Induction to Cynthia's Revels, first acted in the year 1600, also alludes to the ordinary use of horses by visitors to theatres (Workes, ed. 1616, p. 184); so does Decker in his Guls Horne-book, 1609; and a later reference to the practice occurs in Brome's Court Beggar, a comedy acted at Drury-Lane Theatre in the year 1632. Many writers have rejected the tradition mainly on the ground that, although it was known to Rowe, he does not allude to it in his Life of Shakespeare, 1709; but there is no improbability in the supposition that the story was not related to him until after the publication of that work, the second edition of which in 1714 is a mere reprint of the first. Other reasons for the omission may be suggested, but even if it be conceded that the anecdote was rejected as suspicious and improbable, that circumstance alone cannot be decisive against the opinion that there may be a particle of truth in it. This is, indeed, all that is contended for. Few would be disposed to accept the story literally as related by Cibber, but when it is considered that the tradition must be a very early one, that its genealogy is respectable, and that it harmonizes with the general old belief of the great poet having, when first in London, subsisted by "very mean employments," little doubt can fairly be entertained that it has at least in some way or other a foundation in real occurrences. It should also be remembered that horse-stealing was one of the very commonest offences of the period, and one which was probably stimulated by the facility with which delinquents of that class obtained pardons. The safe custody of a horse was a matter of serious import, and a person who had satisfactorily fulfilled such a trust would not be lightly estimated. The theatres of the suburbs, observes a puritanical Lord Mayor of London in the year 1597, are "ordinary places for vagrant persons, maisterles men, thieves, *horse-stealers,* whoremongers, coozeners, conycatchers, contrivers of treason and other idele and daungerous persons to meet together and to make theire matches, to the great displeasure of Almightie God and the hurt and annoyance of her Majesties people, which cannot be prevented nor discovered by the governors of the Citie for that they ar owt of the Citiees jurisdiction," City of London MSS.

No one has recorded the name of the first theatre with which Shakespeare was connected, but if, as is almost certain, he came to London some few years before the notice of him by Greene in 1592, there were at the time of his arrival only two theatres in the metropolis, both of them on the north of the Thames. The earliest theatre on the south was the Rose, the erection of which was contemplated about the year 1586, but it would seem from Henslowe's Diary that the building was not opened till early in 1592. The circus at Paris Garden, though perhaps occasionally used for dramatic performances, was not a regular theatre. Admitting, however, the possibility that companies of players could have hired the latter establishment, there is good reason for concluding that Southwark was not the locality alluded to in the Davenant tradition. The usual mode of transit for those Londoners who desired to attend theatrical performances in Southwark, was certainly by water. The boatmen of the Thames were perpetually asserting at a somewhat later period that their living depended on the continuance of the Southwark, and the suppression of the London, theatres. Some few of the courtly members of the audience, perhaps for the mere sake of appearances, might occasionally have arrived at their destination on horseback, having taken what would be to most of them the circuitous route over London Bridge; but the large majority would select the more convenient passage by boat. The Southwark audiences mainly consisted of Londoners, for in the then sparsely inhabited condition of Kent and Surrey very few could have arrived from those counties. The number of riders to the Bankside theatres must, therefore, always have been very limited, too much so for the remunerative employment of horseholders, whose services would be required merely in regard to the still fewer persons who were unattended by their lackeys. The only theatres upon the other side of the Thames, when the poet arrived in London, were the Theatre and the Curtain, for, notwithstanding some apparent testimonies to the contrary, the Blackfriars' Theatre, as will be afterwards shown, was not then in existence. It was to the Theatre or to the Curtain that the satirist alluded when he speaks of the fashionable youth riding "into the fieldes playes to behold." Both these theatres were situated in the parish of Shoreditch, in the fields of the Liberty of Halliwell, in which locality, if the Davenant tradition is in the slightest degree to be trusted, Shakespeare must have commenced his metropolitan career. This Liberty, at a later period termed Holywell, derived its name from a sacred (A.-S. halig) well or fountain which took its rise in the marshy grounds situated to the west of the high street leading from Norton Folgate to Shoreditch Church,—*mora in qua fons qui dicitur Haliwelle oritur*, charter of A.D. 1189 printed in Dugdale's Monasticon Anglicanum, ed. 1682, p. 531. In Shakespeare's time, all veneration or respect for the well had disappeared. Stow speaks of it as "much decayed and marred with filthinesse purposely layd there for the heighthening of the ground for garden plots," Survay, ed. 1598, p. 14. It has long disappeared, but it was in existence as recently as 1745, its locality being marked in the first accurate survey of the parish of St. Leonard, Shoreditch, made in that year by Chassereau. At that period the well was situated in a field which was on the east of the Curtain Road and a little to the north of the junction of the Willow Walk with that road. The present Bateman's Row takes its name from the then owner of that field, and the site of the well is now one chain to the south of that Row and two chains to the east of the Curtain Road.

The lands in which the holy fountain was situated belonged for many generations to the Priory of Holywell, more frequently termed Halliwell Priory in the Elizabethan documents. This institution was suppressed and its church demolished in the time of Henry the Eighth, but the priory itself, converted into private residences, was suffered to remain. The larger portion of these buildings and some of the adjoining land were purchased by one Henry Webb in 1544, and are thus described in an old MS. index to the Patent Rolls preserved in the Record Office,—"unum messuagium cum pertinenciis infra scitum Prioratus de Halliwell, gardina cum pertinenciis, domos et edificia

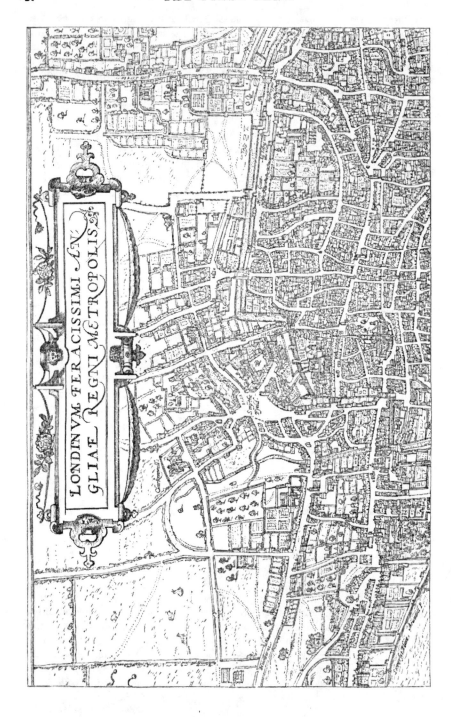

cum pertinenciis, et tota domos et edificia vocata *le Fratrie*, claustrum vocatum *le Cloyster* et terram fundum et solum ejusdem, gardina vocata *the Ladyes Gardens*, unum gardinum vocatum *le Prioresse Garden* et unum columbare in eodem, ortum vocatum *le Covent Orchard* continentem unam acram, et omnia horrea, domos, brazinas etc. in tenura Johannis Foster, terram fundum et solum infra scitum predictum et ecclesie ejusdem et totam terram et solum totius capelle ibidem, totum curtilagium et terram vocata *le Chappell Yard*, et omnia domos, edificia et gardina in tenura predicti Johannis Foster, domum vocatum *le Washinghouse* et stabulum ibidem, et totum horreum vocatum *le Oatebarne*, parcella ejusdem Prioratus de Halliwell." A small portion of this estate, that in which the Theatre was afterwards erected, belonged in the year 1576 to one Giles Allen. It was at this period that " James Burbage of London joyner" obtained from Allen a lease, dated 13 April, 1576, of houses and land situated between Finsbury Field and the public road from Bishopsgate to Shoreditch Church. The boundary of the leased estate on the west is described as "a bricke wall next unto the feildes commonly called Finsbury Feildes." James Burbage, by trade a joiner, but at this time a leading member of the Earl of Leicester's Company of Players, was the originator of theatrical buildings in England, for the successful promotion of which his earlier as well as his adopted profession were exactly suited. He obtained the lease referred to with this express object, Allen covenanting with him that, if he expended two hundred pounds upon the buildings already on the estate, he should be at liberty "to take downe and carrie awaie to his and their owne proper use all such buildinges and other thinges as should be builded, erected or sett upp, in or uppon the gardeines and voide grounde by the said indentures graunted, or anie parte therof, by the said Jeames his executors or assignes either for a theatre or playinge place or for anie other lawefull use for his or their commodities," Answer of Giles Allen in the suit of Burbage v. Allen, Court of Requests, 6 Febr. 42 Eliz. The lease was signed on April 13th, 1576, and Burbage must have commenced the erection of his theatre immediately afterwards. It was the earliest fabric of the kind ever built in this country, and emphatically designated The Theatre. By the summer of the following year it was a recognized centre of theatrical amusements. On the first of August, 1577, the Lords of the Privy Council directed a letter to be forwarded "to the L. Wentworth, Mr. of the Rolles, and Mr. Lieutenaunt of the Tower, signifieng unto them that for thavoiding of the sicknes likelie to happen through the heate of the weather and assemblies of the people of London to playes, her Highnes plesure is that as the L. Mayor hath taken order within the Citee, so they imediatlie upon the receipt of their ll. lettres shall take order with such as are and do use to play without the liberties of the Citee within that countie, as the Theater and such like, shall forbeare any more to play untill Mighelmas be past at the least, as they will aunswer to the contrarye," MS. Register of the Privy Council. The county here alluded to is Middlesex. This is the earliest notice of the Theatre yet discovered.

There is no ancient view of the district leased to Burbage in which the Theatre is introduced, but a general notion of the aspect of the locality may be gathered from the portion of the map of Aggas in which it is included. The perspective and measurements of that plan are unfortunately inaccurate, as may be ascertained by comparing it with the more correct but far less graphic delineation of the same locality in Braun's map, 1574, here reproduced. Both Aggas and Braun undoubtedly made use of one and the same earlier plan, but the work of the latter appears in some respects to be more scientifically executed. It is clear from Braun's map, tested by the later survey completed by Faithorne in 1658, that the eastern boundary of Finsbury Field was much nearer the highway to Shoreditch than might be inferred from the position assigned to it by Aggas. That boundary was also nearly parallel with the highway, and part of it seems to be the road or sewer which, in Aggas's map, extends from an opening on the right of the Dog-house to the lane near the spot where is to be observed a rustic with a spade on his shoulder walking towards Shoreditch. That part of the map which I have here termed a road or sewer may have been and most likely was a line of way by the side of an open ditch, that which was afterwards the Curtain Road; a supposition all but confirmed by a survey of the bounds of Finsbury Manor, taken in 1586, where the eastern boundary of that manor hereabouts is mentioned as the "common sewer and waye" which "goethe to the playehowse called the Theater." If this be the case, the north end of this ditch was the commencement of Holywell Lane, and the brick wall on the west of the Priory buildings was exactly opposite, the position of that wall being incorrectly represented in Aggas's map. Finsbury Field certainly included the meadow in which the three windmills were situated, as appears from a survey of the manor taken in 1567 printed in Stow's Survey of London, ed. 1633, p. 913; and it also extended to the vicinity of the Dog-house, as I find from a notice of it in Rot. Pat. 35 Hen. VIII. pars 16. The portion of the Field which joined Burbage's estate was of course much nearer the village of Shoreditch. At the time of the erection of the Theatre there were, as will be presently seen, more houses in the neighbourhood of the Priory than are shown in either of the early plans of Braun and Aggas. Others were erected by Burbage in the immediate vicinity of the Theatre. Witnesses were asked in 1602, "whither were the said newe howses standing in the said greate yarde, and neere and alonge the late greate howse called the Theater;" and one of them deposed that "the newe houses standing in the greate yard neere and along the Theatre, and also those other newe builded houses that are on the other syde of the sayd greate yard over and against the sayd former newe builded houses, were not at the costes and charges of Gyles Allen erected, builded or sett up, as he hath heard, but were so builded by the said James Burbage about xxviij. yeares agoe." There can be no doubt that Aggas's plan was completed some years before the erection either of these houses or of the Theatre. The portion of it which is here engraved is a minutely faithful copy from the original preserved at the Guildhall. In this plan the Royal Exchange, not completed till 1570, is introduced, but this clearly appears to be the result of an alteration made in the original block some years after the completion of the latter. A similar variation is to be observed in some copies of Braun's plan, in one of which, 1574, in my collection, that building is inserted evidently in the same plate from which other copies of that date, in which it does not occur, were taken. It should be borne in mind that great caution is requisite in the study of all the early London maps. Those of Aggas, Braun and Norden are the only plans of the time of Queen Elizabeth which are authentic, and care must be taken that reliable editions are consulted, there being several inaccurate copies and imitations of all of them.

Burbage gave a premium of £20 for the lease of 1576, the term being for twenty-one years at the annual rent of £14, and it was covenanted that if the lessee expended £200 on the property in certain specified directions he should, at any time before the expiration of ten years, be entitled to claim from Allen a new lease for

THE FIRST PART.

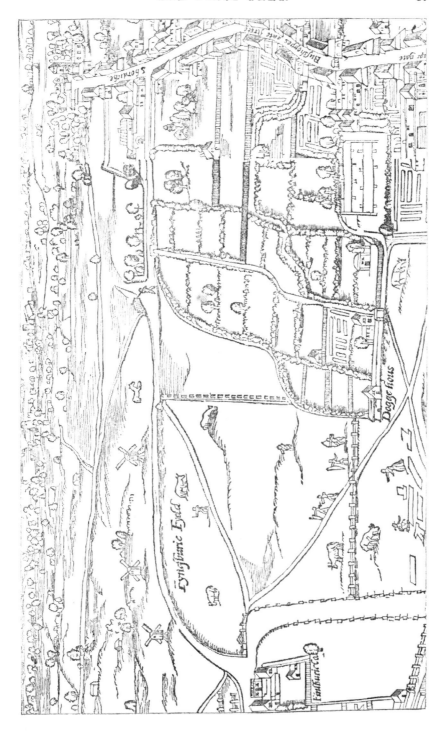

twenty-one years commencing from the date of the latter. A lease carrying out these terms, dated 1 November, 27 Elizabeth, 1585, was accordingly prepared by Burbage and submitted on that day to Allen, who, however, declined to execute. The extent of the property must have been comparatively limited, consisting merely of two gardens, four houses and a large barn, as appears from the following rather curious and minute description of parcels which occurs in the proposed deed of 1585,—"all thos two howses or tenementes with thappurtenaunces which, att the tyme of the sayde former demise made, weare in the severall tenures or occupacions of Johan Harrison, widowe, and John Dragon; and also all that howse or tenement with thappurtenances together with the gardyn grounde lyinge behinde parte of the same beinge then likewise in the occupacion of William Garnett, gardiner, which sayd gardyn plott dothe extende in bredthe from a greate stone walle there which doth inclose parte of the gardyn then or latlye beinge in the occupacion of the sayde Gyles unto the gardeyne ther then in the occupacion of Ewin Colfoxe, weaver, and in lengthe from the same howse or tenement unto a bricke wall ther next unto the feildes commonly called Finsbury Feildes; and also all that howse or tenemente with thappurtenances att the tyme of the sayde former demise made called or knowne by the name of the Mill-howse, together with the gardyn grounde lyinge behinde parte of the same, also att the tyme of the sayde former dimise made beinge in the tenure or occupacion of the foresayde Ewyn Colefoxe or of his assignes, which sayde gardyn grounde dothe extende in lengthe from the same house or tenement unto the forsayde bricke wall next unto the foresayde feildes; and also all those three upper romes with thappurtenaunces next adjoyninge to the foresayde Mill-house also beinge att the tyme of the sayde former dimise made in the occupacion of Thomas Dancaster, shomaker, or of his assignes; and also all the nether romes with thappurtenances lyinge under the same three upper romes and next adjoyninge also to the foresayde house or tenemente called the Mill-house, then also beinge in the severall tenurs or occupacions of Alice Dotridge, widowe, and Richarde Brockenburye or of ther assignes, together also with the gardyn grounde lyinge behynde the same, extendynge in lengthe from the same nether romes downe unto the forsayde bricke wall nexte unto the foresayde foildes, and then or late beinge also in the tenure or occupacion of the foresayde Alice Dotridge; and also so much of the grounde and soyle lyeinge and beinge afore all the tenementes or houses before graunted as extendethe in lengthe from the owtwarde parte of the foresayde tenementes beinge at the tyme of the makinge of the sayde former dimise in the occupacion of the foresayde Johan Harryson and John Dragon unto a ponde there beinge nexte unto the barne or stable then in the occupacion of the Right Honorable the Earle of Rutlande or of his assignes, and in bredthe from the foresayde tenemente or Mill-house to the midest of the well beinge afore the same tementes; and also all that great barne with thappurtenances att the tyme of the makinge of the sayde former dimise made beinge in the severall occupacions of Hughe Richardes, inholder, and Robert Stoughton, butcher; and also a little peece of grounde then inclosed with a pale and next adjoyninge to the foresayde barne, and then or late before that in the occupacion of the sayde Roberte Stoughton, together also with all the grounde and soyle lyinge and beinge betwene the sayde neyther romes last before expressed and the foresayde greate barne and the foresayde ponde, that is to saye, extendinge in lengthe from the foresayde ponde unto a ditche beyonde the brick wall nexte the foresayde feildes; and also the sayde Gyles Allen and Sara his wyfe doe by thes presentes dimise, graunte and to farme lett, unto the sayde Jeames Burbage all the right, title and interest, which the sayde Gyles and Sara have, or ought to have, of, in or to all the groundes and soile lyeinge betwene the foresayde greate barne and the barne being at the tyme of the sayde former dimise in the occupacion of the Earle of Rutlande or of his assignes, extendeinge in lengthe from the foresayde ponde and from the foresayde stable or barne then in the occupacion of the foresayde Earle of Rutlande or of his assignes downe to the foresayde bricke wall next the foresayde feildes; and also the sayde Gyles and Sara doe by thes presentes demise, graunt and to fearme let, to the sayde Jeames all the sayde voide grounde lieynge and beinge betwixt the foresayde ditche and the foresayde brickwall extendinge in lenght* from the foresayde brick wall which incloseth parte of the foresayde garden beinge att the tyme of the makinge of the sayde former demise or late before that in the occupacion of the sayde Giles Allen unto the foresayde barne then in the occupacion of the foresayde Earle or of his assignes." This description is identical with that given in the lease of 1576, as appears from a recital in the Coram Rege Rolls, Easter 44 Elizabeth, R. 257.

There is no doubt that the estate above described formed a portion of that which was purchased by Webb in 1544, and belonged to Allen in 1576, for in a paper in a suit instituted many years afterwards respecting "a piece of void ground" on the eastern boundary of the property leased to Burbage we are informed that Henry the Eighth granted to Henry Webb "a greate parte of the scite of the said Pryorie, and namely amongst other thinges all those barnes, stables, bruehowses, gardens and all other buildinges whatsoever, with theire appurtenaunces, lyinge and beinge within the scite, walles and precincte of the said Pryorye, on the West parte of the said Priorye, within the lower gate of the said Pryorye, and all the ground and soyle by any wayes included within the walles and precincte of the said priorye extendinge from the said lower gate, of which ground the sayd yarde or peece of void ground into which it is supposed that the said Cuthbert Burbage hath wrongfully entered is parcell." This important evidence enables us to identify the exact locality of the Burbage estate, the southern boundary of which extended from the western side of the lower gate of the Priory to Finsbury Fields, the brick wall separating the latter from Burbage's property being represented in Aggas's map in a north-east direction from Holywell Lane on the west of the Priory buildings, though, as previously stated, the wall is placed in that map too near Shoreditch. The rustic with the spade on his shoulder who, in Aggas's view, is represented as walking towards Holywell Lane, is at a short distance from the south-western corner of Burbage's property. Somewhere near that corner the Theatre was undoubtedly situated. This opinion is confirmed by Stow, who, in his Survay of London, ed. 1598, p. 349, thus writes, speaking of the Priory,—"the Church being pulled downe, many houses have bene their builded for the lodgings of noblemen, of straungers borne and other; and neare thereunto are builded two publique houses for the acting and shewe of comedies, tragedies and histories, for recreation, whereof the one is called the Courtein, the other the Theatre, both standing on the south-west side towards the Field," that is, Finsbury Field. The "lower gate," mentioned in the record above quoted, was on the north side of Holywell Lane, and in a deposition taken in 1602, it is stated that the " Earle of Rutland and his assignes did ordinarily at theire pleasures chayne and barre up the lane called Holloway Lane leading from the greate streete of Shordich towardes the fieldes along before the gate of the said Pryory, and so kept the same so cheyned and barred up as a private foote way, and that the same lane then was not used as a common highway for carte or carriage." Other witnesses assert that no one was allowed "to passe with horse or carte" unless he had the Earl's special permission. It is, perhaps, not to be concluded from these statements that persons were not allowed to drive carts through the lane, but simply that the Earl took the ordinary precautions to retain it legally as a private road. The lower gate, though indistinctly rendered, may be observed in Aggas's map on the south of the west end of the Priory buildings, and upon land situated to the north-west of this gate the Theatre was erected. All this locality is now so completely altered, it being a dense assemblage of modern buildings, that hardly any real archæological interest attaches to it. The position of the Theatre, however, can be indicated with a near approach to accuracy. The ruins of the Priory were still visible in the last century in King John's Court on the north of Holywell Lane, and were incorrectly but popularly known as the remains of King John's Palace (Maitland's History of London, ed. 1739, p. 771). The ruins have disappeared, but the Court is still in existence, a circumstance which enables us to identify the locality of the Priory. It appears, therefore, from the evidences above cited, that the Theatre must have been situated a little to the north of Holywell Lane as nearly as possible on the site of what is now Deanes Mews. In digging recently for the foundations of a railway, which passes over some of the ground upon which the Priory stood, there were discovered the remains of the stone-work of one of the ancient entrance-doors. These few relics, now (1873) deposited outside an adjoining cottage, are most probably the only vestiges remaining of what was once the thriving and somewhat important Priory of Holywell.

Although the Theatre must have been situated near some of the houses on the Burbage estate, it was practically "in the fields," as is ascertained from indisputable evidences. Stockwood, in August, 1578, speaks of it as "the gorgeous playing place erected in the fieldes." Fleetwood, writing to Lord Burghley in June, 1584, says,—"that night I retorned to London, and found all the wardes full of watches; the cause thereof was for that *very nere* the Theatre or Curten, at the tyme of the playes, there laye a prentice sleping *upon the grasse*, and one Challes alias Grostock dyd turne upon the too upon the belly of the same prentice, wherupon the apprentice start up, and after wordes they fell to playne blowes," MS. Lansd. 41. The neighbourhood of the Theatre was occasionally visited by the common hangman, a circumstance which proves that there was an open space near the building. In the True Report of the Inditement &c. of Weldon, Hartley and Sutton, who suffred for High Treason in severall Places about the Citie of London on Saturday the Fifth of October, 1588, it is stated that "after Weldons execution the other prisoners were brought to Hollywell, nigh the Theater, where Hartley was to suffer." In Tarlton's Newes Out of Purgatorie, 1590, that celebrated actor is represented as knowing that the performance at the Theatre was finished when he "saw such concourse of people through the Fields;" and when Peter Streete removed the building in 1599, he was accused by Allen of injuring the neighbouring grass to the value of fourty shillings. There is a similar allusion to the *herba Cutberti* in proceedings in Burbage v. Ames, Coram Rege Roll, Hil. 41 Elizabeth, a suit respecting a small piece of land in the immediate locality. The Theatre was originally built on enclosed ground, but a pathway or road was afterwards made from it into the open fields. A witness deposed in 1602 that "shee doth not knowe anie ancient way into the fieldes but a way used after the building of the Theatre, which leadeth into the fieldes." Finally, there is the testimony of Gerard, who, in his pleasing work, the Herball, 1597, p. 804, after describing the ordinary crowfoot, adds,—"the second kind of crowfoot is like unto the precedent, saving that his leaves are fatter, thicker and greener, and his small twiggie stalkes stand upright, otherwise it is like; of which kinde it chanced that, walking in the fielde next unto the Theater by London, in company of a worshipfull marchant named master Nicholas Lete, I founde one of this kinde there with double flowers, which before that time I had not seene." Thus Shakespeare's observation of our wild flowers was not necessarily limited, as has been supposed, to his provincial experiences, the principal theatres existing in the earlier period of his metropolitan career having been situated in a rural suburb, and green fields being then within an easy walk from any part of London.

The quotation above given from Tarlton's Newes out of Purgatorie, 1590, shows that the usual access to the Theatre was through Finsbury Fields. There was certainly no regular path to it through the Lower Gate of the Priory, the old plans of the locality exhibiting its site as enclosed ground; and according to one witness, whose evidence was taken in 1602, Allen, previously to the erection of the Theatre, had no access to his premises from the south, but merely from the east and north. The testimony here alluded to was given in reply to the following interrogatory,— "whither had not the said Allen his servauntes, and such other tenauntes as he had, before those said newe buildinges were sett up and before the Theater was builded their ordinarie waie of going and coming in and out to his howse onely through that place or neere or over againste that place wheare the Theater stood into feildes and streetes, and not anie other waie, and how long is it since he or his did use anie other waie as you knowe or have heard." Mary Hobblethwayte of Shoreditch, who gave her age as 76 or thereabouts, deposed "that the said Allen his servauntes and tenentes, before those newe buildinges were sett up, and before the Theatre was builded, had theire ordinary way of going and coming to and from his house onely through a way directly towardes the North, inclosed on both sydes with a brick wall, leading to a Crosse neere unto the well called Dame Agnes a Cleeres Well, and that the way made into the fieldes from the Theatre was made since the Theatre was builded, as shee remembreth, and that the said Allen his servauntes and tenauntes had not any other way other then the way leading from his house to the High Streete of Shordich." On the other hand, there were witnesses examined at the same time who asserted that Allen had access to the fields by a path through or near the site of the Theatre before that building was erected. Leonard Jackson, aged 80, declared "that the said Allen his servauntes and others his tenauntes had, before those newe buildinges were sett up, and before the Theatre was builded, the ordinary way of going and comming in and out to his house through that place, or neere or over against that place where the Theatre stoode, and that he and they had also another way through his greate orchard into the High Streete of Shorditch, and that he hath used that way some xxx. yeares or xxxv. yeares or thereaboutes." Still more in detail but to a like effect is the deposition of John Rowse, aged 55, who stated that "the saide Allen his servauntes and other tenauntes there had, before those his newe buildinges were sett up and before the Theatre was builded, theire ordinary waie coming and going in and out to his house onely through that place, or neere or over against that place where the saide Theatre stoode into the fieldes, and that nowe and then he and some of his tenauntes did come in and out at the greate gate, and he doth remember this to be true, bycause that the said Allen nowe and then at his going into the country from Hollowell did give this examinates father, being appointed Porter of the house by his Lord Henry Earle of Rutland, for his paines, sometymes iij. *s*, sometymes iiij. *s*, and further he saieth that he hath knowne the said Allen and his servauntes use another way from his house through his long orchard into Hollowell Streete or Shorditch Streete, and this waie as he this examinate remembreth some xxx.ty yeares or thereaboutes." It must be borne in mind that the property affected by the rights of way investigated in these evidences consisted of the whole of Allen's estate before Burbage was his lessee.

It appears from Hobblethwayte's evidence that, after the Theatre was built, there was a road or path made from it on the west side into the fields. This road or path must have been made through the brick wall on the eastern boundary of Finsbury Fields, as is ascertained from a clause in the proposed lease from Allen to Burbage, 1585, and from an unpublished account of the boundaries of Finsbury Manor written in 1586, in which, after mentioning that the bounds of the manor on the south passed along the road which divided More Field from Mallow Field, the latter being the one to the east of the grounds of Finsbury Court, the writer proceeds to describe them as follows,—"and so alonge by the southe ende of the gardens adjoyninge to More Feld into a diche of watter called the Common Sewer which runnethe into More Diche, and from thence the same diche northewarde alonge one theaste side the gardens belonginge to John Worssopp, and so alonge one theaste side of twoo closes of the same John Worssopp nowe in the occupacion of Thomas Lee thelder, buttcher, for which gardens and closses the said John Worssopp payed the quit rent to the mannor of Fynsbury, as aperethe by the recorde, and so the same boundes goe over the highe waye close by a barren lately builded by one Niccolles, includinge the same barren, and so northe as the Common Sewer and waye goethe to the playehowse called the Theater and so tournethe by the same Common Sewer to Dame Agnes the Clere." The evidence of Hobblethwayte is confirmed by the testimony of Anne Thornes of Shoreditch, aged 74, who deposed,—"that shee cannott remember that Allen his servauntes or tenauntes had, before the said new buildinges were sett up or before the said Theatre was builded, theire ordinary way of going and comming unto his house onely through that place where the Theatre stoode into the fieldes or neere or over against that place; but shee hath heard that, since the building of the Theatre, there is a way made into the fieldes, and that the said Allen and his tenauntes have for a long tyme used another way out of the sayd scite of the Priory that the said Allen holdeth into the High Streete of Shorditch." Rowse's evidence proves that there could have been no regular access to the locality of the Theatre through the Lower Gate of the Priory in Holywell Lane, and very few indeed of the audience could have used the path which entered Allen's property to the north from the well of St. Agnes le Clair, which latter was not in the direction of any road used by persons coming from London. It follows that, in Shakespeare's time, the chief if not the only line of access to the Theatre was across the fields which lay to the west of the western boundary wall of the grounds of the dissolved Priory, and through those meadows, therefore, nearly all the visitors to the Theatre would arrive at their destination, most of them on foot but some no doubt riding "into the fieldes playes to behold," Davis's Epigrammes, 1599. This question of their route is not a subject of mere topographical curiosity, the conclusion here reached increasing the probability of there being some foundation for the tradition recorded by Davenant.

The Theatre appears to have been a very favourite place of amusement, especially with the more unruly section of the populace. There are several allusions to its crowded audiences and to the license which occasionally attended the entertainments, the disorder sometimes penetrating into the City itself. "By reason no playes were the same daye, all the Citie was quiet," observes the writer of a letter in June, 1584, MS. Lansd. 41. Stockwood, in a Sermon Preached at Paules Crosse the 24 of August, 1578, indignantly asks,—"wyll not a fylthye playe wyth the blast of a trumpette sooner call thyther a thousande than an houres tolling of a bell bring to the sermon a hundred?—nay, even heere in the Citie, without it be at this place and some other certaine ordinarie audience, where shall you finde a reasonable company?—whereas, if you resorte to the Theatre, the Curtayne and other places of playes in the Citie, you shall on the Lords Day have these places, with many other that I cannot recken, so full as possible they can throng;" and, in reference again to the desecration of the Sunday at the Theatre, he says,—"if playing in the Theatre or any other place in London, as there are by sixe that I know to many, be any of the Lordes wayes, whiche I suppose there is none so voide of knowledge in the world wil graunt, then not only it may but ought to be used; but if it be any of the wayes of man, it is no work for the Lords sabaoth, and therfore in no respecte tollerable on that daye." It was upon a Sunday, two years afterwards, in April, 1580, that there was a great disturbance at the same establishment, the only record of which that has come under my notice is in a letter from the Lord Mayor of London to the Privy Council dated April 12th,—"where it happened on Sundaie last that some great disorder was committed at the Theatre, I sent for the undershireve of Middlesex to understand the cercumstances, to the intent that by myself or by him I might have caused such redresse to be had as in dutie and discretion I might, and therefore did also send for the plaiers to have apered afore me, and the rather because those playes doe make assembles of cittizens and their familes of whome I have charge; but forasmuch as I understand that your Lordship with other of hir Majesties most honorable Counsell have entered into examination of that matter, I have surceassed to procede further, and do humbly refer the whole to your wisdomes and grave considerations; howbeit, I have further thought it my dutie to informe your Lordship, and therewith also to beseche to have in your honorable rememberance, that the players of playes which are used at the Theatre and other such places, and tumblers and such like, are a very superfluous sort of men and of suche facultie as the lawes have disalowed, and their exersise of those playes is a great hinderaunce of the service of God, who hath with His mighty hand so lately admonished us of oure earnest repentance," City of London MSS. The Lord Mayor here of course alludes to the great earthquake which had occurred a few days previously. In June, 1584, there was a disturbance just outside the Theatre, thus narrated in a letter to Lord Burghley,—"uppon Weddensdaye one Browne, a serving man in a blew coat, a shifting fellowe, havinge a perrelous witt of his owne, entending a sport if he cold have browght it to passe, did at Theater doore querell with certen poore boyes, handicraft prentises, and strooke somme of theym; and lastlie he, with his sword, wondeid and maymed one of the boyes upon the left hand, whereupon there assembled nere a thousand people;—this Browne dyd very cuninglie convey hymself awaye." The crowds of disorderly people frequenting the Theatre are thus alluded to in Tarlton's Newes out of Purgatorie, 1590,—"upon Whitson monday last I would needs to the Theatre to see a play, where, when I came, I founde such concourse of unrulye people that I thought it better solitary to walk in the fields then to intermeddle myselfe amongst such a great presse." In 1592, there was an apprehension that the London apprentices might indulge in riots on Midsummer-night, in consequence of which the following order was issued by the Lords of the Council,—"moreover for avoydinge of thes unlawfull assemblies in those quarters, yt is thoughte meete yow shall take order that there be noe playes used in anye place nere thereaboutes, as the Theator, Curtayne or other usuall places there where the same are comonly used, nor no other sorte of unlawfull or forbidden pastymes that drawe togeather the baser sorte of people, from henceforth untill the feast of St. Michaell," MS. Register of the Privy Council, 23 June, 1592. Another allusion to the throngs of the lower orders attracted by the entertainments at the Theatre occurs in a letter from the Lord Mayor of London to the Privy Council dated 13 September, 1595,—"Among other inconvenyences it is not the least that the refuse sort of evill disposed and ungodly people about this Cytie have oportunitie hearby to assemble together and to make their matches for all their lewd and ungodly practizes, being also the ordinary places for all maisterles men and vagabond persons that haunt the high waies to meet together and to recreate themselfes, whearof wee begin to have experienc again within these fiew daies since it pleased her highnes to revoke her comission graunted forthe to the Provost Marshall, for fear of home they retired themselfes for the time into other partes out of his precinct, but ar now retorned to their old haunt, and frequent the plaies, as their manner is, that ar daily shewed at the Theator and Bankside, whearof will follow the same inconveniences, whearof wee have had to much experienc heartofore, for preventing whearof wee ar humble suters to your good Ll. and the rest to direct your lettres to the Justices of Peac of Surrey and Middlesex for the present stay and finall suppressing of the said plaies as well at the Theator and Bankside as in all other places about the Cytie." It is clear from these testimonies that the Theatre attracted a large number of persons of questionable character to the locality, thus corroborating what has been previously stated respecting the degree of responsibility attached to those who undertook the care of the horses belonging to the more respectable portion of the audience.

Two years afterwards, the inconveniences attending the large numbers of people resorting to the Shoreditch theatres culminated in an order of the Privy Council for their removal, a decree which, like several others of a like kind emanating from the same body, was disregarded. The order appeared in the form of a letter to the Justices of Middlesex dated July 28th, 1597, the contents of which are recorded as follows in the Council Register,—"A lettre to Robert Wrothe, William Fleetwood, John Barne, Thomas Fowle and Richard Skevington esquire, and the rest of the Justices of Middlesex nerest to London; Her Majestie being informed that there are verie greate disorders committed in the common playhouses both by lewd matters that are handled on the stages, and by resorte and confluence of bad people, hathe given direction that not onlie no plaies shal be used within London or about the Citty or in any publique place during this tyme of sommer, but that also those playhouses that are erected and built only for suche purposes shal be plucked downe, namelie the Curtayne and the Theatre nere to Shorditch, or any other within that county; theis are therfore in her Majesties name to chardge and commaund you that you take present order there be no more plaies used in any publique place within three myles of the Citty untill Alhallontide next, and likewyse that you do send for the owner of the Curtayne Theatre or anie other common playhouse, and injoyne them by vertue hereof forthwith to plucke downe quite the stages, galleries and roomes that are made for people to stand in, and so to deface the same as they maie not be ymploied agayne to suche use, which yf they shall not speedely performe you shall advertyse us that order maie be taken to see the same don according to her Majesties pleasure and commaundment." This order appears to have been issued in consequence of representations made by the Lord Mayor in a letter written on the same day to the Privy Council, in which he observes,—" wee have fownd by th'examination of divers apprentices and other servantes whoe have confessed unto us that the saide staige playes were the very places of theire randevous appoynted by them to meete with such otheir as wear to joigne with them in theire designes and mutinus attemptes, beeinge allso the ordinarye places for maisterles men to come together to recreate themselves, for avoydinge wheareof wee are nowe againe most humble and earnest suitors to your honors to dirrect your lettres as well to ourselves as to the Justices of Peace of Surrey and Midlesex for the present staie and fynall suppressinge of the saide stage playes as well at the Theatre, Curten and Banckside, as in all other places in and abowt the Citie," City of London MSS. The players wisely erected all their regular theatres in the suburbs, the Mayor and Corporation of the City having been virulently opposed to the drama throughout the reigns of Elizabeth and James.

The crowds which flocked to places of entertainment were reasonably supposed to increase the danger of the spread of infection during the prevalence of an epidemic, and the Theatre and Curtain were sometimes ordered to be closed on that account. The Lord Mayor of London in a letter to Sir Francis Walsingham, dated May 3rd, 1583, thus writes in reference to the plague,—"Among other we finde one very great and dangerous inconvenience, the assemblie of people to playes, beare-bayting, fencers and prophane spectacles at the Theatre and Curtaine and other like places, to which doe resorte great multitudes of the basist sort of people and many enfected with sores runing on them, being out of our jurisdiction, and some whome we cannot descerne by any dilligence and which be otherwise perilous for contagion, biside the withdrawing from Gods service, the peril of ruines of so weake byldinges and the avancement of incontinencie and most ungodly confederacies," City of London MSS. In the spring of the year 1586 plays at the Theatre were prohibited on account of the danger of infection, as appears from the following note in the Privy Council Register under the date of May 11th,—"A lettre to the L. Maior; his l. is desired, according to his request made to their Lordshippes by his lettres of the vij.th of this present, to geve order for the restrayning of playes and interludes within and about the Cittie of London, for th'avoyding of infection feared to grow and increase this tyme of sommer by the comon assemblies of people at those places, and that their Lordshippes have taken the like order for the prohibiting of the use of playes at the Theater and th'other places about Newington out of his charge,"—MS. Register preserved at the Privy Council Office.

The preceding document of July, 1597, contains the latest notice of the Theatre in connexion with dramatic entertainments which has yet been discovered. It is alluded to in Skialetheia, published in the following year, 1598, as being then closed,—" but see yonder == One, like the unfrequented Theater, == Walkes in darke silence and vast solitude." James Burbage on September 17th, 1579, assigned his Shoreditch estate to one John Hyde, who held it till June 7th, 1589 (Coram Rege Rolls, 44 Eliz.), upon which day the latter surrendered his interest in it to Cuthbert Burbage. The assignment to Hyde may have been a security for a loan. At all events, James Burbage appears to have retained the legal estate and to have continued to deal with the property, so far as litigation was concerned, as if it were his own, and at the time of his death, which took place early in 1597, he was involved in a law-suit respecting the estate, this circumstance so embarrassing his successors that they found it difficult to carry on the management of the Theatre. According to the statement made by the family to Lord Pembroke in 1635, James Burbage "was the first builder of playhowses, and was himselfe in his younger yeeres a player; the Theater hee built with many hundred poundes taken up at interest; hee built this house upon leased ground, by which meanes the landlord and hee had a great suite in law, and, by his death, the like troubles fell on us, his sonnes." See the petition given in the Appendix, p. 90, being one of a curious series of papers enrolled in a contemporary volume amongst the Lord Chamberlain's manuscripts, the fac-simile of a leaf of which here annexed includes the passage just quoted. There is some difficulty in reconciling the various statements respecting the devolution of the estate, but the one most likely to be correct is that made by Allen, who asserted that James Burbage, previously to his decease, made a deed of gift of the property to his two sons, Cuthbert and Richard.

It is worth recording that, shortly before the death of the elder Burbage in 1597, negociations were pending with Allen for a considerable extension of the lease, with a stipulation, however, assigning a limited period only for the continuation of theatrical amusements. Allen's statement is that "the said Jeames Burbage grewe to a newe agreement that the said Jeames Burbage should have a newe lease of the premisses conteyned in the former lease for the terme of one and twenty yeares to beginne after the end and expiracion of the former lease for the yearlie rent of foure and twentie powndes, for the said Jeames Burbage, in respect of the great proffitt and commoditie which he had made and in time then to come was further likelye to make of the Theatre and the other buildinges and growndes to him demised, was verye willinge to paie tenn powndes yearelye rent more then formerlie he paid; and it was likewise further agreed betweene them, as the defendant hopeth he shall sufficientlie prove, that the said Theatre should continue for a playinge place for the space of five yeares onelie after the expiracion of the first terme and not longer, by reason that the defendant sawe that many inconveniences and abuses did growe therby, and that after the said five yeares ended it should be converted by the said Jeames Burbage and the complainant or one of them to some other use," Answer of Gyles Allen in the suit of Burbage v. Allen, Court of Requests, 42 Eliz. Cuthbert Burbage, in his Replication, denies that his father consented to entertain the suggestion "that the said Theater should contynue for a playinge place for the space of fyve yeres onelie after the first terme and no longer." In confirmation, however, of Allen's version of the facts, there is the testimony of a witness named Thomas Nevill, who positively declared that "there was an agreemente had betweene them, the said complainante and the said defendantes, for the howses and growndes with the Theatre which were formerlye demised unto Jeames Burbage, the father of the said complainante, with an increasinge of the rente from fourteene powndes by the yeare unto foure and twentye

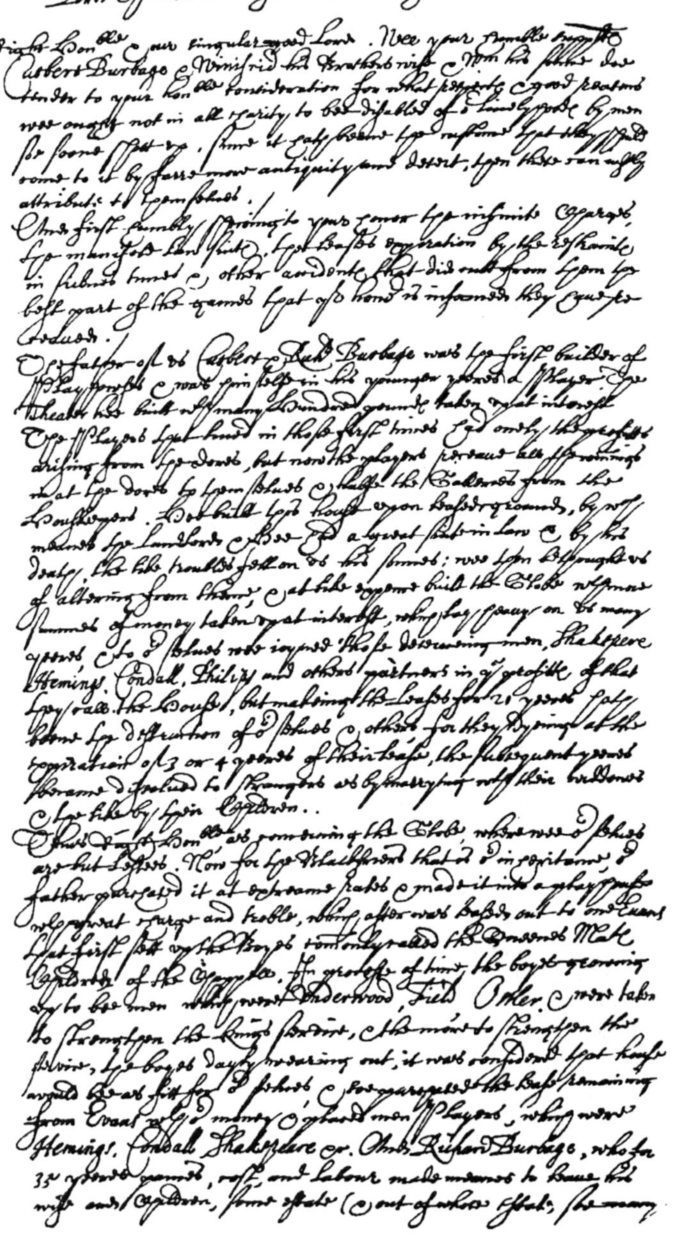
To ye Right Honble Philip Earle of Pembroke & Montgomery
Lord Chamberlaine of his Mats Houshold.

Facsimile of the Commencement of the Petition of the Burbages to the Earl of Pembroke and Montgomery, in the year 1635, respecting Shares in the Globe and Blackfriars' Theatres. From a contemporary Transcript preserved in the Lord Chamberlain's Office.

powndes by the yeare, which lease should beginn at the expiracion of the ould lease made unto the said complainantes father and should continue for the space of one and twentye yeares; and this deponente further saieth that the said defendant was at the firste verrye unwillinge that the said Theatre should continue one daie longer for a playinge place, yet neverthelesse at the laste he yealded that it should continue for a playinge place for certaine yeares, and that the said defendante did agree that the said complainante should after those yeares expired converte the said Theatre to his beste benifitt for the residue of the said terme then to come, and that afterward it should remaine to the onelye use of the defendante," MS. Depositions in the Suit of Burbage v. Allen taken at Kelvedon, co. Essex, in August, 1600.

The year 1597 was a critical one for the Burbages in respect to their Shoreditch estate. The original lease given by Allen expired in the Spring, and they could not succeed in obtaining a legal ratification of the additional ten years covenanted to be granted to the lessee, although they were still permitted to remain as tenants. Bewildered by this uncertainty of the tenure, they resolved in the following year not only to abandon the Theatre, but to take advantage of a condition in the original lease and remove it with the whole of the materials, a step which had at least the advantage of throwing the initiative of further litigation upon Allen. The stipulation in the lease of 1576 here mentioned was to the effect that if Burbage, at any time during the first ten years of the term, expended the sum of £200 upon the improvement of the estate, he should be at liberty "to have, take downe and carie awaye to his and their owne proper use for ever all suche buildinges and other thinges as should be builded, erected or sette uppe in or uppon the gardeins and voyde growndes by the saide indenture graunted, or anie parte therof, by the saide James his executors or assignees, either for a theator or playinge place, or for anie other lawfull use for his or their comodities," lease of 1576 as quoted in a Bill of Complaint, Burbage v. Allen, 42 Eliz. Streete expressly declares that it was originally agreed that the same clause should form a part of the extended lease,—"et ulterius predictus Egidius Alleyn et Sara uxor ejus convenerunt et concesserunt, pro seipsis heredibus executoribus et assignatis suis, et quilibet eorum separatim convenit et concessit prefato Jacobo Burbage, executoribus et assignatis suis, quod licitum foret eidem Jacobo, executoribus seu assignatis suis, in consideratione impenditionis et expositionis predictis ducentarum librarum, modo et forma predicta, ad aliquod tempus et tempora ante finem predicti termini viginti et unius annorum per predictam indenturam concessi, aut ante finem predicti termini viginti et unius annorum post confectionem indenture predicte, virtute ejusdem indenture concedendi, habere, diruere et abcariare ad ejus aut eorum proprium usum imperpetuum, omnia talia edificia et omnes alias res qualia edificata erecta aut supposita forent, Anglice *sett upp*, in et super gardino et locis vacuis, Anglice *the growndes*, per indenturam predictam concessa, aut aliqua parte inde, per predictum Jacobum executores vel assignatos suos, aut pro theatro vocato *a theater or playinge place*, aut pro aliquo alio licito usu pro ejus aut eorum commoditate." It is accordingly found that the stipulation is inserted as follows in the proposed lease of 1585,—"and further the sayde Gyles Allen and Sara his wyfe for them, their heres, executors and administrators, doe covenante and graunte, and every of them severally covenanteth and graunteth, to and with the sayde Jeames Burbage his executors and assignes by thes presentes, that yt shall or may be lawfull for the sayde Jeames Burbage his executors or assignes, in consideracion for the imployinge and bestowinge of the foresayde some of cc.*li*. mencioned in the sayde former indenture, at any tyme or tymes before the ende of the sayde terme of xxj. yeares by thes presentes granted, to have, take downe and carrye awaye, to his and their owne proper use for ever, all such buildinges and other thinges as are alredye builded, erected and sett upp, and which hereafter shal be builded erected or sett upp in or upon the gardings and voyde grounds by thes presentes graunted or any parte therof by the sayde Jeames, his executors or assignes, eyther for a theater or playinge place, or for any other lawfull use for his or theire comodityes." It is unnecessary to enter further into a discussion on the legal intricacies which arose in the suits between the parties, the only topics of present interest in the voluminous proceedings being those which throw light on the history of the Theatre. It was Allen's intention, to use his own words, "seeing the greate and greevous abuses that grewe by the Theater, to pull downe the same and to converte the wood and timber therof to some better use;" but in this design he was anticipated by the Burbages, who engaged one Peter Streete, a builder and carpenter, to remove the building, which operation was accordingly effected in December, 1598, or in January, 1599.

The narrative given by Allen of the demolition of the Theatre and the removal of the "wood and timber" to Southwark, where the materials were afterwards used in the construction of the Globe, is particularly interesting. As has just been stated, Allen had himself contemplated the destruction of the Theatre and the conversion of its materials to some other use, but Cuthbert Burbage, anticipating the design,—"unlawfullye combyninge and confederating himselfe with the sayd Richard Burbage and one Peeter Streat, William Smyth and divers other persons, to the number of twelve, to your subject unknowne, did aboute the eight and twentyth daye of December in the one and fortyth yeere of your Highnes raygne, and sythence your highnes last and generall pardon by the confederacye aforesayd, ryoutouslye assemble themselves together, and then and there armed themselves with dyvers and manye unlawfull and offensive weapons, as, namelye, swordes, daggers, billes, axes and such like, and soe armed, did then repayre unto the sayd Theater, and then and there, armed as aforesayd, in verye ryotous, outragious and forcyble manner, and contrarye to the lawes of your highnes realme, attempted to pull downe the sayd Theater; whereuppon divers of your subjectes, servauntes and farmers, then goinge aboute in peaceable manner to procure them to desist from that their unlawfull enterpryse, they the sayd ryotous persons aforesayd notwithstanding procured* then therein with greate vyolence, not onlye then and there forcyblye and ryotouslye resisting your subjectes, servauntes and farmers, but allso then and there pulling, breaking and throwing downe the sayd Theater in verye outragious, violent and riotous sort, to the great disturbance and terrefyeing not onlye of your subjectes sayd servauntes and farmers, but of divers others of your Majesties loving subjectes there neere inhabitinge; and having so done, did then alsoe in most forcible and ryotous manner take and carrye awaye from thence all the wood and timber therof unto the Bancksyde in the parishe of St. Marye Overyes, and there erected a newe playehowse with the sayd timber and woode," Bill of Complaint, Allen v. Burbage, 44 Eliz.

The date here assigned to the removal of the Theatre is December 28th, 1598; but, according to another authority, the event took place on January 20th, 1599, the possibility being that the operation was not completed on the first occasion. The other account to which reference is here made is in the following terms,—"Egidius

Aleyn armiger queritur de Petro Strete, in custodia marescalli marescallie domine Regine coram ipsa Regina existenti, de eo quod ipse, vicesimo die Januarij anno regni domine Elizabethe nunc Regine Anglie quadragesimo primo, vi et armis &c. clausum ipsius Egidii vocatum *the Inner Courte Yarde*, parcellum nuper monasterii prioratus de Hallywell modo dissoluti apud Hallywell, fregit et intravit, et herbam ipsius Egidii ad valenciam quadraginta solidorum adtunc in clauso predicto crescentem pedibus suis ambulando conculcavit et consumpsit; et quandam structuram ipsius Egidii ibidem fabricatam et erectam vocatam *the Theater* ad valenciam septingentarum librarum adtunc et ibidem diruit, divulsit, cepit et abcariavit, et alia enormia ei intulit contra pacem dicte domine Regine ad dampnum ipsius Egidii octingentarum librarum," Coram Rege Rolls, 42 Eliz. The Inner Court Yard was situated to the west of the Lower Gate, as appears from other evidences. In an Answer filed in a suit in the Court of Requests, February, 42 Elizabeth, Allen declares that he was absent in the country at the time of the removal of the building, the date of that event which is given in this Answer certainly being erroneous. According to the Defendant's statement, Cuthbert Burbage "sought to take occasion when he might privilie and for his best advantage pull downe the said Theatre, which aboute the Feast of the Nativitie of our Lord God in the fourtith yeare of her Majesties raigne he hath caused to be done without the privitie or consent of the defendant, he beinge then in the countrie." A mistake is here made in the number of the regnal year. There can be no doubt of the fact that it was in the course of the month of December, 1598, or January, 1599, that the greater portion at least of the Theatre was removed. It may be questioned if Burbage's agents had succeeded in carrying away the whole of the materials of the structure. At all events, in January, 1600, he speaks of having taken away only "parte of the building." In his Bill against Allen in the Court of Requests, speaking of the expectation that the Defendant intended ultimately to renew the original lease for ten years, he observes,—"by reason wherof your subjecte did forbeare to pull downe and carie awaye the tymber and stuffe ymployed for the said Theater and playinge house at the ende of the saide first tearme of one and twentie yeares, as by the directe covenaunte and agreemente expressed in the saide indenture he mighte have done, but after the saide firste tearme of one and twentie yeares ended the saide Alleyne hathe suffred your subjecte to contynue in possession of the premisses for diverse yeares, and hathe accepted the rente reserved by the saide indenture from your subjecte, wheruppon of late your saide subjecte, havinge occasion to use certayne tymber and other stuffe which weare ymploied in makinge and errectinge the saide Theator uppon the premisses, beinge the cheefeste proffitte that your subjecte hoped for in the bargayne therof, did to that purpose, by the consente and appointmente of Ellen Burbadge, administratrix of the goodes and chattells of the saide James Burbage, take downe and carie awaye parte of the saide newe buildinge, as by the true meaninge of the saide indenture and covenauntes lawfull was for him to doe, and the same did ymploye to other uses." In another part of the same Bill, however, he alludes to Peter Streete, who by his "direction and comaundment did enter uppon the premisses and take downe the saide buildinge;" and Streete himself admitted the fact in his Answer to a suit of trespass brought against him by Allen early in 1599,—" et quoad venire vi et armis, ac tot et quicquid quod est suppositum fieri contra pacem dicte domine Regine, nunc, preter fractionem et intracionem in clausum predictum et herbe predicte conculcationem et consumptionem, necnon diruptionem, divulsionem, captionem et abcariationem predicte structure vocate *the Theater*, idem Petrus dicit quod ipse in nullo est inde culpabilis." The second statement of Cuthbert Burbage on the subject, in his Replication in the suit of Burbage v. Allen, April, 1600, which perhaps may be considered of better authority than his previous account, seems to confirm the evidence given by Streete,—"and this complainant doth not denie but that he hathe pulled downe the said Theatre, which this complainant taketh it was laufull for him so to do, beinge a thinge covenaunted and permitted in the said former leas." Whether any remains of the Theatre were left standing or not, it is certain that the building, so far as it is connected with the history of the stage, may be considered to have been removed by the month of January, 1599.

A few of the dramas which were performed at the Theatre are mentioned by contemporary writers. Gosson, in his Schoole of Abuse, 1579, speaks of,—"the Blacksmiths Daughter and Catilins Conspiracies, usually brought in to the Theater; the firste contayning the trechery of Turkes, the honourable bountye of a noble minde, and the shining of vertue in distresse; the last, bicause it is knowen too be a pig of myne owne sowe, I will speake the lesse of it, onely giving you to understand that the whole marke which I shot at in that woorke was too showe the rewarde of traytors in Catilin, and the necessary government of learned men in the person of Cicero, which forsees every danger that is likely to happen and forstalles it continually ere it take effect." The Play of Plays, a moral drama in defence of plays, was acted at the same establishment in February, 1581-2,—"the Playe of Playes showen at the Theater the three and twentieth of Februarie last," Gosson's Playes Confuted in Five Actions, n. d. Another kind of performance had been selected on the previous day, as appears from the following obscure notice in a contemporary journal preserved in MS. Addit. 5008,—"1582. Feb. 22, we went to the Theater to se a scurvie play set owt al by one virgin, which ther proved a fyemarten without voice, so that we stayd not the matter." A marginal note describes this mysterious entertainment as "a virgin play." About this period "the history of Cæsar and Pompey and the playe of the Fabii" were acted at the same place, as we are told by Gosson in his Playes Confuted; and mention is made in the same work of "that glosing plaie at the Theater which profers you so faire," but in which there was "enterlaced a baudie song of a maide of Kent and a litle beastly speach of the new stawled roge, both which I am compelled to burie in silence, being more ashamed to utter them then they; for as in tragedies some points are so terrible that the poets are constrayned to turne them from the peoples eyes, so in the song of the one, the speache of the other, somewhat is so dishonest that I cannot with honestie repeate it," sig. D. 6. Some years afterwards, Lodge, in his Wits Miserie, 1596, speaks of one who "looks as pale as the visard of the ghost which cried so miserally[*] at the Theator, like an oister-wife, *Hamlet, revenge.*" This passage refers to the old play of Hamlet, which Shakespeare might have seen performed at Shoreditch soon after his arrival in London.

According to the account previously quoted from Stow's Survay of London, ed. 1598, p. 349, the Curtain Theatre and the building removed in 1599, the latter distinctively termed the Theatre, were in the same locality. They are both described as being near the site of the dissolved priory, and "both standing on the south-west side towards the Field." The Curtain Theatre, however, was situated on the southern side of Holywell Lane, a little to the westward of the two trees which are seen in Aggas's view in the middle of a field adjoining Holywell Lane. In a document preserved at the Privy Council Office, dated in 1601, this theatre is spoken of as "the Curtaine in Moorefeildes," which shows that it was on the south of that lane. Stow, ed. 1598, p. 351, speaks of Moorfields as extending in ancient times to Holywell, but what were usually called the Moorfields in the days of Shakespeare did not reach so far to the north, so that the description of 1601 must be accepted with some qualification. The Curtain Theatre, as is ascertained by Stow's decisive testimony, could not possibly have stood much to the south of the lane. It must in fact have been situated in or near the place which is marked as Curtain Court in Chassereau's plan of Shoreditch, 1745. This Court was afterwards called Gloucester Row, and it is now known as Gloucester Street.

This theatre derived its name from a piece of ground of considerable size termed the Curtain, which anciently belonged to Holywell Priory. The land is mentioned under that name in a lease of 29 Henry VIII., 1538,—"Sibilla Newdigate, priorissa dicti nuper monasterii sancti Johannis Baptiste de Halliwell predicti, et ejusdem loci conventus, per aliam indenturam suam sigillo eorum conventuali sigillatam, datam primo die Januarij dicto anno vicesimo nono predicti nuper patris nostri, unanimi eorum assensu et consensu dimiserunt, tradiderunt et ad firmam concesserunt prefato nuper Comiti Rutland totam illam mansionem sive mesuagium cum gardino adjacenti, scituatam, jacentem et existentem infra muros et portas ejusdem nuper monasterii, cum illa longa pergula ducente a dicto mesuagio usque ad capellam ; ac duo stabula et unum fenile supra edificatum, scituata et existentia extra portas ejusdem nuper monasterii prope pasturam dicte nuper Priorisse vocatam *the Curten*," Rot. Pat. 27 Eliz., Pars 14. The phrase *extra portas* shows that the Curtain ground was on the southern side of Holywell Lane, the entrance to the priory having been on the north of that road. At a later period there were several buildings, including a large one specially mentioned as the Curtain House (Shoreditch Register), erected upon this land, and one or more were known as being situated in the Curtain Garden. In March, 1581, one William Longe sold to Thomas Harberte,—"all that the house, tenemente or lodge commonlie called the Curtayne, and also all that parcell of grounde and close walled and inclosed with a bricke wall on the west and northe partes, and in parte with a mudde wall at the west side or ende towardes the southe, called also the Curtayne Close, sometyme apperteyning to the late Priorie of Halliwell nowe dissolved, sett, lyeng and being in the parishe of Sainte Leonarde in Shortedytche alias Shordiche in the countie of Middlesex, together with all the gardeyns, fishepond, welles and brick-wall to the premisses or any of them belonginge or apperteyning; and also all and singuler other mesuages, tenementes, edifices and buildinges, with all and singuler their appurtenaunces, erected and builded uppon the saide close called the Curtayne or uppon any parte or parcell thereof, or to the same nere adjoyning, nowe or late in the severall tenures or occupacions of Thomas Wilkinson, Thomas Wilkins, Roberte Medley, Richard Hickes, Henrie Lanman and Roberte Manne, or any of them, or of their or any of their assigne or assignes, and also all other mesuages, landes, tenementes and hereditamentes with their appurtenaunces sett, lyeng and being in Halliwell Lane in the saide parishe of Sainte Leonard," Rot. Claus. 23 Eliz. The Curtain House was either in or near Holywell Lane. "John Edwardes being excommunicated was buried the vij.th of June in the Kinges high waie in Hallywell Lane neare the Curtayn," Register of St. Leonards, Shoreditch, 1619. In some Chancery papers of the year 1591 it is described as the "howse with the appurtenaunces called the Curtayne," and it is stated that " the grounde there was for the most parte converted firste into garden plottes, and then leasinge the same to divers tenauntes caused them to covenaunt or promise to builde uppon the same, by occasion wherof the buildinges which are there were for the most parte errected and the rentes encreased." The name is still retained in the locality in that of the well-known Curtain Road, which must have been so called either from the Curtain Theatre or from the land above described.

The earliest notice of the Curtain Theatre by name, which has yet been discovered, occurs in Northbrooke's Treatise on Dicing, &c., licensed in December, 1577; but it is also probably alluded to, with the Theatre, by one Thomas White, in a Sermon Preached at Pawles Crosse on Sunday the Thirde of November, 1577, in which he says,—"looke but uppon the common playes in London, and see the multitude that flocketh to them and followeth them; beholde *the sumptuous theatre houses,* a continuall monument of Londons prodigalitie and folly." The Queen's Players seem to have acted at the Curtain as well as at the neighbouring theatre. At all events, Tarlton, who belonged to that company, played there, if we may confide in an allusion in one of the Jests (see Appendix, p. 104). If any credit may be given to the blundering evidences of Aubrey, Ben Jonson also was at one time an actor at the Curtain. According to that biographer, he "acted and wrote, but both ill, at the Green Curtaine, a kind of nursery or obscure play-house somewhere in the suburbes, I thinke towards Shoreditch or Clarkenwell." Aubrey is the only authority for the theatre ever having been known as the Green Curtain, one probably of that writer's numerous misstatements.

It has been usually stated, on the authority of a paper dated April 9th, 1604, preserved at Dulwich College (see p. 115), that, on the accession of James, Prince Henry's Company occupied the Curtain; but the wording of that document is ambiguous, and the order in which the theatres are named in it may not necessarily follow that of the companies. According to more precise evidences, Prince Henry's Players in 1606 were acting at the Fortune, and in 1609 the Servants of Queen Anne were certainly performing at " theire nowe usuall houses called the Redd Bull in Clarkenwell and the Curtayne in Hallowell," Rot. Pat. 7 Jac. I., pars 39. In a contemporary rough draft of the licence to Queen Anne's Company the places in which they were acting are mentioned as their " now usuall howsen called the Curtayne and the Bores Head within our county of Middlesex," the latter being no doubt one of the numerous taverns which were then used for dramatic performances. Heath, in his Epigrams, 1610, alludes to the Fool's part in dramas performed at that time at the Globe, Fortune and Curtain. In 1615 was published the "Hector of Germanie or the Palsgrave Prime Elector, a new Play, an honourable Hystorie, as it hath beene publikely acted at the Red Bull and at the Curtaine by a Companie of young Men of this Citie," that is, of this City of London. "A new play called the Duche Painter and the French Branke was allowed to be acted by the Prince's Servants at the Curtayne," Herbert's Diary, 10 June, 1622, cited by Chalmers, Supplemental Apology, 1799, p. 213. It would appear from Vox Graculi, 1623, that the Red Bull and Curtain were famous for the production of " new playes." A story in the Banquet of Jests, 1639, referring no doubt to a period much earlier than the date of that book, thus commences,—" a handsome young fellow having seene a play at the Curtaine comes to William Rowley after the play was done, and entreated him, if his leisure served, that he might give him a pottle of wine to be better acquainted with him." William Rowley was one of the Prince's actors in 1610 when Charles was Duke of York, and he continued to remain in the same company until the death of James the First (account of the King's funeral, MS. in the Lord Chamberlain's Office). No mention of dramatic performances at the Curtain after the accession of Charles the First has been discovered.

Is there decisive evidence that the Lord Chamberlain's Servants acted at the Curtain Theatre previously to the erection of the Globe in 1599? The reply to this question depends upon the interpretation given to the words "Curtaine plaudeties" in the well-known lines on stage-struck Luscus in Marston's Scourge of Villanie, 1598; whether the word *Curtaine* refers to the playhouse, or whether it is merely a synonyme for *theatrical* in reference to the curtains of the stage. The latter explanation appears to be somewhat forced, while the former and more natural one is essentially supported by the fact that Pope and Underwood, both of them belonging to the Lord Chamberlain's Company, were sharers in the Curtain. If the supposition that Marston speaks of the Curtain Theatre be correct, and no doubt can be fairly entertained on that point, it is certain that Shakespeare's tragedy of Romeo and Juliet was there "plaid publiquely by the Right Honourable the L. of Hunsdon his Servants," title-page of ed. 1597. Luscus is represented as infatuated with this play, and the allusion to his "courting Lesbia's eyes" out of his theatrical commonplace-book can but refer to Romeo's impassioned rhapsody on the eyes of Juliet. See the whole of Marston's interesting lines on the subject in the Appendix, p. 121. It may then be safely assumed that Shakespeare's Romeo and Juliet was acted at the Curtain Theatre some time between July 22nd, 1596, the day on which Lord Hunsdon, then Lord Chamberlain of the Household, died, and April 17th, 1597, when his son, Lord Hunsdon, was appointed to that office (Privy Council Register). During those nine months the Company was known as Lord Hunsdon's, but as the same body of actors continued throughout to serve those two noblemen, for the sake of convenience they are here alluded to as the Lord Chamberlain's Servants when that brief interval has been under consideration. The changes which took place in that office are not likely to have affected their occupancy of the Curtain; but any allusion, if there be one, to the Lord Chamberlain's Servants bearing date between August 6th, 1596, and March 5th, 1597, would refer to a company under the patronage of Lord Cobham, who was the Lord Chamberlain during that period. That the members of the other Lord Chamberlain's Company transferred their services to Lord Hunsdon on the death of his father in July, 1596, is shown by the following entry in the accounts of the Treasurer of the Chamber to Queen Elizabeth,—" to John Hemynge and George Bryan, servauntes to the late Lorde Chamberlayne and now servauntes to the Lorde Hunsdon, upon the Councelles warraunte dated at Whitehall xxj. mo die Decembris, 1596, for five enterludes or playes shewed by them before her Majestie on St. Stephans daye at nighte, the sondaye nighte followeing, Twelfe Nighte, one St. Johns daye and on Shrovesunday at nighte laste, the some of xxxiij. *li.* vj. *s.* viij. *d*, and by waye of her Majesties rewarde, xvj. *li.* xiij. *s.* iiij. *d*, in all the some of l. *li.*"

The earliest authentic notice of Shakespeare as a member of the Lord Chamberlain's Company which has hitherto been published is that which occurs in the list of the actors who performed in the comedy of Every Man in his Humour in 1598; but that he was a leading member of that company four years previously, and acted in two plays before Queen Elizabeth in December, 1594, appears from the following interesting memorandum which I had the pleasure of discovering in the accounts of the Treasurer of the Chamber,—"to William Kempe, William Shakespeare and Richarde Burbage, servauntes to the Lord Chamberleyne, upon the Councelles warrant dated at Whitehall xv. to Marcij, 1594, for twoe severall comedies or enterludes shewed by them before her Majestie in Christmas tyme laste paste, viz., upon St. Stephens daye and Innocentes daye xiij. *li.* vj. *s.* viij. *d,* and by waye of her Majesties rewarde vj. *li.* xiij. *s.* iiij. *d,* in all xx. *li.*" This evidence is decisive, and its great importance in several of the discussions respecting Shakespeare's early literary and theatrical career will hereafter be seen. For the present, it is merely considered in reference to the early history of the Lord Chamberlain's Company, the investigation of which is attended with the great difficulty accompanying the scantiness of material. Henry Lord Hunsdon held the post of Lord Chamberlain from the year 1583 until his decease on July 22nd, 1596. As early as 1586 his Company, in conjunction with that of the Lord Admiral, acted at Court before the Queen. "To the servantes of the Lo. Admirall and the Lo. Chamberlaine, uppon the Counsells warrant dated at Grenwich ultimo Januarij, 1585, for a plaie by them presented before her Majestie one Twelfe daie laste paste, x. *li.*," Accounts of the Treasurer of the Chamber, MS. These two companies of players appear to have long continued in the habit of acting together, or at least in friendly connexion with each other in theatrical matters. Henslowe thus distinguishes a list of dramatic performances which commenced in June, 1594,—"In the name of God, amen; begininge at Newington, my Lord Admeralle men and my Lorde Chamberlen men, as folowethe, 1594," MS. at Dulwich College. These words do not necessarily imply that the two companies acted jointly on the same days, or the word *together* would perhaps have been added, as it is in a previous entry in the same manuscript. It may, however, be safely concluded that the Lord Chamberlain's Company of players did act, either jointly with the other company or separately, at Newington in June, 1594, but their engagement with Henslowe could not have been of long duration, for Lord Hunsdon, addressing a letter to the Lord Mayor of London from Nonsuch on October 8th, 1594, thus writes concerning them,—"where my nowe® companie of players have byn accustomed, for the better exercise of their qualitie and for the service of her Majestie if need soe requier, to plaie this winter time within the Citye at the Crosse Kayes in Gratious Street, these are to require and praye your Lordship to permitt and suffer them soe to doe, the which I praie you the rather to doe for that they have undertaken to me that where heretofore they began not their plaies till towardes fower a clock, they will now begin at two and have don betwene fower and five, and will nott use anie drumes or trumpettes att all for the callinge of peopell together, and shal be contributories to the poore of the parishe where they plaie accordinge to their habilities." This interesting notice shows that the Company, which a few weeks afterwards and probably then included Shakespeare, Kemp and Burbage, had been in the habit of playing in the winter time at the Cross Keys in Gracechurch Street and desired to renew their performances at that tavern in the season of 1594-5. It also establishes the fact that they had continued in the habit of acting before the Queen, who bestowed her special patronage on the companies of the Lord Chamberlain and the Lord Admiral. This latter circumstance appears from the following letter addressed by the Lords of the Council "to the Master of the Revelles and Justices of Peace of Middlesex and Surrey," dated February 19th, 1598,—"whereas licence hath bin graunted unto two companies of stage players retayned unto us, the Lord Admyrall and Lord Chamberlain, to use and practise stage playes, whereby they might be the better enhabled and prepared to shew such plaies before her Majestie as they shal be required at tymes meete and accustomed, to which ende they have bin cheeflie licensed and tollerated as aforesaid; and whereas there is also a third company who of late, as wee are informed, have by waie of intrusion used likewise to play, having neither prepared any plaie for her Majestie, nor are bound to yow, the Masters[®] of the Revelles, for perfourming such orders as have bin prescribed and are enjoyned to be observed by the other two companies before mencioned; wee have therefore thought good to require yow upon receipt heereof to take order that the aforesaid third company may be suppressed, and none suffered heereafter to plaie but those two formerlie named belonging to us, the Lord Admyrall and Lord Chamberlaine, unles yow shall receave other direccion from us," MS. Register of Privy Council. There were thus abundant opportunities for the development of the appreciation in which Shakespeare, as we know from other sources, was held by Queen Elizabeth.

There must have been an alteration in the constitution of the Lord Chamberlain's Company at some time between May, 1593, and December, 1594, and there are reasons for believing that the change was one of considerable extent, even if there were not an absolute transfer to it of the actors belonging to another patron. When the Rose Theatre was opened early in 1592, it was occupied by the Servants of Ferdinando Lord Strange, amongst whom was the celebrated Edward Alleyn, who was also at the same time one of the Lord Admiral's Company. Lord Strange's Players were engaged during the Christmas holydays the same year at Hampton Court to act before the Queen,—" a warrant to Sir Thomas Henneage knight, Tresurer of her Majesties Chamber, to paie or cause to be paide to the servantes of the L. Straunge for presenting to[®] three severall plaies before her Majestie at Hampton Courte, viz., the one upon St. John night, the second upon Newe Yeares Eave at night, and the third upon Newe Yeares Day at night, the some of twentie poundes, and by waie of rewarde for the said three plaies the some of tenn poundes, and this shall be your sufficient warrant in that behalf," Privy Council Register, 7 March, 1592-3. In the spring of the following year all actors were forbid to play in the metropolis on account of the plague, and on May 6th, 1593, the following precept was entrusted to Lord Strange's Company by the Lords of the Privy Council,—"whereas it was thought meet that during the time of the infection and continewaunce of the sicknes in the citie of London there shold no plaies or enterludes be usd, for th'avoiding of th'assemblies and concourse of people in anie usual place apointed nere the said Citie; and though the bearers hereof, Edward Allen, servaunt to the right honorable the L. Highe Admiral, William Kemp, Thomas Pope, John Heminges, Augustine Philipes and George Brian, being al one companie, servantes to our verie good the* lord the Lord Strainge, ar restrained their exercize of playing within the said citie and liberties therof, yet it is not therby ment but that they shal and maie, in regard of the service by them don and to be don at the Court, exercize their quallitie of playing comodies, tragedies and such like, in anie other cities, townes and corporacions where the infection is not, so it be not within seaven miles of London or of the Court, that they maie be in the better readines hereafter for her Majesties service whensoever they shal be therunto called; theis therfore shal be to wil and require yow that they maie without their* lett or contradiccion use their said exercize at their most convenient times and places, the accustomed times of devine praiers excepted." Supported by this authority, the Servants of Lord Strange made a theatrical itinerary through the provinces during the summer of 1593. In July they were at Bristol, and it would seem from a letter from Alleyn to his wife, preserved at Dulwich College, that Richard Cowley, who had then arrived at that city from London, may also have belonged to that Company. They were shortly afterwards at Shrewsbury, and apparently acted there jointly with the Lord Admiral's Company. "Item, paid and yeven to my L. Strange and my L. Admyralls players, xl. s," Shrewsbury Corporation MSS., 1593. Now it is certain that Kemp had joined the Lord Chamberlain's Company before Christmas, 1594, and that all the other Servants of Lord Strange, with the exception of Alleyn, who are named in the warrant of May 6th, 1593, were afterwards distinguished members of the former Company, so there appears to be the strongest probability that the main body of Lord Strange's Company transferred their services to Lord Hunsdon, probably on the death of Ferdinando Lord Derby in April, 1594. This nobleman had borne the title of Lord Strange till within a few months of his decease, having succeeded Henry, the fourth earl, in 1593. It may also be worth notice that Lord Strange's Company used sometimes to perform at the Cross Keys in the winter time, the same tavern which is afterwards alluded to as having been selected by the Lord Chamberlain's Servants for their performances at that season.

When Shakespeare acted before Queen Elizabeth in December, 1594, the Court was at Greenwich Palace. "For making ready at Grenewich for the Qu. Majestie against her Highnes coming thether, by the space of viij. daies mense Decembr. 1594, as appereth by a bill signed by the Lord Chamberleyne, viij. li. xiij. s. iiij. d," Accounts of the Treasurer of the Chamber. "To Tho: Sheffeilde, under keaper of her Majesties house at Grenewich for thallowaunce of viij. labourers there three severall nightes, at xij. d the man, by reason it was night woorke, for making cleane the greate chamber, the Presence, the galleries and clossettes, mense Decembr. 1594, xxiiij. s," MS. ibid. The view of the Palace here introduced is taken from one on a much larger scale which was engraved by Basire from an ancient drawing, and published in 1767. This is believed to be the only authentic representation of the building as it appeared at the time of Shakespeare's visit. There are views of the Palace belonging to other periods, and an engraving of modern date purporting to represent it, but the last is really a sketch of a large Elizabethan mansion which stood in the neighbourhood and was removed about twenty years ago.

In the early part of the year 1600 arrangements were made for the erection of the Fortune Theatre near Golden Lane, a spot which was at no considerable distance, not much more than half a mile, from the Curtain Theatre. It was considered by the opponents of theatrical amusements that the permission to establish a new theatre in that part of London should be conditional upon the removal of the older one. Strenuous efforts were accordingly made to induce the Privy Council to insist upon the demolition of the Curtain, and orders were given in June, 1600, to that effect; but, like the previous injunction of 1597, they proved to be altogether inoperative. The Lords of the Council seem indeed to have been aware of the possibility of this result, for, in their letters to the Lord Mayor of London and the Justices of Middlesex, they observe,—"as wee have done our partes in prescribinge the orders, so, unlesse yow perfourme yours in lookinge to the due execution of them, we shall loose our labor, and the wante of redresse must be imputed unto yow and others unto whome it apperteyneth," Privy Council Register, 22 June, 1600. Copies of the Lords' order and their letters will be found in the Appendix, pp. 107, 108, and it appears from the former that Tylney, the Master of the Revels, had stated to the Council "that the house nowe in hand to be builte by the saide Edward Allen is not intended to encrease the number of the playhouses, but to be insteede of another, namely the Curtayne, which is ether to be ruyned and plucked downe or to be put to some other good use." It is not improbable that Allen was anxious for the suppression of the Curtain as a theatre, and was exerting his influence to accomplish that object. The prospects of the new establishment would of course have been improved had the efforts in this direction been successful, but the combined influences of the City authorities and the Privy Council were ineffectual. On the last day of the following year, 1601, the Lords of the Council made another strenuous but fruitless attempt to persuade the magistrates to enforce their order for the suppression of all but the two selected theatres, the Globe and the Fortune.

In the same year in which the Curtain Theatre was ordered to be abolished, some actor who was in the habit of taking the Clown's part at that establishment published a quaint little tract entitled,—" Quips vpon Questions, or a Clownes conceite on occasion offered, bewraying a morallised metamorphoses of changes vpon interrogatories; shewing a litle wit, with a great deale of will: or indeed more desirous to please in it, then to profite by it. Clapt vp by a Clowne of the towne in this last restraint, hauing litle else to doe to make a litle vse of his fickle Muse, and carelesse of carping. By *Clunnyco de Curtanio Snuffe*.—Like as you list, read on and spare not,== Clownes iudge like Clownes, therefore I care not. *Or thus*,—Floute me, Ile floute thee: it is my profession,==To iest at a Iester, in his transgression.—Imprinted at London for W. Ferbrand, and are to be sold at the signe of the Crowne ouer against the Mayden head neare Yeldhall. 1600." There is an edition of 1601 mentioned in the Catalogus Bibliothecæ Harleianæ, 1745, v. 213, and another of 1602 is also noticed in the same work, 1744, iii. 357. The title-page is nearly the most curious part of the book, which consists mainly of dull questions with replies equally unentertaining, both written in verse. There is a burlesque dedication, subscribed *Clunnico Snuffe*, addressed to "the right worthy Sir Timothie Truncheon alias Bastinado, ever my part-taking friende, Clunnico de Curtanio sendeth greeting." In the spring of the following year, 1601, complaints were made that the actors at the Curtain Theatre had covertly satirized living individuals of good position in some of their plays. It is not known to which of the companies they belonged. With the view of terminating these irregularities the Lords of the Privy Council addressed the following letter to "certaine Justices of the Peace in the county of Middlesex" on May 10th, 1601, —" wee do understand that certaine players, that use to recyte their playes at the Curtaine in Moorefeildes, do represent upon the stage in their interludes the persons of some gent. of good desert and quallity that are yet alive under obscure manner, but yet in such sorte as all the hearers may take notice both of the matter and the persons that are meant thereby. This beinge a thinge very unfitte, offensive and contrary to such direccion as have bin heretofore taken that no plaies should be openly shewed but such as were first perused and allowed, and that might minister no occasion of offence or scandall, wee do hereby require you that you do forthwith forbidd those players to whomsoever they appertaine that do play at the Courtaine in Moorefeildes to represent any such play, and that you will examine them who made that play and to shew the same unto you, and as you in your discrecions shall thincke the same unfitte to be publiquely shewed to forbidd them from henceforth to play the same eyther privately or publiquely; and yf upon veiwe of the said play you shall finde the subject so odious and inconvenient as is informed, wee require you to take bond of the cheifest of them to aunswere their rashe and indiscreete dealing before us," MS. Register of the Privy Council. The performances at the Curtain were no doubt of a very miscellaneous character. Wither, in his Abuses Stript and Whipt, 1613, describing a paltry braggadocio, says, perhaps in contempt of the plays there exhibited,—" His poetry is such as he can cull,==From plaies he heard at Curtaine or at Bull." In the same work there is an allusion to the jigs or ludicrous ballads for which the Curtain Theatre appears to have been celebrated,—" And undeserv'd base fellowes, whom meere time==Hath made sufficient to bring forth a rime,==A Curtaine jigge, a libell or a ballet,=For fidlers or some roagues with staffe and wallet=To sing at doores." Performances of the legitimate drama were, however, undoubtedly sometimes exhibited at the Curtain Theatre. Guilpin, in his Skialetheia, 1598, writes,—" or if my dispose=Perswade me to a play, I'le to the Rose,=Or Curtaine, one of Plautus Comedies,=Or the patheticke Spaniards tragedies." In the last line the author may allude to the celebrated Spanish Tragedy.

The puritanical writers of the time of Shakespeare were indignant at the erection of regular theatrical establishments, and the Theatre and Curtain were the special objects of their invective. They are continually named together as sinks of all wickedness and abomination. In Northbrooke's Treatise, 1577-8, Youth asks,— "doe you speake against those places also whiche are made uppe and builded for such playes and enterludes, as the Theatre and Curtaine is, and other suche lyke places besides?" By "other *suche lyke* places," that is, similar places, the writer perhaps alludes to houses or taverns in which interludes were performed, speaking of such buildings generally, the construction of the sentence not necessarily implying that he refers to other edifices built especially for dramatic representations. Age replies,— " yea, truly, for I am persuaded that Satan hath not a more speedie way and fitter schoole, to work and teach his desire to bring men and women into his snare of concupiscence and filthie lustes of wicked whoredome, than those places and playes and theatres are, and therefore necessarie that those places and players shoulde be forbidden and dissolved and put downe by authoritie, as the brothell houses and stewes are." The effects of the great earthquake of April, 1580, were felt generally throughout London as well as at the theatres, but Stubbes affects to consider it a "fearfull judgement of God" on the wickedness of the stage,—" the like judgement almost did the Lord shewe unto them a little before, beyng assembled at their theaters to see their baudie enterludes and other trumperies practised, for He caused the yearth mightely to shake and quaver as though all would have fallen downe, wherat the people, sore amazed, some leapt down from the top of the turrets, pinacles and towers where thei stood to the grounde, whereof some had their legges broke, some their armes, some their backes, some hurt one where, some another, and many sore crusht and brused, but not any but thei went awaie sore afraied and wounded in conscience," Anatomie of Abuses, 1583. The allusion to "turrets, pinacles and towers" would seem to be a metaphorical flourish. In the Refutation of the Apology for Actors, 1615, pp. 43, 44, where the narrative of Stubbes is quoted, the passage in question is thus altered,—"some leapt downe to the ground from the tops of turrets and galleries where they sate." According to Munday,—"at the play-houses the people came running foorth, supprised* with great astonishment," View of Sundry Examples, 1580. "The earthquake that hapned in the yeere 1580 on the sixt of April, that shaked not only the scenicall Theatre but the great stage and theatre of the whole land," Gardnier's Doomes-day Booke, 1606. At the time of this earthquake the only theatres in England were situated in Shoreditch, and there is evidence that the effects of it were felt in that locality. "Also in Shordiche and other places fell chymneys, as at Mr. Alderman Osburns in Fyllpot Lane fell a pece of a chymney," MS. Diary, 6 April, 1580. Again, when Field wrote his Godly Exhortation upon the accident which occurred at Paris Garden in January, 1583, he could not resist the introduction of adverse criticism on the Shoreditch theatres,—"surely it is to be feared, beesides the distruction bothe of bodye and soule that many are brought unto by frequenting the Theater, the Curtin and such like, that one day those places will likewise be cast downe by God himselfe, and being drawen with them a huge heape of such contempners and prophane persons utterly to be killed and spoyled in their bodyes." This is, however, moderate language in comparison with the exaggerated invective of Stubbes in the same year. After alluding to the Theatre and Curtain as "Venus pallaces," he writes, here speaking generally of plays and theatres,—"doe they not maintaine bawdrié, insinuat foolerie and renue the remembraunce of Heathen idolatrie? Doe thei not induce whoredome and uncleannesse? Nay, are thei not rather plaine devourers of maidenly virginitie and chastitie? For proofe whereof but marke the flockyng and runnyng to Theaters and Curtens daylie and hourelie, night and daie, tyme and tide, to see playes and enterludes, where suche wanton gestures, such bawdie speeches, suche laughyng and flearyng, suche kissyng and bussyng, suche clippyng and culling, such wincking and glauncing of wanton eyes and the like is used as is wonderfull to beholde," Anatomie of Abuses, ed. 1583. This passage is introduced, with variations, in the Refutation of the Apology for Actors, 1615, p. 61. Rankins, in his Mirrour of Monsters, 1587, observes that "the Theater and Curtine may aptlie be termed for their abhomination, the chappell adulterinum." It was not surprising that these attacks provoked retaliation, so the absurdities of the Martin Marprelate clique were unmercifully ridiculed at the Theatre, as appears from a marginal note, *The Theater*, to the following passage in Martins Months Minde, 1589,— "as first, drie beaten and therby his bones broken; then whipt, that made him winse; then wormd and launced, that he tooke verie grievouslie to be made a Maygame upon the stage." It is afterwards stated that "everie stage plaier made a jest of him." Some of these theatrical satires were so virulent that their performance was forbidden. "Would those comedies might be allowed to be plaid that are pend, and then I am sure he would be decyphered and so perhaps discouraged," Pappe with an Hatchet, n. d. The Theatre and Curtain are again named together by Rainolds, in his Overthrow of Stage Playes, 1599, written in 1593, but there merely in reference to male actors being permitted to wear the costume of the other sex.

Although the denunciations of the Puritans were grounded upon exaggerated statements, there can be little doubt that both these theatres were frequented by some disreputable characters. "In the playhouses at London," observes Gosson in his Playes Confuted, sig. G. 6,—"it is the fashion of youthes to go first into the yarde and to carry theire eye through every gallery; then like unto ravens, where they spye the carion thither they flye and presse as nere to the fairest as they can; instead of pomegranates they give them pippines, they dally with their garments to passe the time, they minister talke upon al occasions, and eyther bring them home to theire houses on small acquaintance or slip into taverns when the plaies are done. He thinketh best of his painted sheath, and taketh himselfe for a jolly fellow, that is noted of most to be busyest with women in all such places." The independent testimony of the author of the Newes from the North, 1579, is to a similar effect,—"I have partely shewed you heere what leave and libertie the common people, namely youth, hath to followe their owne lust and desire in all wantonnes and dissolution of life; for further proofe wherof I call to witnesse the Theaters, Courtaines, heaving houses, rifling boothes, bowling alleyes and such places where the time is so shamefully mispent, namely the Sabaoth dayes, unto the great dishonor of God and the corruption and utter destruction of youth." In Anthony Babington's Complaint, written by R. Williams, the former, who was executed in 1586, is represented as saying,—"to bee a good lawier my mynde woulde not frame,=I addicted was to pleasure and given so to game;=But to the Theatre and Curtayne woulde often resorte,=Where I mett companyons fittinge my disporte," MS. Arundel 418. It appears from Nash's Pierce Penilesse, 1592, and several other authorities, that the neighbouring village of Shoreditch was distinguished by the number of houses which were inhabited by the frail sisterhood. In Skialetheia, 1598, mention is made of an old citizen, "who, comming from the Curtaine, sneaketh in=To some odde garden noted house of sinne;" and West, in a rare poem, the Court of Conscience, 1607, tells a libertine,—"Towards the Curtaine then you must be gon,=The garden alleyes paled on either side;=Ift be too narrow walking, there you slide." Compare also a line in a poem of the time of James I. in MS. Harl. 2127,—" Friske to the Globe or Curtaine with your trull."

Little is known respecting the dimensions and structure of either the Theatre or the Curtain. In Stockwood's Sermon Preached at Paules Crosse the 24 of August, 1578, they are alluded to as having been erected at a large cost, while the former is termed a "gorgeous" playing-place,—"what should I speake of beastlye playes againste which out of this place every man crieth out? have we not houses of purpose built with great charges for the maintainance of them, and that without the Liberties, as who woulde say,—there, let them saye what they will say, we wil play. I know not how I might with the godly learned especially more discommende the gorgeous playing place erected in the fieldes than to terme it, as they please to have it called, a Theatre, that is, even after the maner of the olde heathnish theatre at Rome, a shew place of al beastly and filthie matters, to the which it can not be chosen that men should resort without learning thence muche corruption." The Theatre is mentioned in 1601 as "the late greate howse," and that it was correctly so designated would appear from the proceedings of a Chancery Suit, Braynes v. Burbage, 1590, in which it is stated that James Burbage at the time of its erection had borrowed the sum of £600 for the express object of defraying the greater portion of the cost. This agrees with an assertion made by Burbage's descendants in 1635 that "the Theater hee built with many hundred poundes taken up at interest." Allen, the freeholder, stated in 1601 his belief that the Theatre was "erected att the costes and charges of one Braynes, and not of James Burbage, to the value of one thousand markes," that is, between £600 and £700, a large sum at the period at which it was built. When the Theatre was removed in 1599, Allen (see p. 26) estimated the value of the building at £700. This Braynes was the father-in-law of James Burbage. The consideration given for the money advanced by this person must have sadly interfered with the profits derived by Burbage from the Theatre, which was doubtlessly a good speculation in itself. Allen, indeed, speaks of a profit of £2000 having been realized from it. "And further whereas the complainant," observes Allen, referring to Cuthbert Burbage, "supposeth that the said Jeames Burbage his father did to his great chardges erecte the said Theatre, and therby pretendeth that there should be the greater cause in equitie to releive him, the complainant, for the same, hereunto the defendant saieth that, consideringe the great proffitt and benifitt which the said Jeames Burbage and the complainant in their severall times have made therof, which, as the defendant hath credibilie hard, doth amounte to the somme of twoe thousand powndes at the least, the defendant taketh it they have been verie sufficientlye recompensed for their chardges which they have bestowed uppon the said Theatre or uppon anie other buildinges there," Answer of Gyles Allen in the suit of Burbage v. Allen, Court of Requests, 42 Eliz. Cuthbert Burbage, in his Replication, denies "that the said James Burbadge or this complaynant hathe made twoo thousand poundes proffitt and benefitt by the said theatre." Nothing is here said respecting the material of which the edifice was constructed, but in another paper in the same suit he alludes to "certayne tymber and *other* stuffe ymploied in makinge and erectinge the Theator." That the building was mainly constructed of wood cannot, however, admit of a doubt, it being spoken of continually in the legal papers of more than one of the Burbage suits as a structure of "wood and timber," materials which James Burbage, being a joiner, would naturally have selected. "The said defendant Cuthbert Burbage being well able to justifie the pullinge downe, usinge and disposinge of the woodde and tymber of the saide playehowse," Answer of the Burbages, 44 Eliz. The Lord Mayor, in a letter written in April, 1583, speaks, in reference to the Theatre, of "the weakenesse of the place for ruine," alluding perhaps to the wooden scaffolds inside the building.

Although entertainments took place both at the Theatre and at the Curtain during the winter months, there can be but little doubt that the roof in each of these buildings merely covered the stage and galleries, the pit or yard being open to the sky. This was certainly the case in the latter theatre. The author of Vox Graculi or Jack Dawes Prognostication, 1623, describing the characteristics of the month of April, observes,—"about this time new playes will be in more request then old, and if company come currant to the Bull and Curtaine, there will be more money gathered in one after-noone then will be given to Kingsland Spittle in a whole moneth; also, if, at this time, about the houres of foure and five it waxe cloudy, and then raine downeright, they shall sit dryer in the galleries then those who are the understanding men in the yard."

The charge for admission to the Theatre was a penny, but this sum merely entitled the visitor to standing room in the lower part of the house. If he wanted to enter any of the galleries another penny was demanded, and even then a good seat was not always secured without a repetition of the fee. None who go, observes Lambard, "to Paris Gardein, the Bell Savage or Theatre, to beholde beare baiting, enterludes or fence play, can account of any pleasant spectacle unlesse they first pay one pennie at the gate, another at the entrie of the scaffolde, and the thirde for a quiet standing," Perambulation of Kent, ed. 1596, p. 233, one of the passages in that edition not found in ed. 1576. The author of Pappe with an Hatchet, 1589, speaks of twopence as the usual price of admission "at the Theater," so the probability is that the penny alone was insufficient for securing places which would be endured by any but the lowest and poorest class of auditors, those who stood in the yard or pit and were there exposed to the uncertainties of the weather. Those of the audience who were in the galleries were at least protected from the rain. There were upper as well as lower galleries in the building, the former being mentioned in the following interesting clause of the proposed lease to Burbage of 1585,—"and further that yt shall or maye be lawfull for the sayde Gyles and for hys wyfe and familie, upon law-full request therfore made to the sayde Jeames Burbage, his executors or assignes, to enter or come into the premisses and their[⊗] in some one of the upper romes to have such convenient place to sett or stande to se such playes as shal be ther played, freely without anythinge therefore payeinge, soe that the sayde Gyles, hys wyfe and familie, doe come and take ther places before they shal be taken upp by any others." It appears from this extract that there were seats for the audience as well as standing-room in the galleries.

Neither the Theatre nor the Curtain was used exclusively for dramatic entertainments. "Theater and Curtine for comedies and other shewes," marginal note in Stow's Survay of London, ed. 1598, p. 69. Both these theatres were frequently engaged for matches and exercises in the art of fencing. "Edward Harvie playd his provostes priz the five and twentith daye of August at the Theatour at thre weapons, the two hand sword, the backe sword and the sword and buckeler," 1578, MS. Sloane 2530. "Richarde Fletcher playd his schollers priz at the Curtyn in Holiwell the 25 daye of August at ij. weapons, the longe sworde and the sword and buckeler," 1579, MS. ibid. "Vallentin Longe playd his schollers priz at the Curtyn in Holiwell the iiij.th day of February at two kynde of weapons, that is to say, the longe sword and the sworde and buckeler," 1580-1, MS. ibid. "Androw Bello playd his schollers prize the tenth daye of Maye at the Curtyn in Holiwell at two weapons," 1582, MS. ibid. "Robert Blisse playde his provostes prize at the Theator in Holewell the firste day of Julye at thre weapons," 1582, MS. ibid. "Androwe Bello playd his provostes priz at the Courten in Holiwell the fiveth daye of July, and at thre weapons," 1582, MS. ibid. "Vallentyne Longe playde his provostes priz at the Courten in Holiwell the fiveth daye of August at thre weapons," 1582, MS. ibid. "John Dewell playd by challenge at the Theator in Holiwell agaynste all provostes and free schollers at thre weapons, the longe sword, the sword and buckeler, and the sword and dagger, the tenth day of Auguste, 1582," MS. ibid. "John Harris playd his provostes priz at the Curtine in Holiwell the second day of September, 1582," an entry in the same manuscript, but cancelled as if it were incorrect. "John Norris playd his skollers price the towe and twentye day of Aprill at the Theater in Hollowell at towe weapons," 1583, MS. ibid. "Alexander Reyson playd his maisters prize the laste daye of Aprill, 1583, at the Curteyn in Hollywell, at iiij. kynde of weapons, that is to saye, the longe sworde, the back sworde, the sworde and buckler, and the staffe," MS. ibid. "Androwe Dwellyn playde his masteres pryse the xx. daye and xxvj. daye of Maye, at the Theatur in Hollywell, att fower kynde of wepons, that ys to saye, att the longe sworde, the sworde and buckler, sworde and dagger, and raper and dagger," 1585, MS. ibid. The curious manuscript from which these extracts are taken seems to be a register of a society formed for the advancement of the science of fencing, in which degrees were granted to those who proved themselves to be the most efficient. It would appear from the original manuscript of Stow's Survey that not only fencers, but tumblers and such like, sometimes exhibited at these theatres. Near the buildings of the dissolved Priory, observes Stow, "are builded two howses for the showe of activities, comodies, tragidies and histories, for recreation; the one of them is named the Curteyn in Halywell, the othar the Theatre; thes are on the backesyde of Holywell, towards the filde," MS. Harl. 538. It should, however, be observed that the word *activities* is not in the printed edition.

When the fencers engaged the Theatre they sometimes increased their audience by marching "with pomp" through the City. In July, 1582, the Lord Mayor thus writes to the Earl of Warwick respecting one John David, a fencer in the Earl's service who desired to exhibit his skill at that establishment,—"I have herein yet further done for your servante what I may, that is, that if he may obteine lawefully to playe at the Theater or other open place out of the Citie, he hath and shall have my permition with his companie drumes and shewe to passe openly throughe the Citie, being not upon the sondaye, which is as muche as I maye justefie in this season, and for that cause I have with his owne consent apointed him Monday next," City of London MSS. This permission, as appears from the correspondence, was granted very reluctantly by the Lord Mayor, whose successor in the following year absolutely prohibited any display of the kind. His Lordship thus writes on April 27th, 1583, to one of the Justices of the Peace,—"there ar certain fencers that have set up billes, and meane to play a prise at the Theatre on Tuesday next, which is May eve. How manie waies the same maie be inconvenient and dangerous, specially in that they desire to passe with pomp thorough the Citie, yow can consider; namelie, the statute against men of that facultie, the perill of infection, the danger of disorders at such assemblies, the memorie of Ill May Daie begon upon a lesse occasion of like sort, the weakenesse of the place for ruine, wherof we had a late lamentable example at Paris Garden; for these causes in good discretion we have not only not geven them licence, but also declared to them the dangers, willing them at their perill to forbeare their passing both thorough the Citie and their whole plaieng of such prise."

It would appear, from these notices of the fencing matches which took place at the Theatre and Curtain, that both establishments were accessible to persons who desired to hire them for occasional purposes. The probability is that they were thus engaged by various companies, and a curious narrative given in the following words in a letter from Fleetwood to Lord Burghley, written in June, 1584, seems to confirm this opinion,—" Upon Sonndaie my Lord sent ij. aldermen to the Cowrt for the suppressing and pulling downe of the Theatre and Curten, for all the Lords agreed thereunto, saving my Lord Chamberlen and Mr. Vice-Ch., but we obteyned a lettre to suppresse theym all. Upon the same night I sent for the Quenes players and my Lord of Arundel his players, and they all well nighe obeyed the Lordes lettres. The chiefest of her Highnes players advised me to send for the owner of the Theater, who was a stubburne fellow, and to bynd him. I dyd so. He sent me word that he was my Lord of Hunsdens man and that he wold not comme at me, but he wold in the mornyng ride to my Lord. Then I sent the under-shereff for hym, and he browght hym to me, and, at his commyng, he showtted me owt very justice; and in the end I shewed hym my Lord his masters hand, and then he was more quiet; but, to die for it, he wold not be bound. And then I mynding to send hym to prison, he made sute that he might be bounde to appere at the oier and determiner, the which is to-morowe, where he said that he was suer the court wold not bynd hym, being a counselers man; and so I have graunted his request, where he shal be sure to be bounde, or els ys lyke to do worse," MS. Lansd. 41, art. 13. It is not to be assumed that the person who is here mentioned as "the owner of the Theater" was either Burbage or Hyde. He was more probably a temporary occupier of the building. James Burbage is not known to have ever belonged to the company of actors in the pay of Lord Hunsdon, who was at that time Lord Chamberlain of the Household. It may reasonably be gathered from Fleetwood's letter that at least three companies, those of Queen Elizabeth, Lord Arundel and Lord Hunsdon, were playing in June, 1584, at the Theatre or Curtain; the first and last probably at the Theatre, perhaps acting on alternate days. It is certain that the Queen's Company sometimes performed at the latter, for Laneham and Tarlton, both at one period belonging to that company, are noticed as having acted there. The author of Martins Months Minde, 1589, speaks of "twittle twattles that I had learned in ale-houses and at the Theater of Lanam and his fellowes." Tarlton is alluded to, as an actor at the Theatre, in Nash's Pierce Penilesse, 1592,—"Tarlton at the Theator made jests of him;" and again in Harington's Metamorphosis of Ajax, 1596,—"which worde was after admitted into the Theater with great applause by the mouth of Mayster Tarlton, the excellent comedian." The establishment appears to have been noted for its comic entertainments. "If thy vaine," observes the author of Pappe with an Hatchet, 1589, "bee so pleasaunt and thy witt so so⁕ nimble that all consists in glicks and girds, pen some play for the Theater."

The Theatre and the Curtain were for many years after their erection the only regularly constructed theatres in England situated on the north of the Thames. There have been frequent statements to the contrary, but these have resulted from the assumption that the terms, *houses, theatres* and *playhouses*, were necessarily applied to such edifices. The fact is that inn-yards and other buildings occasionally used for dramatic performances were often so designated by our early writers. When Gosson, in his Playes Confuted, c. 1580, speaks of "Cupid and Psyche plaid at Paules, and a greate many comedies more at the Blacke friers and in every playe house in London," he unquestionably refers to houses or taverns temporarily employed for the performances alluded to. That this was the case appears more distinctly from the following curious passage in Rawlidge's Monster Late Found Out, 1628,—"some of the pious magistrates made humble suit to the late Queene Elizabeth of ever-living memorie and her Privy Counsaile, and obtained leave from her Majesty to thrust those players out of the Citty and to pull downe the dicing houses, which accordingly was affected⁕, and the play-houses in Gracious street, Bishopsgate street, nigh⁕ Paules, that on Ludgate hill, the Whitefriars, were put downe, and other lewd houses quite suppress within the liberties by the care of those religious senators, for they did their best to remove all disorders out of their citties liberties; and surely had all their successors followed their worthy stepps, sinne would not at this day have beene so powerfull and raigning as it is." The "play-houses" in Gracious or Gracechurch Street, Bishopsgate Street and on Ludgate Hill, were the yards respectively of the well-known taverns called the Cross Keys, the Bull and the Belle Savage. There is no good reason for believing that the other "play-houses" mentioned, those near St. Paul's and in the Whitefriars, were, at the period alluded to, other than buildings occasionally used for the representation of plays, not edifices expressly constructed for the purpose; and Flecknoe, in the following interesting notice taken from his Short Discourse of the English Stage, 1664, speaks of "theaters" having been established in the yards of taverns, —"playes, which so flourisht amongst the Greeks, and afterwards amongst the Romans, were almost wholly abolished when their empire was first converted to Christianity, and their theaters together with their temples for the most part demolished as reliques of paganisme, some few onely reserved and dedicate⁕ to the service of the true God, as they had been to their false gods before; from which time to the last age they acted nothing here but playes of the Holy Scripture or saints lives, and that without any certain theaters or set companies till about the beginning of queen Elizabeths reign they began here to assemble into companies and set up theaters, first in the city, as in the inn-yards of the Cross-Keyes and Bull in Grace and Bishopsgate street at this day is to be seen, till that fanatick spirit which then began with the stage, and after ended with the throne, banisht them thence into the suburbs, as after they did the kingdom, in the beginning of our Civil Wars; in which time playes were so little incompatible with religion, and the theater with the Church, as on week-dayes after vespers both the Children of the Chappel and St. Pauls acted playes, the one in White-Friers, the other behinde the Convocation-house in Pauls, till people growing more precise, and playes more licentious, the theatre of Pauls was quite suppresst and that of the Children of the Chappel converted to the use of the Children of the Revels."

There has been a tendency hitherto to antedate the period of the erection of our ancient theatres. The Blackfriars, supposed to have been built in 1576, could not have been commenced until twenty years afterwards, for it was only in February, 1596, that Burbage purchased from Sir William More that portion of the large old building which he converted into a theatre. See the conveyance from Sir W. More to Burbage printed at length in the Appendix, pp. 108-112. "Now for the Blackfriers," said the Burbages in 1635, "that is our inheritance; our father purchased it at extreame rates and made it into a playhouse with great charge and troble," Lord Chamberlain MS. printed in the Appendix, p. 90. In like manner, it has been for many years the accepted belief that the Globe was built in 1594, the only foundation for this opinion being a mere conjecture first suggested in Malone's Inquiry, 1796, p. 87. This theatre was, however, certainly erected in 1599, the materials for its construction having, as has been previously shown, been brought from Shoreditch to the Bankside early in that year; and there being an allusion to the building itself in Shakespeare's play of Henry the Fifth, which is known to have been produced at the Globe (see Chorus to the First Act) and at some time between April and September, 1599, during the absence of the Earl of Essex in Ireland. See also the indenture of January, 1600, printed at p. 81, in which the new theatre is alluded to as "the *late-erected* play-howse on the Bancke in the parish of Saint Saviours called the Globe." Ben Jonson's comedy of Every Man Out of his Humour was another of the dramas which were exhibited before the first year's audience of this theatre, it having been acted by the Lord Chamberlain's Servants in 1599, and the author distinctly appealing to the judgment of "the happier spirits in this faire-fild Globe," ed. 1600. In another place the Presenter addresses the audience as the "thronged round." No company but that of the Lord Chamberlain, known after the time of Elizabeth as the King's Servants, appears to have acted at the Globe. When the Lords of the Privy Council attempted in June, 1600, to limit the number of playhouses to one in Middlesex and one other in Surrey, they observe,—"and for the other house allowed to be on Surrey side, whereas their Lordships are pleased to permitt to the company of players that shall play there to make their owne choice which they will have of divers houses that are there, choosing one of them and no more; and the said company of plaiers, being the servantes of the Lord Chamberlain that are to play there, have made choise of the house called the Globe, it is ordered that the saide house and none other shal be there allowed." Amongst the Shakespearean dramas acted at the old Globe before its destruction by fire in 1613 may be mentioned, Romeo and Juliet, Richard the Second, King Lear, Troilus and Cressida, Pericles, Othello, Macbeth and the Winter's Tale.

It has been generally asserted that the Globe was strictly a summer theatre and that it was closed in the winter time. There is evidence that this was usually the case with the second building, but winter performances certainly took place occasionally in the older theatre. This appears from a note of the examination of Sir Gilly Meyrick, who stated that early in February, 1601, he and several friends "went all together to the and⁹ Globe over the water wher the L. Chamberlens men use to play" and witnessed a representation of the drama of "Kyng Harry the iiij.th and of the Kyllyng of Kyng Richard the Second," State Papers Domest. Eliz. It is very rarely that the exact days of performances at the Globe are recorded. Forman notices one of Macbeth on April 20th, a play of Richard the Second on April 30th, and the Winter's Tale on May 15th, so that at all events the theatre was regularly opened early in the spring, and perhaps used only for occasional performances during the winter. It was a circular wooden building, the centre being open to the sky, but the stage and galleries protected from the weather by thatch. The only authentic representation of this old theatre which I have yet met with is in the foreground of an interesting view of London in the corner of a map of Great Britain

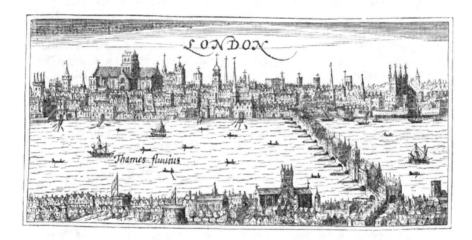

and Ireland, "graven by I. Hondius and are to be solde by I. Sudbury and George Humble in Popes head Alley in London, 1610," and inserted in Speed's Theatre of the Empire of Great Britaine, 1611. The fac-simile of this view here given is carefully taken from a copy of the original edition of 1610. Some of the later impressions of it are of inferior execution and not accurate copies of the original engraving, and there are some old diminutive imitations of the view which are of no value or authority. It would appear from this engraving that there was in the original Globe Theatre a circular sub-structure of considerable size, perhaps constructed of brick or masonry, which probably included a corridor with a passage to the pit or yard and staircases leading to other parts of the house. Upon this sub-structure the two wooden stories, in portions of which were included the galleries and boxes, were erected.—Further observations upon the history and structure of this celebrated theatre are reserved for a future occasion.

The Two Gentlemen of Verona.—The earliest notice of this drama which has yet been discovered is that in the list of Shakespeare's plays given by Meres in his Palladis Tamia, 1598, where it is mentioned as the Gentlemen of Verona. It is not impossible that this latter title was the original designation of the comedy, one by which it was generally known in the profession, and at a later period, Kirkman, who was intimately connected with the stage, inserts it in his list of plays, which first appeared in 1661, as the Gentleman of Verona. As a rule it is unsafe to pronounce a judgment on the period of the composition of any of Shakespeare's dramas from internal evidence, but the general opinion that this play is one of the author's earliest complete dramatic efforts may be followed without much risk of error. Admitting its lyrical beauty, its pathos, its humour and its infinite superiority to the dramas of contemporary writers, there is nevertheless a crudity in parts of the action, one at least being especially unskilful and abrupt, which the more lengthened experience of such a writer could hardly have sanctioned. A few of its incidents occur in the tale of Felix and Felismena, which is introduced in the romance of Diana written in Spanish by George of Montemayor about the middle of the sixteenth century. The story in that romance, Felix corresponding to Proteus and Felismena to Julia, may thus be briefly narrated. A youth named Don Felix falls rapturously in love with Felismena, a young lady who is disposed to reciprocate his affection but is unwilling to acknowledge her inclination. Her maid Rosina, whom he has induced to be the bearer of a letter to her, is at first angrily repulsed; but on a subsequent occasion, she purposely, but as if by accident, drops the missive in the sight of Felismena, who invents an excuse for its perusal. A correspondence then followed which resulted in the complete acknowledgment of the lady's affection. As, however, the course of true love never did run smooth, the father of Don Felix, as might be anticipated, gains intelligence through some officious person of their passion for each other, and, disapproving of the attachment, at once orders him to a foreign court upon the plea that enforced idleness at home was prejudicial to the formation of his character. Felix is upon this decree so overcome with grief that he leaves the object of his affections without acquainting her with his dismissal. Felismena's sorrow at his departure is increased by the jealous apprehension of the possibility of rivals when he was beyond the reach of her personal influence, and as a continued absence from her lover was unendurable, she dons male attire and travels to the same court. Upon her arrival at the town where Felix was sojourning, she takes lodgings in an unfrequented street, and by the invitation of her host experiences the trial of hearing the voice of her lover serenading another mistress. Her next step was soon decided upon. Assuming the name of Valerius, she takes the earliest opportunity of visiting the court, where she ascertained from Fabius, the page of the faithless swain, that Don Felix is enamoured with a lady of the name of Celia, who is described as inferior in beauty to Felismena. It chances that Felix is then in want of another page, and Valerius, secure in her masculine disguise, is speedily engaged. While in this service, she is compelled not only to listen to the outpourings of the love of the perjured Felix for the obdurate Celia, but to become his advocate and the bearer of his love-letters and "tokens." Celia had determined to reject the hand of any one who had deserted another lover in her favour, but she encourages the correspondence and the expectations of her lover for the sake of obtaining interviews with Valerius, with whom she had become desperately enamoured at their first interview. Felismena continues loyally to urge the suit of her master; Celia expires of grief when she discovers that her affection for the page is wholly unrequited, and Don Felix, at the news of her death, leaves the city in an agony of despair. He is pursued by Felismena, who, after many months of fruitless search, finally discovers him in one whom she is the means, through her skilful archery, of saving from destruction in a combat in which he was engaged single-handed against three other knights. Reconciliation and marriage are the natural results of this romantic episode. See the whole of the tale of Felix and Felismena, as translated from the Spanish by Yong in 1582, printed in the Appendix, pp. 91-104.

Montemayor's story, parts of which are graphically written, was in a dramatic form in English at least as early as the year 1585, when it was acted before Queen Elizabeth by her Majesty's Players,—"the history of Felix and Philiomena shewed and enacted before her highnes by her Majesties servauntes on the sondaie next after newyeares daie at night at Grenewiche, whereon was ymploied one battlement and a house of canvas," Revels' Accounts, 1584-5. In the primitive kind of scenery which illustrated the performances of dramas acted before the Queen, a battlement was the conventional representation of any royal or courtly residence. There are a sufficient number of incidents and minute particulars common to the tale above analysed and to Shakespeare's comedy to show that the plot of the latter was partially derived either from Montemayor or from some other work, possibly the old English play just named, in which use had been made of the tale of Felismena; the latter supposition appearing much more likely to be correct than the notion that the great dramatist had perused the Spanish romance previously to the composition of the Two Gentlemen of Verona. There is, indeed, an allusion in the latter which seems to indicate the probability that Shakespeare did not take his story immediately from the Diana, but from some novel or play in which there were correct references to the topography of Milan. Although the poet's instinctive genius enabled him to avoid a serious continuity of anachronism, it is evident from numerous examples that he was indifferent to minute accuracy in trivial matters of detail; so that when, as in this comedy, there is found a mention of St. Gregory's Well at Milan, and it is seen from Braun's Civitates Orbis Terrarum, 1582, where there is an engraving of that holy well, that it was a veritable object in that city, it may fairly be concluded that the notice in the play owes its introduction to a predecessor. Braun's work is one extremely unlikely to have been even seen, much more consulted, by Shakespeare, while the notion of the poet having visited and been well acquainted with Italy is unsupported by evidence or probability. Speed's welcome of Launce to Padua, a city which has no connexion with the plot of the comedy, may perhaps be considered an error originating in some allusion or incident in the older story, which perhaps included something analogous to the action of Valentine and Silvia in combination with that of Proteus and Julia. The drama of Felix and Philiomena is lost. The Diana was not issued in English until after November 28th, 1598, the date of the dedication to Yong's translation. Shakespeare therefore had obviously written the Two Gentlemen of Verona before he could have seen this publication, and no other early English translation which includes the story of Felix and Felismena is known to exist either in print or manuscript. Yong, however, asserts that his version had been completed in manuscript more than sixteen years, so it is just possible, in that age of transcript reading, that the great dramatist had perused it when in that form; more probable that the author of the play of Felix and Philiomena had thence derived the materials of his plot.

According to Tieck, there was an old English play, a German abridgment or mutilated translation of which was acted by English players in Germany about the year 1600, whence some of the materials for the story of the Two Gentlemen of Verona might have been derived. The foreign version alluded to, in which the characters are very coarsely delineated, was first printed in the Englische Comedien vnd Tragedien, 1620, under the title of Tragædia von Julio vnd Hyppolita, but the opinion of some critics that there is a strong resemblance between the plots of the two dramas, the German one and Shakespeare's, seems on examination to be untenable. The clown in the German play is, like Speed, extremely eager after his perquisites; and there is an incident of the tearing of a letter, but it is not in the slightest degree analogous to that in Shakespeare. The story of the play may be briefly stated as follows. Romulus, a Roman, betrothed to Hyppolita, leaves his beloved to the care of his brother Julius whilst he travels to Rome to obtain the consent of his parents to his marriage. Julius, who is secretly in love with Hyppolita, betrays his trust, intercepting the letters of Romulus and substituting others in their place, the latter being of a nature to infuriate Hyppolita and the Prince, her father. The lady, distracted by the conduct of which she presumes Romulus to have been guilty, eventually determines to accept her father's advice and marry Julius; while Romulus, on his return, accidentally discovering the fragments of the spurious letter that Hyppolita, when she received, had torn in pieces, of course ascertains the treachery by which his hopes had been defeated. But the discovery was made too late, Julius and his fair bride being then returning from the Church after their marriage unconscious of the fate that awaited them. Romulus joins in the wedding dance in disguise, stabs Julius and upbraids Hyppolita with perfidy. The latter kills herself in despair and Romulus follows her example, the Prince, overwhelmed by so great a calamity, retiring from the world. It will readily be seen that there is, in all this, nothing which may not have been invented or derived from sources that have no relation to Shakespeare's comedy; and the same observation applies to an incident in Sydney's Arcadia which has been thought to have suggested the scenes in which Valentine is induced to join the outlaws.

The Old English Religious Drama.—There are no indications that the dramatic art of Shakespeare was in the least degree influenced by any of the numerous religious plays the representations of which were so popular in England during the fourteenth, fifteenth and sixteenth centuries, and were not finally discontinued in the provinces until the reign of James the First. As there is, however, a possibility, and a few reasons for believing, that the great dramatist may have witnessed the performances of some of these quaint pageants, a few observations on the subject may be admissible. According to Matthew Paris, the story of St. Catherine was dramatised about the commencement of the twelfth century by one Geoffrey, a learned Norman then in England, and acted at Dunstable at the same period. This is the earliest notice of the drama in this country which has been discovered, but it is not at all likely that the performance was in the English language. It may indeed be safely assumed that all the plays acted in England at this time, and for several generations afterwards, were composed either in Latin or Anglo-Norman, the testimony which assigns the composition of the Chester Mysteries to the thirteenth century being unworthy of credence. The earliest piece in English of a dramatic character known to exist is a metrical dialogue between three persons preserved on a vellum roll in a handwriting of the commencement of the fourteenth century. It is entitled *Interludium de Clerico et Puella*, but there is no evidence to show that it was intended for the stage. It may have been merely an interlocutory poem like the contemporary Harrowing of Hell in MS. Harl. 2253, which has been usually, but perhaps erroneously, considered to be one of the old English mysteries. Dismissing the consideration of these pieces for the obvious reason that there is at least no substantial proof that either of them are connected with the subject, the history of the English drama, so far as can be gathered from the materials which have been preserved, really commences with the plays which were exhibited on moveable stages either by the guilds of towns or by itinerant companies in and after the fourteenth century. Amongst many other places, Chester, York and Coventry may be mentioned as having been then and for long afterwards specially celebrated for these performances, which usually took place at the time of the festival of Corpus Christi or at Whitsuntide; but as Shakespeare, if he were ever present at any of them, no doubt formed one of a Warwickshire audience, observations on the subject will be mainly restricted to those of Coventry. An engraving of that city would have been here introduced, but there is no very reliable view of it with its ancient walls as it appeared in the days of Shakespeare. The sketches engraved by Hollar are certainly not only inaccurate but altogether untrustworthy. It should be remarked that the interesting plays, usually termed the Coventry Mysteries, a transcript of which, made in the fifteenth century, is in MS. Cotton. Vespas. D. 8, were certainly not performed by any of the trading companies of that city, but by itinerant players, probably from Coventry, who acted those dramas in various towns, a fact which clearly appears from the concluding lines of the prologue. Very few of the plays which were acted by the trading companies have been preserved, but there is a curious one at Longbridge House, transcribed in the form in which it was revised by one Robert Croo in the year 1534, which was performed by the guild of the Shearmen and Taylors of Coventry. The subjects of this pageant are the Birth of Christ and the Adoration of the Magi, with the Flight into Egypt and the Murder of the Innocents. It is not impossible that Shakespeare witnessed some late performance of this curious drama, in which the violent character of Herod is depicted with what would now be thought a ludicrous exaggeration, greater perhaps than in any other play in which he is introduced, and strikingly justifying the expression of out-heroding Herod. This braggadocio describes himself as "prynce of purgatorré and cheff capten of hell" and also as "the myghttyst conquerowre that ever walkid on grownd," observing,—"Magog and Madroke bothe did I confownde,=And with this bryght bronde there bonis I brak on sundr." He tells the audience that it is he who is the cause of the thunder, and that the clouds were frequently so disturbed at the sight of his "feyrefull contenance" that "for drede therof the verré yerth doth quake." When the Magi escape his fury knows literally no bounds,—" I stampe, I stare, I loke all abowtt,=Myght I them take I schuld them bren at a glede,=I rent, I rawe, and now run I wode." After this outburst, Herod not merely storms furiously on the platform, but descends from the scaffold and exhibits the violence of his passion in the street, as appears from the following curious stage-direction,— "here Erode ragis in the pagond and in the strete also." The extravagance of rage, which formed one of the main characteristics of this personage, must have made a deep impression on a youthful spectator, and that Shakespeare probably witnessed the representation of this, or some other mystery on the same subject, may fairly be gathered from his several allusions to the character. Those references, however, considered together, would rather favour the conclusion that the play in his recollection was one in which the King was introduced as Herod of Jewry, and in which the children of Bethlehem were barbarously speared, the soldiers disregarding the frantic shrieks of the bereaved mothers. In the collection known as the Coventry Mysteries a soldier appears before Herod with a child on the end of his spear in evidence of the accomplishment of the King's commands, a scene to be remembered, however rude may have been the property which represented the infant. The idea of such a subject being susceptible of exaggeration into burlesque never entered a spectator's mind in those days, and the impression made upon him was probably not slightly increased by the style of Herod's costume. It would seem that the actor of this part wore a painted mask, there being several entries of payments in the accounts of the guilds for mending and painting his head. "Item, to a peyntour for peyntyng the fauchon and Herodes face, x. d," Accounts of the Smiths' Company, 1477, MS. at Longbridge House. "Item, payd to a peynter for peyntyng and mendyng of Herodes heed, iiij. d," Costes on Corpus Christi day, 1516, MS. ibid. "Paid to John Croo for menddyng of Herrode hed and a mytor and other thynges, ij. s," Costes on Corpus Crysty day, 1547, MS. ibid. "Payd to John Hewet, payntter, for dressyng of Errod hed and the faychon, ij. s," Paymentes for the Pagent, 1554, MS. ibid. The faychon here mentioned was a painted sword, in addition to which Herod carried a sceptre and had an ornamented helmet and crest. He wore red gloves, and his clothes appear to have been painted or dyed in a variety of colours, so that, as far as costume could assist the deception, he probably appeared as fierce and hideous a tyrant as could well have been represented. "Item, paid for a gowen to Arrode, vij. s. iiij. d; item, paid for peynttyng and stenyng theroff, vj. s. iiij. d; item, paid for Arrodes garment peynttyng that he went a prossassyon in, xx. d; item, paid for mendyng off Arrodes gauen to a taillour, viij. d; item, paid for mendyng off hattes, cappus and Arreddes creste, with other smale geyr belongyng, iij. s," Accounts of the Smiths' Company, 1490, MS. at Longbridge House. "Item, paid for iij. platis to Heroddis crest of iron, vj. d; item, paid to Hatfeld for dressyng of Hererodes* creste, xiiij. d," Smiths' Accounts, 1495, MS. ibid. "Item, paid for colour and coloryng of Arade, iiij. d," Costes of Corpus day Christi, 1508, MS. ibid.

Besides the allusions made by Shakespeare to the Herod of the Coventry players, there are indications that other grotesque performers in the pageants of that city were occasionally in his recollection, those who with blackened faces acted the parts of the Black Souls. There are several references in Shakespeare to condemned souls being of this colour, and in one place there is an allusion to them in the language of the mysteries. Falstaff is reported to have said of a flea on Bardolph's red nose that "it was a black soul burning in hell," Henry the Fifth, ii. 3. In the Coventry plays, "the Black or Damned Souls had their faces blackened, and were dressed in coats and hose; the fabric of the hose was buckram or canvas, of which latter material nineteen ells were used, nine of yellow and ten of black, in 1556, and probably a sort of party-coloured dress was made for them, where the yellow was so combined as to represent flames," Sharp's Dissertation on the Coventry Mysteries, 1825, p. 70. The following notices of these singular personages are taken from the accounts of the Coventry Guilds as quoted by Sharp in the same work,—"1537. Item, for v. elnes of canvas for shyrts and hose for the blakke soules at v. *d* the elne, ij. *s.* j. *d*; item, for coloryng and makyng the same cots, ix. *d*; item, for makyng and mendynge of the blakke soules hose, vj. *d*." In 1556 there is an entry of a payment which was made "for blakyng the sollys fassys." It is certainly possible that Shakespeare may have derived his notions of Herod and the Black Souls from other sources, but the more natural probability on the whole appears to be that they are recollections of the Coventry plays of his early youth. To the performances at Coventry at the festival of Corpus Christi there was a large resort of people from considerable distances, and thither might the boy Shakespeare have been taken by his parents for a holiday treat. Dugdale, writing about the middle of the following century, says,—" I myselfe have spoke with some old people who had in their younger yeares bin eye-witnesses of these pageants soe acted, from whome I have bin tolde that the yearly confluence of people *from farr and neare* to see that shew was extraordinary great, and which yielded noe small advantage to this citty," original MS. of Dugdale's Antiquities of Warwickshire preserved at Merevale. At the same time it must be borne in mind that perhaps it is not necessary to assume that Shakespeare was present at any dramatic performance in Coventry itself, the players of that city having been in the habit during the years of the poet's boyhood of strolling through the country and acting their plays in various towns, amongst which Stratford-on-Avon would from its position have naturally been included. They are known to have travelled as far as Bristol and to have acted there in the year 1570. "Item, paid to the players of Coventrie by the commaundement of Mr. Mayer and thaldremen, x. *s*," Bristol Corporation MSS., December, 1570. They were at Abingdon in the same year and at Leicester in 1569 and 1571, but there is no record of the nature of their performances. Those at Coventry were no doubt of a more impressive character, the players there having the advantage of somewhat elaborate appliances. In that city the mysteries were performed on moveable scaffolds belonging to the guilds, those scaffolds being moved in succession to various stations, so that several plays were continually being acted at one and the same time in different places, a judicious method of separating the audiences in those days of very narrow streets and of enabling each group to witness a series of performances every day of the festival. These pageants, observes Dugdale in his Antiquities of Warwickshire, ed. 1656, p. 116, "had theaters for the severall scenes very large and high, placed upon wheels and drawn to all the eminent parts of the city for the better advantage of spectators." A more elaborate account of them is given by a clergyman who witnessed some of the later performances of the Chester mysteries, which were no doubt conducted similarly to those of Coventry,—" every company had his pagiant or parte, which pagiants weare a high scafolde with two rowmes, a higer* and a lower, upon four wheeles; in the lower they apparelled themselves, and in the higher rowme they played, beinge all open on the tope, that all behoulders mighte heare and see them; the places where the played them was in every streete; they begane first at the Abay gates, and when the firste pagiante was played, it was wheeled to the Highe Crosse before the mayor, and so to every streete, and soe every streete had a pagiant playinge before them at one time till all the pagiantes for the daye appoynted weare played; and when one pagiant was neere ended, worde was broughte from streete to streete that soe the mighte come in place thereof excedinge orderlye, and all the streetes have their pagiantes afore them all at one time playeinge togeather; to se which playes was great resorte, and also scafoldes and stages made in the streetes in those places where they determined to playe theire pagiantes," MS. Harl. 1948. It has been frequently stated that there were sometimes three rooms in the pageant, the highest representing heaven, the middle one the earth and the lowest the infernal regions. This was the case in some of the continental performances, but there is no good evidence that the English pageant ever contained more than two rooms. That the lower one of the latter was not exclusively used for a tiring-house is, however, certain. There were trap-doors on the floor of the stage out of which the performers ascended and descended, and in some instances the descent was certainly intended to be to the place of torment. A similar contrivance was sometimes adopted on the supplementary scaffolds. "Here xal entyr the Prynse of Dylfs in a stage and helle ondyrneth that stage," stage-direction in Mary Magdalene, Digby Mysteries, ed. 1835, p. 78. In the same mystery the bad angel is represented as entering "into hell with thondyr," no doubt through the grotesquely painted hell-mouth, a favourite property on the ancient English stage. This consisted of a huge mouth constructed of canvas so contrived with a moveable jaw that, when it opened, flames could be seen within the hideous aperture. "The little children were never so afrayd of hell mouth in the old plaies painted with great gang teeth, staring eyes and a foule bottle nose," Harsnet's Declaration, 1603. "Item, payd for payntyng hell hede newe, xx. d; payde for kepynge hell hede, viij. d; item, payd for kepyng of fyer at hell mothe, iiij. d; paid to Jhon Huyt for payntyng of hell mowthe, xvj. d; paid for makyng hell mowth and cloth for hyt, iiij. s," Accounts of the Drapers' Pageant at Coventry, 1554-1567, printed in Sharp's Dissertation, 1825, pp. 61, 73. The "fyer at hell mothe" was probably represented by the skilful management of links or torches held behind the painted canvas. It may be observed that hell-mouth was one of the few contrivances in use in the ancient mysteries which were retained on the metropolitan stage in the time of Shakespeare, it being in the list of properties belonging to the Lord Admiral's Servants in 1599.

The vehicles which Dugdale calls *theaters* were in Shakespeare's time always termed *pageants*. They were not constructed merely for temporary use, but were substantially formed of wood and lasted for years, having been carefully preserved by the guilds in their various pageant-houses, whence they were brought out when the performances of the mysteries were arranged to take place. "Item, reparacion for the pagent and the pagant hows, for a gret burd for the dur of the pagent howse, v. d," Accounts of the Smiths' Company, 1469, MS. Longbridge. "Item, payd for rente of the pagent hows, iiij. s. vj. d; item, payde for the reperacion of the pagente hows, for a sylle and for sparrys and lathe and nayle and warkmanschyp, iiij. s. ij. d," Smiths' Accounts, 1499, MS. ibid. "Item, payd for menddyng the look of the pagent howss dor, j. d; item, payd for mendyng of the chest in the pagent howss, j. d," Smiths' Accounts, 1545, MS. ibid. The pageant-houses were still to be seen at Coventry in the time of Shakespeare. "Paid for a lode of cley for the padgyn howse, vj. d; paid for iij. sparis for the same howse, vj. d; paid to the dawber and his man, xiiij. d; paid to the carpyntur for his worke, iiij. d; paid for a bunche and halfe of lathe, ix. *d*; paid for vj. pennye naiylles, ij. *d*," Accounts of the Smiths' Company, 1571, MS. Longbridge. "Spent at Mr. Sewelles of the company about the pavynge of the pajen house, vj. *d*; payd for the pavynge of the pagen house, xxij. *d*; payd for a lode of pybeles, xij. *d*; for a lode sande, vj. *d*," Smiths' Accounts, 1576, MS. ibid. "Item, paide to James Bradshawe for mendynge the pageant-howse doores, iiij. *d*; item, to Christofer Burne for a key and settynge on the locke on the doore, v. *d*; item, paide to Baylyffe Emerson for halfe yeres rente of the pageant-howse, ij. *s.* vj. *d*; item, gyven to Bryan, a sharman, for his good wyll of the pageante-howse, x. *d*," Smiths' Accounts, 1586, MS. ibid.

The pageant itself may be described as a wooden structure which consisted of two rectangular rooms erected on the floor of a strong wagon, the lower room being enclosed with painted boards, and the upper one open, the latter having a decorated canopy supported by pilasters or columns rising from each corner of the floor and ornamented at the top with banners or other appendages. In the following series of extracts referring to the Coventry pageants the ancient entries respecting them are included, there being no reason for believing that there was any material variation in the appliances or representations of the mysteries from the fifteenth century to the time of Shakespeare. "Item, spend at bryngyng down of the pajent to William Haddons, vj. *d*; item, payed the torchberers, viij. *d*; item, spend in ale uppon them, j. *d*; item, payed for ale to the players in the pajent, xij. *d*; item, for ij. tre hoppis to the pajent whelles, iiij. *d*; item, spend at havyng home the pajent, x. *d*," Accounts of the Smiths' Company, 1450, MS. Longbridge. "Also it is ordenyd that the jorneymen of the seyd crafte schall have ȝerely vj. *s.* viij. *d*, and for that they schall have owte the paggent, and on Corpus Christi day to dryve it from place to place ther as it schal be pleyd, and then for to brynge it geyn into the paggent howse without ony hurte nyther defawte, and they for to put the master to no more coste," Ordinances of the Company of Weavers of Coventry, 1453, MS. "Item, expende at the fest of Corpus Christi yn reparacion of the pagent, that ys to say, a peyre of new whelys, the pryce viij. *s*; item, for naylys and ij. hokys for the sayd pagiente, iiij. *d*; item, for a cord and sope to the sayde pagent, ij. *d*; item, for to have the pagent ynto Gosford strete, xij. *d*," Accounts of the Company of Smiths of Coventry, 1462, MS. Longbridge. "Item, in expenses on Corpus Christi evyn to wasche the pageant, and to have it in and out, and on the day in wyne, ale, rysches and torches beryng and all odur thynges, and to hand in the pageant, xiij. *d*," Smiths' Accounts, 1465, MS. ibid. "Item, in met and drynk on mynstrelles and on men to drawe the pagent, xxij. *d*," Smiths' Accounts, 1467, MS. ibid. "For x. pond yrne for the pagent and the weket, xv. *d*; item, a lachet on the pagent whele, j. *d*," Smiths' Accounts, 1469, MS. ibid. "Item, rysshes to the pagent, ij. *d*; item, ij. clampys of iron for the pagent, viij. *d*; item, ij. legges to the pagent and the warkemanship withall, vj. *d*," Smiths' Accounts, 1470, MS. ibid. "Expenses to brynge up the pagent into the Gosford Strete amonge the felishp, viij. *d*; expenses for burneysshyng and peyntyng of the fanes to the pagent, xx. *d*; item, cloutnayle and other nayle and talowe to the pagent, and for waysshyng of the seid pagent and ruysshes, vj. *d.* ob.; item, at bryngyng the pagent owt of the house, ij. *d*; item, nayles and other iron gere to the pagent, viij. *d.* ob.; expenses to a joyner for workemanshipp to the pagent, vij. *d*," Smiths' Accounts, 1471, MS. ibid. "Inprimis, sope to the pagent wheles and rysschys, j. *d.* ob.," Expenses for

Corpus Christi, 1472, MS. ibid. "Item, a c. cloutenayle to the pagent, iiij. *d*; item, teynturhokes and spykynges, iij. *d*; item, iron bondes and clyppis to the wheles, xiiij. *d*; item, for waysschyng of the pagent, ij. *d*," Smiths' Accounts, 1473, MS. ibid. "Item, for havyng furth the pagent on the Wedonsday, iij. *d*; item, paid for ij. peyre newe whelis, viij. *s*; expenses at the settyng on of hem, vij. *d*; item, for byndyng of thame, viij. *d*; paid to a carpenter for the pagent rowf, vj. *d*," Smiths' Accounts, 1480, MS. ibid. "Item, for the horssyng of the padgeantt and the axyll tree to the same, xvj. *d*; item, for the hawyng of the padgeantt in and out, and wasshyng it, viij. *d*," Smiths' Accounts, 1498, MS. ibid. "Item, paid for ij. cordes for the draught of the paygaunt, j. *d*; item, paid for shope and gresse to the whyles, j. *d*; item, paid for havyng oute of the paygant and swepyng therof and havyng in, and for naylles and ij. claspes of iron, and for mendyng of a claspe that was brokon, and for coterellis and for a bordur to the pagaunte, xix. *d*," Smiths' Accounts, 1499, MS. ibid. "Item, for nayles to the pagente and hokes, iiij. *d*. ob.; item, payd to John Gybbys for byndynge of the welys and clampys to the pagente, xv. *d*; item, spend on the jorneymen in bred and ale for havynge forthe pagente, vj. *d*," Smiths' Accounts, 1500, MS. ibid. "Paid for dryvyng of the pagent, iiij. *s*. iiij. *d*; paid for russys and soop, ij. *d*," Smiths' Accounts, 1547, MS. ibid. The soap was used for greasing the wheels, and the rushes were strewn on the floor of the pageant. "Item, payd to payntter for payntyng of the pagent tope, xxij. *d*," Smiths' Accounts, 1554, MS. ibid. "Item, spent on the craft when the overloked the pagyand, ij. *s*; item, payd for iiij. harneses hyrynge, iij. *s*; item, payd to the players betwene the stages, viij. *d*; item, payd for dressynge the pagyand, vj. *d*; item, payd for kepynge the wynd, vj. *d*; item, payd for dryvyng the pagyand, iiij. *s*; item, payd to the dryvers in drynke, viij. *d*; item, payd for balls, vj. *d*; item, payd to the mynstrell, viij. *d*," Accounts of the Cappers' Company for 1562, delivered in February, 1563, MS. ibid. "Item, paid for a ledge to the scafolde, vj. *d*; item, paid for ij. ledges to the pagiand, viij. *d*; item, paid for grett naylles, vj. *d*; item, for makynge clene the pagiand house, ij. *d*; item, paid for washenge the pagiand clothes, ij. *d*; item, for dryvinge the pagiand, vj. *s*. vj. *d*; item, paid to the players at the second stage, viij. *d*," Pageant Accounts of the Cappers' Company for 1568, MS. ibid. "Paid for laburrars for horssyng the padgang, xvj. *d*; spent abowt the same bessynes, xvj. *d*; for takyng of the yron of the olde whele, x. *d*; paid for poyntes and paper, iij. *d*," Accounts of the Smiths' Company, 1570, MS. ibid. The pageant was sometimes accompanied with what were termed scaffolds or stages, which appear to have been merely pageants of small dimensions appropriated to the use of special characters in the mysteries. These scaffolds were mounted on wheels, and were perhaps attached to the pageant in the transit of the latter to its various stations, but they were certainly sometimes separated from it during the performance, and occasionally scenes of the play, with or without properties and mechanical contrivances, were exhibited in the street between the scaffolds or between the pageant and the scaffolds. Herod, as has been previously mentioned, sometimes "raged" in the street as well as on the platform. Some of the actors occasionally descended from the latter and mounted their steeds, while others came on horseback to the pageant, according to the necessities of the history which was represented.

The panelled or boarded sides of the lower room which were visible to the audience were sometimes if not always painted, most likely with designs illustrative of the action of that mystery which was appropriated to the owners of the pageant. Two or three of the sides of the upper room were ornamented with painted cloths, which answered the purpose of a rude kind of scenery. The Smiths' Company in 1440 paid three shillings and sixpence halfpenny for "cloth to lap abowt the pajent." On another occasion sixpence was invested in "halfe a yard of rede sea," Smiths' Accounts, 1569, MS. Longbridge. Two "pajiont clothes of the Passion" are mentioned in an inventory of the goods of the Cappers' Company in the time of Henry the Eighth, and in a list of the theatrical appliances of another trading company, 1565, are included "three paynted clothes to hang abowte the pageant." Some of the pageant accounts include payments "for curten ryngus." It is probable that curtains were sometimes placed across the stage, so that a new scene might by their withdrawal be instantaneously presented to the audience. "Payd for makyng of the hooke to hang the curten on, iiij. d," Accounts 2 Edward VI., MS. ibid. There was frequently at the back of the stage a raised platform to which there was an ascent by steps from the floor of the pageant, and sometimes an important part of the action of the mystery was enacted upon it. Some of the properties, however rude, must have been of large dimensions. They were generally made of wood which was invariably painted, but some appear to have been constructed of basket-work covered over with painted cloths. Amongst the larger ones must have been the cities with pinnacles and towers, kings' palaces, temples, castles and such like, which are named in the ancient inventories, some probably not very unlike decorated sentry-boxes. Noah's Ark must have been a magnificent example of this class of properties, as may be gathered from the following stage-direction in the Chester mystery of the Flood,—"then Noy shall goe into the Arke with all his famylye, his wife excepte; the Arke must be borded rounde about, and upon the bordes all the beastes and fowles hereafter rehearsed must be painted, that there wordes maye agree with the pictures," MS. Harl. 2013, fol. 23. Amongst the miscellaneous properties may be named "a rybbe colleryd red," which was no doubt used in the mystery of the Creation. Clouds were represented by painted cloths so contrived that they could open and show angels in the heavens. Artificial trees were certainly introduced, and so were beds, tombs, pulpits, ships, ladders and numerous other articles. One of the quaintest contrivances was that which was intended to convey the idea of an earthquake, which seems to have been attempted by means of some mechanism within a barrel. In the lower room, connected with pulleys in the upper part of the pageant, was a windlass used for the purpose of lowering or raising the larger properties, and for various objects for which moveable ropes could be employed. Some of the other machinery were evidently of an ingenious character, but their exact nature has not been ascertained.

The costumes of many of the personages in the mysteries were of a grotesque and fanciful description, but in some instances, as in those of Adam and Eve, there was an attempt to make the dresses harmonize with the circumstances of the history. Some writers, interpreting the stage-directions too literally, have asserted that those characters were introduced upon the pageant in a state of nudity. This was certainly not the case. When they were presumed to be naked they appeared in dresses made either of white leather or of flesh-coloured clothes, over which at the proper time were thrown the garments of skins. "Adam and Eve aparlet in whytt lether," stage-direction in the old Cornish mystery of the Creation of the World. "Two cotes and a payre hosen for Eve stayned; a cote and hosen for Adam steyned," inventory of pageant costumes, 1565. There were no doubt some incidents represented in the old English mysteries which would now be considered indecorous, but it should be borne in mind that every age has, within certain limits, its own conventional and frequently irrational sentiments of toleration and propriety. Adam and Eve attired in white leather and personified by men, for actresses were then unknown, scarcely could have realized to the spectator even a generic idea of the nude, but at all events there was nothing in any of the theatrical costumes of the early drama which can be fairly considered to be of an immodest character, although many of them were extravagantly whimsical. The quaint costume worn by the personator of Herod has already been described. The Devil was another important character, who was also grotesquely attired and had a mask or false head which frequently required either mending or painting. Masks were worn by several other personages, though it would appear that in some instances the operation of painting the faces of the actors was substituted. "Item, paid for gloves to the pleyares, xix. d; item, paid for pyntyng*® off ther fasus, ij. d," Accounts of the Smiths' Company, 1502, MS. Longbridge. "Payd to the paynter for payntyng the players facys, iiij. d," Paymentes on Corpus Crysty day, 1548, MS. ibid. Wigs of false hair, either gilded or of red, yellow and other colours, were also much in request.

There were occasional performances of the mysteries at Coventry during all the time of Shakespeare's boyhood. In 1567 the following were the "costes and charges of the pagiand" of the Cappers' Company,—"Item, payd for a cloutt to the pagiand whelle, ij. d; item, payd for a ponde of sope to the pagiand, iij. d; item, payd to the players at the second stage, viij. d; item, payd for balles, viij. d; item, payd to the mynstrell, viij. d; item, payd to Pilat for his gloves, ij. d; item, payd for assyden for Pilat head, ij. d; item, payd to Jorge Loe for spekyng the Prologue, ij. d," Accounts delivered in January, 1568, MS. Longbridge. In 1568 there was another account of a similar character for the same Company's pageant,—"Item, paid for balles, viij. d; item, paid for Pylatt gloves, iiij. d; item, paid for the spekynge of the Prologe, ij. d; item, paid for prikynge the songes, xij. d; item, paid for makyng and coloringe the ij. myters, ij. s. iiij. d; item, paid for makynge of hell-mothe new, xxj. d," MS. ibid. There was also a performance in the next year by the Cappers' Company, and in 1571 their accounts for the pageant are thus recorded,—"Item, paid for mendynge the pagiand geyre, iij. d; item, paid for a yard of bokeram, xij. d; item, paid for payntynge the demons mall and the Maris rolles, vj. d; item, for makynge the roles, ij. d; item, paid to the players att the second stage, viij. d," MS. ibid. Pilate appears to have been the leading character in this pageant, and it seems from other entries that he was attired in a green cloak and carried a huge club stuffed with wool. In 1572 the following were the "charges for the padgand" of the Smiths' Company,—"Paid for canvys for Jwdas coote, ij. s; paid for the makyng of hit, x. d; paid to too damsselles, xij. d; paid for a poollye and an yron hoke and mendyng the padgand, xvj. d; paid for cowntters and a lase and pwyntes for Jwdas, iij. d," MS. Longbridge. The same Company first performed in this year, 1572, their "new play," either in conjunction with or after the older pageant, as appears from the original accounts. This new drama was unquestionably an imitation of the ancient mystery. The expenses of this performance in 1573 are thus stated,—"Paid for pleyng of Petur, xvj. d; paid for Jwdas parte, ix. d; paid for ij. damsylles, xij. *d*; paid to the deman, vj. *d*; paid to iiij. men that bryng yn Herod, viij. *d*; paid to Fastoun for hangyng Jwdas, iiij. *d*; paid to Fawston for coc-croyng, iiij. *d*; paid for Mr. Wygsons gowne, viij. *d*," MS. Longbridge. It seems from the following account of the expenses of the same play in 1574 that the last entry was a payment made for the loan of a gown to be worn by the person who acted the part of Herod,—" Paid for pleynge of Petur, xvj. *d*; paid for Jwdas, ix. *d*; paid for ij. damselles, xij. *d*; paid to the deman, vj. *d*; paid to iiij. men to bryng yn Herode, viij. *d*; paid to Fawston for hangyng Jwdas and cock-croyng, viij. *d*; paid for Herodes gowne, viij. *d*," MS. ibid. In 1576 there was a payment of eighteenpence "for the gybbyt of Jezie." In 1577 the old mystery and the "new pley" were again performed by the Smiths' Company, and threepence was paid "for a lase for Jwdas and a corde" used in the latter. The expenses of the old pageant are stated as follows,—" Paid to the plears at the fyrst reherse, ij. *s.* vj. *d*; paid for ale, iiij. *d*; paid for sent Marye Hall to reherse there, ij. *d*; paid for mendyng the padgand howse dore, xx. *d*; paid for too postes for the dore to stand upon, iiij. *d*; paid to the carpyntur for his labur, iiij. *d*; paid to James Beseley for ij. plattes on the post endes, vj. *d*; for great naylles to nayle on the hynge, ij. *d*; paid to vj. men to helpe up with the dore, vj. *d*," Accounts of the Smiths' Company for 1577, MS. Longbridge. There was a repetition of both these performances in the following year, when the following expenses were incurred for the new play,—" Paid for the cokcroing, iiij. *d*; paid to Thomas Massy for a trwse for Judas, ij. *s.* viij. *d*; paid for a new hoke to hange Judas, vj. *d*; paid for ij. new berars of yron for the new seyt in the padgand, xij. *d*," Accounts, 1578, MS. ibid. These must have been amongst the last performances at Coventry of the genuine old English mystery, which appears to have been suppressed in that city and in some other places in the year 1580; but the dramatic spirit survived, and in 1584 the Smiths' Company brought out, under the sanction of the Corporation, an entirely new pageant entitled the Destruction of Jerusalem, a tragedy partially founded on events recorded by Josephus, which it may be presumed was composed with the express object of retaining the attractions of the older performances in a form that would meet the objections of the authorities to the latter. This pageant was also acted by other Companies, and appears to have been the only one allowed to be performed. It was written by John Smith, a native of Warwickshire, then a member of St. John's College, Oxford, who received what was in those days a liberal sum for his work. "Paid to Mr. Smythe of Oxford the xv. th daye of Aprill, 1584, for hys paynes for writing of the tragidye, xiij. *li.* vj. *s.* viij. *d*," Coventry Municipal MSS. The Destruction of Jerusalem, with its Chorus and large number of characters, must have been a more elaborate production than any of the ancient English mysteries, but it was acted on the pageant vehicle and no doubt with appliances similar to those used in the performances of the older dramas. The accounts of the expenses incurred in the production of this tragedy in 1584 are sufficiently curious to be quoted at length,—" Imprimis, payd to the players for a reherse, ij. *s.* vj. *d*; item, payde to Jhon Grene for wrytynge of the playe-booke, v. *s*; item, payde to the trumpeter for soundynge in the pagent, v. *s*; item, payde to hym that playde on the flute, ij. *s.* vj. *d*; item, payde to Jhon Foxall for the hyer of Irysshe mantylles, viij. *d*; item, gyvyn to the dryvers of the pagent to drynke, iiij. *d*; item, payde for sope for the pagent wheles, iiij. *d*; item, payde for a boorde for the pagente, vj. *d*; item, payde to Cookeson for makynge of a whele to the skaffolde, viij. *d*; item, payde to the carpenter for mendynge the pagente and for nayles, ij. *d*; item, payde to William Barrat his men for a berrage, iiij. *d*; item, payde for a iron pynne and a cotter for the skaffolde whele, iiij. *d*; item, spent on the Companye at Mr. Smythes on the pley even, ij. *s*. viij. *d*; paid to Jhon Deane and Fosson for theyre dyner on the playe daye, vj. *d*; item, payde to Williams for makynge of ij. payre of galleyes, ij. *s*; item, paid for the masters breakfast on the playe daye, xx. *d*; item, paid for the players drynke to the pagente, ij. *s*; item, paid for starche to make the storme in the pagente, vj. *d*; item, paid for carryenge of our aperaill from pagent to pagent, vj.*d*; item, paid for drynke at Walkers for the muzizions, ij. *d*; item, paid to Hewette for fetchynge of the hoggesheaddes, vj. *d*; item, paid to the souldyers for waytynge on the captaynes, ij. *s*. vj. *d*; item, paid for a pottell of wyne to the pagente, x. *d*; item, paid to the muzicions for playenge on theyre instrumentes in the pagent, v. *s*; item, paid for the masteres and the players sowper, viij. *s*. vj. *d*; item, paid to Jhon Deane for hys sowper and drynkynge, vj. *d*; item, paid to William Longe for russhes, packthryd and tenterhookes, viij. *d*; item, paid to ij. drumme-players, x. *d*; item, paid to the dryvers of the pagente, iiij. *s*; item, paid to Hewet for hys paynes, ij. *d*; item, paid to Reignolde Headley for playenge of Symon and Phynea, v. *s*; item, paid to Gabryell Foster for playenge of Justus, Ananus, Eliazar and the Chorus, vj. *s*. viij. *d*; item, paid to Jhon Bonde for playenge of the Capteyne, Jhoannes and the Chorus, vj. *s*. viij. *d*; item, paid to William Longe for playenge of Merstyars, Jacobus, Hippenus and the Chorus, v. *s*; item, paid to Jhon Hoppers for playenge of Jesus and Zacharyas, iij. *s*; item, paid to Henry Chamberleyne for playenge of Pristus, a pece of Ananus and Zilla, iij. *s*. iiij. *d*; item, paid to Jhon Grene for playenge of Mathias and Esron, ij. *s*; item, paid to John Copestake for playeng of Esron his parte, xx. *d*; item, paid to Lewes Pryce for playenge of Niger his parte, xvj. *d*; item, paid to Frauncys Cocckes for playenge of Solome, xij. *d*; item, paid to Richard Fitzharbert and Edward Platte for playeinge Chyldren to Solome, xij. *d*; item, paid to Christofer Dyglyne for hys ij. drummes, vj. *s*. viij. *d*; item, paid to the awncyente berer, xij. *d*; item, paid to Robert Lawton for kepynge of the booke, ij. *s*; item, paid to Edmund Durrant for payntynge, ij. *s*; item, paid to Thomas Massye for the Temple and for his beardes, iij. *s*; item, payd to the players at the fyrst reherse, vij. *d*; item, payd moore to them at the second reherse, xx. *d*; item, payd unto the muzicyons the same tyme, vij. *d*; item, payd unto Cristopher Dyglyn the same tyme in earnest, iiij. *d*; item, payd to the players at the reherse on the Monday en Whytson wycck, ij. *s*; item, payd unto Cocckam in earnest for to playe on his bagpypes, iiij. *d*; item, payd to the players at the last reherse in Sent Nycholas hall, iij. *s*; item, payd for havynge the pageaunt owte, viij. *d*; item, spent at the Panyer at the fyrst reherse, ij. *s*; item, spent at Rychard Turners at the secund reherse, viij. *d*; item, payd to Henrye Chamberleyne for ij. beardes, vj. *d*; item, payd for a clampe of iron weyng viij. *li* for the pageant, xx. *d*; item, payd for nayles to fasten the said clampe, ij. *d*; item, payd for a iron pynne to the pageant, iiij. *d*; item, payd for a iron to hold uppe the stremer, iiij. *d*; item, payd for the pageant howse rente, v. *s*; item, payd to Jhon Deane for takyng paynes abowte the pageant, ij. *s*. vj. *d*," MS. Longbridge. It may be doubted, however, if the Destruction of Jerusalem, notwithstanding the pains bestowed upon its production and though it was probably superior as a work of art to the old mysteries, ever achieved the popularity of the latter. The new drama does not appear to have been exhibited again until the year 1591, when it was played with the unanimous consent of the Corporation. "It is also agreed by the whole consent of this house that the Distruccion of Jerusalem, the Conquest of the Danes or the Historie of K. E. the 4, at the request of the comons of this cittie, shal be plaid on the pagens on Midsomer Daye and St. Peters Daye next in this cittie and non other playes; and that all the meypoles that nowe are standing in this cittie shal be taken downe before Whitsonday next, and non hereafter to be sett up in this cittie," MS. Council-Book of Coventry, 19 May, 1591. The merry England of Shakespeare's youth was now in the course of a rapid transformation so far as the favourite recreations of the country people were concerned, and these performances in 1591 were the last representations of the Coventry pageants. Several of the companies had disposed of their pageants and pageant-houses some years previously. Those of the Smiths' Company were parted with in 1586. "Item, recievyd of Mr. Pyle for the pageant-howse, xx. s; item, recievyd of Henry Bankes for the pageant, xl. s," Accounts of the Smiths' Company for 1586, MS. Longbridge. The Weavers sold their pageant in the following year for the same amount. The properties and dresses, however, belonging to some of the companies, were preserved by them for years after the termination of the performances. An inventory of the goods of the Cappers' Company, taken in 1597, includes,—"ij. pawles, sixe cressittes, ij. streamars and the poles, ij. bisshopes myters, Pylates dublit, ij. curtaynes, Pylates head, fyve Maries heades, one coyff, Mary Maudlyns gowne, iij. beardes, sixe pensils, iiij. rolles, iij. Marye boxes, one play-boke, the giandes head and clubbe, Pylates clubbe, hell-mowth, Adams spade, Eves distaffe," MS. ibid. It may perhaps be inferred from the preservation of these relics that some of the companies still cherished the hope that the Coventry pageants would be revived. It is certain that mysteries, similar to those which had been acted in that city when Shakespeare was a boy, lingered in some parts of England till the reign of James the First. Weever, after mentioning the eight-day play in London in 1409 (see Stow's Survay, ed. 1598, p. 69), observes,—"the subject of the play was the Sacred Scriptures from the creation of the world; they call this Corpus Christi Play in my countrey, which I have seene acted at Preston and Lancaster, and last of all at Kendall in the beginning of the raigne of King James, for which the townesmen were sore troubled, and upon good reasons the play finally supprest not onely there but in all other townes of the kingdome," Ancient Funerall Monuments, 1631, p. 405. The mystery of the Passion acted at Ely House in the same reign (Prynne's Histrio-Mastix, 1633, p. 117) was probably one of the more modern and elaborate religious dramas which so long maintained their popularity with the Catholics. A collection of these later compositions is preserved in a manuscript of the early part of the seventeenth century in the library of Stonyhurst College. It is not likely that any of the legitimate ancient English mysteries were performed in London at so late a period.

It is scarcely necessary to observe that the English drama in its earlier stages was chiefly intended to serve as a medium of religious instruction. In days when education of any kind was a rarity and spiritual religion an impossibility or at least restricted to very few, appeals to the senses in illustration of theological subjects were wisely encouraged by the Church. The impression made on the rude and uninstructed mind by the representations of incidents in sacred history and religious tradition by living characters must have been far more profound than any which could have been conveyed by the skill of the sculptor or painter, or by the eloquence of the priest. Notwithstanding therefore the opposition that these performances encountered at the hands of a small section of churchmen, who apprehended that the introduction of the comic element into them would ultimately tend to feelings of irreverence, it is found that, in spite of some abuses, they long continued to be one of the most effectual means of spreading a knowledge of scriptural history and of inculcating belief in the doctrines of the Church. In the Hundred Mery Talys there is a story of a village priest in Warwickshire who preached a sermon on the Articles of the Creed, telling the congregation at the end of his discourse,—"these artycles ye be bounde to beleve, for they be trew and of auctoryté; and yf you beleve not me, then for a more suerté and suffycyent auctoryté go your way to Coventré, and there ye shall se them all playd in Corpus Cristi playe." Although this is related as a mere anecdote, it well illustrates the value which was attached to the teachings of the ancient stage. Even as lately as the middle of the seventeenth century there could have been found in England an example of a person whose knowledge of the Scriptures was limited to his recollections of the performance of a mystery. The Rev. John Shaw, who was the temporary chaplain in a village in Lancashire in 1644, narrates the following curious anecdote respecting one of its inhabitants,—"one day an old man about sixty, sensible enough in other things, and living in the parish of Cartmel, coming to me about some business, I told him that he belonged to my care and charge, and I desired to be informed in his knowledge of religion. I asked him how many Gods there were; he said, he knew not. I, informing him, asked him again how he thought to be saved; he answered he could not tell, yet thought that was a harder question than the other. I told him that the way to salvation was by Jesus Christ, God-man, who, as he was man, shed his blood for us on the crosse, &c. Oh, sir, said he, I think I heard of that man you speake of once in a play at Kendall called Corpus Christi Play, where there was a man on a tree and blood ran downe, &c., and after he professed he could not remember that ever he heard of salvation by Jesus but in that play." It is impossible to say to what extent even the Scriptural allusions in the works of Shakespeare himself may not be attributed to recollections of performances of the mysteries, for in one instance at least the reference by the great dramatist is to the history as represented in those plays not to that recorded in the New Testament. The English mysteries indeed never lost their position as religious instructors, a fact which, viewed in connexion with that of a widely spread affection for the old religion, appears to account for their long continuance in a practically unaltered state while other species of dramas were being developed by their side. From the fourteenth century until their suppression in the reign of James the First they remained the simple poetic versions in dialogue of religious incidents of various kinds, enlivened by the occasional admission of comic scenes,—"Interminglinge therewith, onely to make sporte,—Some thinges not warranted by any writt," Banes to the Chester Plays. In some few instances the theological narrative was made subservient to the comic action, but as a rule the mysteries were designed to bring before the audience merely the personages and events of religious history. Allegorical characters had been occasionally introduced, and about the middle of the fifteenth century there appeared a new kind of English dramatic composition, apparently borrowed from France, in which the personages were either exclusively or almost exclusively of that description. When the chief object of a performance of this nature was to inculcate a moral lesson, it was sometimes called either a Moral or a Moral-play, terms which continued in use till the seventeenth century and were licentiously applied by some early writers to any dramas which were of an ethical or educational character. Some of the moral-plays were nearly as simple and inartificial as the mysteries, but others were not destitute of originality or even of the delineation of character and manners. There is an interesting account of a genuine Moral of the time of Shakespeare's boyhood which no doubt belonged to a class of plays the great dramatist saw acted in his native town. The title of this piece was the Cradle of Security, performed at Gloucester about the year 1572. The writer of the following description and Shakespeare were born in the same year, 1564, so that, when he gives an account of the performance from personal recollection, it requires no great exertion of the imagination to believe it possible that the poet himself could have related the narrative in similar terms, especially as it is ascertained from other sources that the Cradle of Security was extremely popular, and it was therefore very likely to have been acted at Stratford-on-Avon in the same season and by the same company who produced it in the neighbouring county,—" *Upon a Stage-play which I saw when I was a child.* In the city of Gloucester the manner is, as I think it is in other like corporations, that when players of enterludes come to towne they first attend the Mayor to enforme him what noble-mans servants they are, and so to get licence for their publike playing; and if the Mayor like the actors, or would shew respect to their lord and master, he appoints them to play their first play before himselfe and the Aldermen and Common Counsell of the city; and that is called the Mayors play, where every one that will comes in without money, the Mayor giving the players a reward as hee thinks fit to shew respect unto them. At such a play my father tooke me with him and made mee stand betweene his leggs as he sate upon one of the benches, where wee saw and heard very well. The play was called the Cradle of Security, wherin was personated a king or some great prince, with his courtiers of severall kinds, amongst which three ladies were in speciall grace with him; and they, keeping him in delights and pleasures, drew him from his graver counsellors, hearing of sermons and listning to good counsell and admonitions, that in the end they got him to lye downe in a cradle upon the stage, where these three ladies joyning in a sweet song rocked him asleepe that he snorted againe; and in the meane time closely conveyed under the cloaths wherewithall he was covered a vizard, like a swines snout, upon his face, with three wire chaines fastned thereunto, the other end whereof being holden severally by those three ladies, who fall to singing againe, and then discovered his face that the spectators might see how they had transformed him, going on with their singing. Whilst all this was acting, there came forth of another doore at the farthest end of the stage two old men, the one in blew with a serjeant at armes his mace on his shoulder, the other in red with a drawn sword in his hand and leaning with the other hand upon the others shoulder; and so they two went along in a soft pace round about by the skirt of the stage, till at last they came to the cradle, when all the court was in greatest jollity; and then the foremost old man with his mace stroke a fearfull blow upon the cradle, whereat all the courtiers, with the three ladies and the vizard, all vanished; and the desolate prince starting up bare-faced, and finding himselfe thus sent for to judgement, made a lamentable complaint of his miserable case, and so was carried away by wicked spirits. This prince did personate in the Morall the Wicked of the World; the three ladies, Pride, Covetousnesse and Luxury; the two old men, the End of the World and the Last Judgement. This sight tooke such impression in me that, when I came towards mans estate, it was as fresh in my memory as if I had seen it newly acted," Willis's Mount Tabor or Private Exercises of a Penitent Sinner, published in the yeare of his age 75, Anno Dom. 1639, pp. 110-113. Moral-plays were not only performed in Shakespeare's day but continued to be a recognized form of dramatic composition. There was in fact no consecutive or systematic development of either the mystery into the moral or the moral into the historical and romantic drama, although there are examples in which the specialities of each are curiously intermingled. Each species of the early English drama appears for the most part to have pursued its own separate and independent career.

The allegorical was the first deviation from the purely religious drama. The introduction of secular plays quickly followed, after which, from the close of the fifteenth century to the time of Shakespeare, there was a succession of interludes and other theatrical pieces in great variety, in many of which some of the characters were abstract personifications similar to those introduced into the moral-plays. The most ancient English secular drama which is known to exist was written about the year 1480, and afterwards printed by Rastell under the title of,—"Here is conteyned a godely interlude of Fulgeus Cenatoure of Rome, Lucres his daughter, Gayus Flaminius and Publius Cornelius, of the disputacyon of noblenes, and is deuyded in two partyes to be played at ii. tymes. Compyled by mayster Henry Medwall, late Chapelayne to the ryght reuerent Fader in God Iohan Morton cardynall, Archebysshop of Caunterbury." Medwall was the author of at least two other lengthy pieces, in both of which, however, the characters were mainly allegorical, and he appears to have been the first writer who introduced a prose speech into an English play. His works, however dull, are superior both in construction and versification to those of his predecessors, and he may almost be said to be really the founder of our national drama;—but this is a digression. The history of that branch of our literature previously to the reign of Elizabeth is consistently left to abler hands. The subject is beyond the latitude of the present work, for although it is most likely that Shakespeare witnessed representations of some of our ancient mysteries and interludes, a probability which has sanctioned these few observations, there are no reasons for believing that his dramatic art was influenced in a direct manner by any plays which were composed anterior to that period. Neither was the Shakespearean drama the termination of a progressive development from the ancient mystery.

Unconnected Shakespeares.—It will be convenient to arrange under this title a few remarks on the surname of Shakespeare and on persons of that name who, so far as is at present known, were not even remotely connected with the family of the great dramatist. The name probably arose in the thirteenth century, when surnames derived from personal occupations first came into general use in this country, and it appears to have rapidly become a favourite patronymic. The origin of it is sufficiently obvious. Some, says Camden, are named "from that which they commonly carried, as Palmer, that is, Pilgrime, for that they carried palme when they returned from Hierusalem; Long-sword, Broad-speare, Fortescu, that is, Strong-shield, and in some such respect, Breake-speare, Shake-speare, Shot-bolt, Wagstaffe," Remaines, ed. 1605, p. 111. "Breakspear, Shakspear and the lyke, have bin surnames imposed upon the first bearers of them for valour and feates of armes," Verstegan's Restitution of Decayed Intelligence, ed. 1605, p. 294. Drawsword was another old English surname of similar formation. The name of our poet's family was certainly known as early as the thirteenth century, there having been a John Shakespere, living, apparently in Kent, in the year 1279, who is mentioned in Plac. Cor. 7 Edw. I. Kanc. In the fourteenth and fifteenth centuries there were Shakespeares residing in several English counties both in the north and south, and in the two following centuries there were families of the name to be found in nearly every part of England. It cannot be said that during the latter period the surname was anywhere an excessively rare one, but from an early date Shakespeares abounded most in Warwickshire. In the fifteenth century they were to be found in that county at Coventry, Wroxhall, Balsall, Knowle, Meriden and Rowington; in the sixteenth century, at Berkswell, Snitterfield, Lapworth, Haseley, Ascote, Rowington, Packwood, Salford, Tanworth, Barston, Warwick, Tachbrook, Haselor, Rugby, Budbrook, Wroxhall, Norton-Lindsey, Wolverton, Hampton-in-Arden, Knowle, Hampton Lucy and Alcester; and in the seventeenth century, at Weston, Haseley, Henley-in-Arden, Kenilworth, Wroxhall, Nuneaton, Tardebigg, Charlcote, Kingswood, Knowle, Flekenho, Coventry, Rowington, Hatton, Ansley, Solihull, Lapworth, Budbrook, Arley, Packington, Tanworth, Warwick, Longbridge, Kington, Fillongley, Little Packington, Meriden, Long Itchington, Claverdon and Tachbrook. It is not probable that this list, which has been compiled almost exclusively from records inspected by myself, is by any means a complete one, but it is sufficiently extensive to show how very numerous formerly were Shakespeares in Warwickshire, and how dangerous it must be, in the absence of direct evidence, to assume that early notices of persons of that name relate to members of the poet's family. Thus it has happened that more than one John Shakespeare has been erroneously identified with the father of the great dramatist. There was an agriculturist of that name who in 1570 was in the occupation of a small farm, situated in the parish of Hampton Lucy near Stratford-on-Avon, which was described as "one other meadowe with thappurtenaunces called or knowen by the name of Ingon alias Ington meadowe, conteynynge by estymacion fouretene acres, be it more or lesse, then or late in the tenure or occupacion of John Shaxpere or his assignes," Rot. Claus. 23 Eliz. This individual has always been considered to have been the John Shakespeare of Henley Street, but that he was a different person who resided at Ingon appears from the following entry in the Hampton Lucy register under the date of 1589,—"Joannes Shakespere of Yngon was buried the xxv. th of September." It has also been supposed that the poet's father resided about the year 1583 at Clifford, a village at a short distance from Stratford-on-Avon, but that this conjecture is groundless may be confidently inferred from the fact of the John Shakespeare of Clifford having been married there in 1560 to a widow of the name of Hobbyns. "1560, 15 Octobris, John Shaxspere was maryed unto Julian Hobbyns vidua," MS. Register in Clifford Church. Even when there are documents which yield notices referring apparently to one individual in one locality, identification should not be assumed in the absence of corroborative evidence or at least of circumstances inducing a high degree of probability; but when, as in the instances just discussed, there are merely the facts of persons of the same Christian and surname living about the same period in neighbouring but different parishes, conjecture of

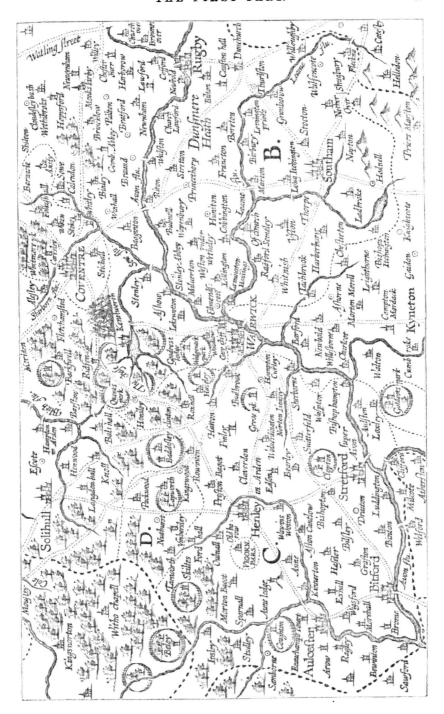

identity, without such confirmation, ought to be inadmissible. Neither would any interest attach to the volumes which might be compiled on the numerous ancient branches of the Shakespeares, and at the same time be destitute of a single morsel of real evidence to connect them in any degree of consanguinity with those of Stratford-on-Avon.

Amongst the multitude of Shakespeare families who were settled in Warwickshire in the sixteenth and seventeenth centuries the Shakespeares of Rowington are those most frequently noticed in the records of those times. It is no exaggeration to say that at least fifty pages of this work could be filled even with the materials regarding them which have been collected by myself, and these are certainly not exhaustive. If any connexion, however slight, had existed between the Shakespeares of Rowington and those of Stratford-on-Avon during that period, it is all but impossible that some indication of the fact should not be discovered in one or other of the numerous wills, law papers and other documents of the Rowington family. There is nothing of the kind. The conjecture that Richard Shakespeare of Snitterfield, who was very likely the poet's grandfather and was living there as lately as 1560, removed some time after that year to Rowington and was the same person as the Richard Shakespeare of the latter village who died in or about 1592, is one of those gratuitous speculations which unfortunately embarrass most discussions on genealogical subjects. Richard had been a Christian name in the Rowington family at least as early as the time of Henry the Eighth, as appears from the subsidy rolls of that reign, and it frequently occurs in the Rowington Shakespeare documents from that period to the close of the seventeenth century. There is no reason for believing that any person of the name migrated to Rowington after the year 1560, much less any evidence that he arrived there from Snitterfield. It is not probable, however, that the idea of a connexion between the Shakespeares of Rowington and the poet's family would have arisen, had it not been assumed from the fact of Shakespeare having been a copyholder under the manor that he was also connected with the parish. This was not necessarily the case. Singularly enough there were two very small properties at Stratford-on-Avon held under the manor of Rowington, but it does not follow from the mere circumstance of Shakespeare purchasing one of these estates that he was connected in any way with that village or even that he was ever there. Rowington and Stratford-on-Avon are in the same Hundred, but they were about twelve miles distant from each other by the nearest road, and there was very little communication between the two places in Shakespeare's time. Their relative situations will be best observed in the map of Warwickshire engraved in 1603, in which the indirect roads between them are delineated. More than one person of the name of William Shakespeare resided at Rowington in the times of Elizabeth and the first James. Richard Shakespeare of Rowington, who died in 1560, mentions his son William in a will dated in the same year. It appears from the will of another Richard Shakespeare of Rowington, 1591, that his youngest son was also named William. There was a William Shakespeare who signs his name with a mark, something like a small letter a,—"the mark of William Shakespere,"—in a roll of the customs of the manor of Rowington which were confirmed in 1614, this person being one of the jury sworn on that occasion. The eldest son of a Richard Shakespeare of Rowington, who died in 1614, was also called William, as appears from his will and from the papers of a Chancery suit of 1616. This individual may or may not have been the marksman of the customs-roll. He was over forty years of age in 1614, as is ascertained from the Chancery records just mentioned. Which of these William Shakespeares was the trained soldier of Rowington in the muster-roll of 1605 is a matter of no consequence, it being certain that the latter was not the great dramatist, who, in such a list, would undoubtedly have been described as belonging to Stratford-on-Avon not to a place in which he never resided. A reference to the original muster-roll will set the question at rest, a list of the trained soldiers at Stratford-on-Avon appearing not only in a different part of the manuscript but in another division of the Hundred and including no person of the name of Shakespeare.

Shakespeare's Mulberry-Tree.—The mere circumstance of Shakespeare having planted a mulberry-tree at New Place would scarcely have been worth recording had it not been an evidence of the interest taken by the poet in his garden. It thus becomes a testimony of value in the history of his tastes and pursuits. If the tradition which associates this celebrated tree with the great dramatist could not be traced to a period anterior to the Jubilee of 1769, grave suspicions might be entertained respecting its genuineness, but it was not until that festival was in contemplation that there was a tendency towards the fabrication of Shakespearean anecdotes and relics at Stratford-on-Avon. From the time that Garrick succeeded in creating a general public interest in the birth-town of Shakespeare to the present day, all kinds of deception have been practised in these matters; but there is no reason for believing that this was the case previously to the celebration of the Jubilee. The tree was cut down in or about 1758, and early in the following year, if not before, tobacco-stoppers made of its wood were publicly sold as Shakespearean relics by one Moody, a toy-seller at Birmingham; Hull's Select Letters, 1778, i. 251. The gift of one of these relics made by Percy through Shenstone to a mutual friend in 1759 was the occasion of a silly hoax practised upon the credulity of the latter, Shenstone accompanying the present with a forged correspondence respecting the tree. There can therefore be no doubt that long before the Jubilee, and very soon after the tree was felled, it was known as Shakespeare's mulberry-tree and relics made from it exposed for sale. It may be observed in confirmation of this that in the following year, 1760, the Corporation presented an inkstand made of the wood to the Steward of the Court of Record, who thus expresses his thanks in a letter to the Town-Clerk dated August 2nd, 1760,—"I really want words to express the sense I have of this great instance of regard which the Corporation of Stratford have honoured me with by their Chamberlain. I do not know any present that could have been so agreeable to me—not only as a testimony of respect to me from the Corporation, which I shall always pride myself upon, but also as it falls in with what, if I had known how to have wished, I should most certainly have wished for. The standish of Shakspeare's planting is the fittest ornament for an hermitage." A person named Sharp owned a large quantity of the wood of the mulberry-tree and his original bill against the Corporation for the portions supplied on this and on some other similar occasion is preserved in their archives, and the date of it being of importance in the present enquiry, it is here given in facsimile. A lady who visited Stratford-on-Avon in the spring of the same year, 1760, after quoting the epitaph on Shakespeare's monument, that part of it referring to "envious death," proceeds to say,—"death, however, in taking Shakespear from the world so early, is, I think, far outdone by a man now living in or near this town; for there was till lately the house in which Shakespear lived and a mulberry-tree of his planting; the house large, strong and handsome; the tree so large that it would shade the grass-plat in your garden, which I think is

> The Gentlemen of the Borough of Stratford &c.
> 1760   to Thos Sharp
>   £ s d
> Augst For Mulberry Wood to make a tea Chest   0 =12= 0
>   2d   Ditto for Canisters —   —   —   0 = 3= 0
>   one Ink Stand —   —   —   0 = 7= 6
>   Silver furniture for the Ink Stand   0 = 5= 0
>   Expences and loss in sending for }
>   the Silver furniture for the tea Chest } 0 = 7= 0
>   1 =14= 0
> 1761 Recvd the Contents of the above   1 =11= 6
> Jany
> 25th   Thos Sharp

more than twenty yards square, and supply the whole town with mulberries every year. As the curiosity of this house and tree brought much fame and more company and profit to the town, this man, on some disgust, has pulled the house down so as not to leave one stone upon another, and cut down the tree and piled it as a stack of firewood, to the great vexation, loss and disappointment of the inhabitants. However, an honest silversmith bought the whole stack of wood, and now makes many odd things of this wood for the curious." These evidences show that the wood was highly esteemed almost immediately after the destruction of the tree. There is a story that Sharp merely bought the remains for firewood, and that, shortly after the purchase, some of the wood being seen on the fire, a gentleman happening to be present and suggesting the profit that could be made by converting it into saleable relics, Sharp seized the hint directly and even snatched away the log that was burning. This anecdote was related to me in 1863 by Thomas Gibbs, who was for many years one of Sharp's assistants, and so had an opportunity of being well-informed on the subject. If Sharp really did buy the remains of the tree at a firewood price, the fact is undoubted that he very soon discovered their importance and that the Corporation as early as 1760 acknowledged the value of his purchase. A few years afterwards he was accused of having used spurious wood, and the report was deemed of sufficient moment to be contradicted in the year 1768 by the special declaration of a person from whom he was said to have purchased it. Sharp, in an affidavit, states that Gastrell "cut down the mulberry-tree and cleft it as firewood, when the greatest part of it was purchased by me the said Thomas Sharp, who employed one John Luckman to convey it to my own premises, where I have worked it into many curious toys and usefull articles from the same." Notices of mulberry-tree relics dated between the years 1760 and 1768 are exceedingly rare, but after the latter date they are "as plenty as blackberries." A history of these relics might be compiled at great length, but would hardly be of interest to any but the owners of such memorials. What has been already stated suffices to establish the only fact after the removal of the tree which is of any biographical value. That its wood was venerated at the time of that event adds to the probability of the tradition that the tree was planted by Shakespeare.

Sir Hugh Clopton, who resided at New Place during the first half of the last century, died in 1751, and in 1756 the estate was sold by his representatives to the Rev. Francis Gastrell, who, in 1759, pulled the modern building, not Shakespeare's house, down to the ground. Previously to the removal of this structure the reverend owner of New Place had felled the mulberry-tree to the great annoyance of the inhabitants of the town. The late R. B. Wheler tells us that he recollects his father saying that, when a boy, he assisted in breaking Gastrell's windows in revenge for the fall of the tree, which latter act, however, may be accounted for without attaching wilful blame to Gastrell, a person who obviously had little sympathy with Shakespearean enthusiasts. Several accounts agree in stating that it had attained a great magnitude with overhanging boughs, the trunk being in a state of decay, and indeed it is most probable that a tree of a century and a half's growth would have been of a very considerable size, the soil of Stratford being peculiarly favourable to the luxuriant growth of the mulberry. If planted at all near the house, its boughs would certainly have overshadowed some of the rooms at the back. Davies, in his Life of Garrick, the first edition of which appeared in 1780, expressly asserts that "the mulberry-tree planted by the poet's own hand became an object of dislike to this tasteless owner of it because it overshadowed his window, and rendered the house, as he thought, subject to damps and moisture." Here is a plausible reason given for the removal of the tree, which may have been accomplished somewhat thoughtlessly, without a presentiment of the indignation the act would excite at Stratford; and the statement made by Davies is supported by the fact that the mulberry-tree was situated in the small garden at the back of New Place, the one near the house. One Charles Oakes, in an affidavit made in a lawsuit in 1807, supported by recollections of Stratford extending to the period of Gastrell's residence there, says that the garden which was opposite the vicar's garden wall, the latter near the Chapel and in Chapel Lane, "was called the Shakespeare Garden, being the garden on the north side of the lane, and so called from the mulberry-tree planted by Shakespeare growing therein." At this time the site of the tree had been generally forgotten, and most people took it for granted that the mulberry-tree planted in the Great Garden was in the situation of the old one. In a plan of Stratford made in 1802 the "spot on which grew Shakspeare's mulberry" is marked as being in the Great Garden, but apparently at some little distance westward from the present tree. There is evidence of what was the belief at Stratford-on-Avon only twenty years after the tree was cut down, in a paper accompanying a letter from the Rev. Richard Jago, vicar of Snitterfield, to the Town-clerk of Stratford, written in 1778, in which he gives an extract from a pretended work entitled, Acts and Monuments of the Fairies, consisting of a decree from King Oberon to his loving fairy subjects respecting their revels held in the poet's garden,—"And whereas by the wilful and malicious destruction of the said mulberry-tree, as before recited, and other damage at New Place, late the mortal residence of the said William Shakespear of immortal memory, the sports and recreations of our good subjects have been grievously disturbed and interrupted, now we, taking the same into our serious consideration, have ordered and ordained, and by these presents do order and ordain, that the said sports and recreations formerly kept and held by our good people under the said mulberry-tree *do forthwith cease at the place where the said mulberry-tree stood*, and that from henceforth they be duely celebrated and observed with accustomed rites *in the piece of ground next thereunto adjoining*, being part or parcel of the terrestrial estate of the said William Shakespear, and now belonging to our beloved William Hunt, of whose affection for us and our people we have undoubted assurance, as likewise of his care to cultivate the same with all manner of productions agreeable to us, and to cause the same to be laid in proper places with clean and close-binding gravel, and the grass thereof to be neatly and frequently mowed for the better accommodation of our good subjects in celebrating the said rites; and our royal will and pleasure further is that a part of the said ground lying nearest to the river Avon, and appropriated hereby to the celebration of the said rites, shall henceforth be called Fairy Lawn, and that a fair pedestal or tablet of stone shall be erected in the centre of the said lawn, and an inscription, recording our affection and regard for the said William Shakespear, and our determination herein, engraven thereon." This document, written by a person well acquainted with the locality for the amusement of one who must have been familiar with all the Stratford testimony on the subject, furnishes conclusive evidence that the site of the original tree was in the smaller garden. The one now in the Great Garden is said to have been raised from a scion of Shakespeare's tree, but this tradition is at least doubtful. Enquiries have not succeeded in tracing its existence previously to William Hunt's tenancy, some considerable time after the removal of the older tree, and that Gastrell took sufficient interest in the matter to plant a sapling from the latter is improbable, nor is there any record to that effect. It is obvious that if Gastrell had cared in the least for the preservation of a Shakespearean relic, he would never have committed the vandalic act of cutting down the original tree. The late R. B. Wheler, who was better acquainted with the subject than any one else, distinctly asserts that—"it is well-known that neither of these trees (that at New Place and one in Old Town), nor that growing in the Lion garden, nor any other reported as such, ever sprung from Shakespeare's tree; many people are willing enough to affirm their own as a scion from the celebrated tree, but unfortunately their tales are foolish and improbable when examined."

- No record of Shakespeare's mulberry-tree has been discovered of a date previously to its destruction, but there is a story, resting on the testimony of a very old man, that Sir Hugh Clopton entertained friends under it about the year 1744. The statement has been repeated in many works with slight variations, but the only good authority for it appears to be an unpublished letter from Malone to Davenport, dated in April, 1788, in which he says,—"old Mr. Macklin the player, who is now playing with wonderful vigour in the eighty-eighth year of his age, informs me that Mr. Garrick and he paid a visit to Stratford about the year 1744, and were hospitably entertained by Sir Hugh Clopton, then a very old gentleman; his memory, however, is by no means accurate." Malone, referring to the mulberry-tree in another part of the same letter, adds,—"old Mr. Macklin says he was entertained under it by one of the Clopton family in 1744." It has also been generally stated that Denis Delane the actor was in company with Garrick and Macklin on the occasion, the earliest authority for which statement seems to be a passage in Ireland's Views, 1795, p. 201. Then there is the testimony of Jordan saying that "the mulberry-tree in the garden of New Place, planted by Shakespeare, was grown to a very large size with wide spreading boughs that shaded many yards of ground, under which were placed benches to sit on in the shade, and which I have heard Sir Hugh Clopton took great delight in shewing to the nobility and gentry whose curiosity excited them to visit the last memorial of immortal Shakespeare;" MS. at Stratford-on-Avon, repeated in nearly the same words in another MS. by the same writer. There appears to be little doubt of the fact that Sir Hugh Clopton, who, as is known from the evidence of Theobald, took an interest in the traditions respecting New Place, valued the mulberry-tree on account of its having been planted by Shakespeare. Thomas Sharp, the relic-carver, in a declaration made upon oath shortly before his death in 1799, asserted,—"that I was personally acquainted with Sir Hugh Clopton, knight, barrister at law and one of the Heralds at Arms, who was son of Sir John Clopton, knight, that purchased a certain messuage or house near the Chapel in Stratford, called the New Place, of the executors of Lady Elizabeth Barnard, and grand-daughter of Shakespear; and that I have often heard the said Sir Hugh Clopton solemnly declare that the mulberry-tree, which growed in his garden, was planted by Shakespear, and he took pride in shewing it to and entertaining persons of distinction whose curiosity excited them to visit the spot known to be the last residence of the immortal bard." The story told to Malone by Davenport, on the information of one Hugh Taylor, is so inconsistent with known facts that it cannot be received. "The Rev. Mr. Davenport," observes Malone, "informs me that Hugh Taylor, who is now (1790) eighty-five years old, and an alderman of Warwick, says, he lived when a boy at the next house to New Place; that his family had inhabited the house for almost three hundred years; that it (the fact of Shakespeare planting the tree) was transmitted from father to son during the last and the present century; that this tree, of the fruit of which he had often eaten in his younger days, some of its branches hanging over his father's garden, was planted by Shakespeare; and that, till this was planted, there was no mulberry-tree in that neighbourhood. Mr. Taylor adds that he was frequently when a boy at New Place, and that this tradition was preserved in the Clopton family as well as in his own," Life of Shakespeare, ed. 1790, p. 118. There was a family of the name of Taylor living in the same ward, but not in the house adjoining New Place, at the time here named, so that the old man's memory must have failed him. It is not impossible that he may have been, when a boy, on some occasion in the garden of Nash's house, and eaten of the mulberries from the branches of the New Place tree overhanging that garden.

The tradition respecting the mulberry-tree is the only evidence which has reached us of any sort of interest taken by the great dramatist in horticulture. It has indeed been attempted to prove his attachment to rural pursuits by various allusions in his works, but no inferences can be safely drawn from any number of such references. So marvellous was Shakespeare's all but intuitive perception of nearly every variety of human thought and knowledge, the result of an unrivalled power of rapid observation and deduction, if once the hazardous course of attempting to realize the personal characteristics or habits of the author through his writings be indulged in, there is scarcely an occupation he might not be suspected of having adopted at one period or other of his life. That Shakespeare was familiar with and fondly appreciated the beauty of our wild flowers; that he was acquainted with some of the cultivated plants and trees; that he had witnessed and understood a few of the processes of gardening;—these facts may be admitted, but they do not prove that he was ever a botanist or a gardener. Neither are his numerous allusions to wild flowers and plants, not one of which appears to be peculiar to Warwickshire, evidences, as has been suggested, of the frequency of his visits to Stratford-on-Avon. One writer advises us to "note as much as possible the chronology of Shakespeare's use of country terms and similes;" adding that "the prevalence of them in his earliest work, the Venus and Adonis, when he had just left Stratford, and in his latest Winter's Tale, after he had retired for good to his native town, is most striking." There is no evidence that the Winter's Tale was his latest play, nor are its rural allusions in any way the result of its having been composed at Stratford-on-Avon. To judge in that manner from those allusions it might be inferred that the play must have been written in London, for there is no proof that a specimen of one of the flowers therein mentioned, the crown-imperial, could have been seen at Stratford, whereas there is Gerard's excellent authority that it had "been brought from Constantinople amongst other bulbus rootes and made denizons in our London gardens," Herball, ed. 1597, p. 154. All inductions of this kind must be received with the utmost caution. Surely the poet's memory was not so feeble that it is necessary to assume that the selection of his imagery depended upon the objects to be met with in the locality in which he was writing. Even were this extravagant supposition to be maintained, no conclusion can be derived from it, for it is not probable that London would have had the exclusive possession of any cultivated flower, while it is certain that Stratford had not the monopoly of any wild one. It should be recollected that the line of demarcation between country and town life was not strongly marked in Shakespeare's day. The great dramatist may be practically considered never to have relinquished a country life during any part of his career, for even when in the metropolis he must always have been within a walk of green fields, woods and plant-bordered streams, and within a few steps of some of the gardens which were then to be found in all parts of London not even excepting in the limited area of the City. Wild plants, as has been previously observed (see p. 17), were to be seen in the immediate vicinity of the Shoreditch theatres, and there is perhaps not a specimen mentioned by Shakespeare which was not to be observed in or near the metropolis; but even were this not the case, surely the fact of his having resided in Warwickshire during at least the first eighteen years of his life is sufficient to account for his knowledge of them. Then again at a later period he must, in those days of slow and leisurely travel, have been well acquainted with the rural life and natural objects of many other parts of the country which were traversed by him when the members of the Lord Chamberlain's Company made their professional tours, and with the district between London and Stratford-on-Avon he must of course have been specially familiar. A consideration of these simple facts will render any further discussion on the subject unnecessary.

The New Place.—There is a vellum roll, which was written in the year 1483, in which mention is made of a tenement at Stratford-on-Avon *juxta Capellam modo Hugonis Clopton generosi*; but the earliest distinct notice of the large house in that town, situated at the corner of Chapel Street and Chapel Lane, generally referred to in the old records as the New Place, the term *place* being used in old English in the sense of residence or mansion, occurs in the will of Sir Hugh Clopton, an eminent citizen and mercer of London in the fifteenth century. In this will, dated on September 14th, the day before the testator's death, and proved in October, 1496, the building is devised in the following terms,—"to William Clopton I bequeith my grete house in Stratford-upon-Avon and all other my landes and tenementes being in Wilmecote, in the Brigge Towne and Stratford, with reversion and servyces and duetes thereunto belonginge, remayne to my cousin William Clopton, and for lak of issue of hym to remayne to the right heires of the lordship of Clopton for ever being heires mailes." That the "grete house" refers to New Place clearly appears from the inquisition upon Sir Hugh Clopton's death, taken at Stratford-on-Avon in 1497, in which he is described as being seized "de uno burgagio jacente in Chapell Strete in Stretford predicta *ex oposito Capelle ex parte boriali.*" Sir Hugh, shortly before his death, had granted a life-interest in the estate to one Roger Paget, in whose possession it was vested in 1496. The William Clopton, to whom the reversion in fee was bequeathed in the same year, was the son of John Clopton, and the grandson of Thomas Clopton, the brother of Sir Hugh. He was consequently the testator's great-nephew. Livery of seizin in respect to New Place was granted to him in July, 1504, probably after the death of Paget; Rot. Pat. 19 Hen. VII. He died in 1521, bequeathing all his lands and tenements in Stratford-upon-Avon to his wife Rose for her life. The words of the will are,—"I will that the said Rose my wel-beloved wif shall have for terme of hir lif and to hir assignes my manors of Ruyn Clyford and Brygtown with thappurtenaunces, and all my landez and tenementes with their appurtenauncez in Stratford-upon-Haven in the countie of Warwyke, and all other my landez, tenementes, rentes, revercions and servicez, with all and singler theire membres and appurtenaunces in Ruyn Clyfforde, Briggetown and Stratford-upon-Haven in the foresaid countie of Warwyke which nowe be, or at eny tyme were or have bene reputed, taken or knowen as percell of any of the said maners, or letten or taken to and with the said maners, or any of theym." In the inquisition taken on his death, held in September, 1521, he was found to be possessed of one tenement in Chapel Street situated to the north of the Chapel of the Guild,—"necnon de et in uno burgagio jacente in strata vocata Chapel Strete in Stratford super Avene ex parte boriali Capelle Sancte Trinitatis in Stratford predicta," Inq. 13 Henry VIII. William Clopton, in the same will, leaves "all such maners, londes and tenementis which were sumtyme of thenheritance of myne auncettours havyng the name and names of Clopton to those of the heirez males of my body commyng, and for defaulte of suche heire male of my body comyng, to the use of the heires malez of my said auncettours of the name of the Cloptones, accordyng to the old estates of intaylez and willis hertofore therof had, made and declared by my said auncettours, or any of theym." This devise seems to include New Place, otherwise there would be no provision for its descent after the death of Rose Clopton. The will is dated in May, 1521, and was proved in the following June. After Rose Clopton's death in 1525, New Place became the property of William Clopton, son of the above-named William. It is alluded to as his freehold estate in an inquisition taken on his death in 1560, and as consisting of one tenement or burgage with the appurtenances in Chapel Street, now or late in the tenure of William Bott,—"de et in uno tenemento sive burgagio cum pertinentiis in Stratford-super-Aven in dicto comitatu Warwici, in vico ibidem vocato *le Chappell strete* modo in tenura sive occupacione Willielmi Bott," Escheat. 2 Eliz.

Leland, who visited Stratford-on-Avon about the year 1540, describes New Place as an elegant house built of brick and timber. His words are,—" There is a right goodly chappell in a fayre street towardes the south ende of the towne, dedicated to the Trinitye; this chappell was newly re-edified by one Hugh Clopton, major of London; this Hugh Clopton builded also by the north syde of this chappell a praty house of bricke and tymbre wherin he lived in his latter dayes and dyed." Leland perhaps means that upright and cross pieces of timber were used in the construction of the house, the intervening spaces being filled in with brick. The situation of New Place in respect to the Chapel will be observed from the accompanying engraving, in which the excavations on the site of the house are seen at the

corner of Chapel Street and Chapel Lane. The Chapel narrowly escaped destruction at the time of the Reformation, notwithstanding the favourable report of Edward the Sixth's commissioners in 1547,—"yt is also a thinge very mete and necessary that the Guild Chappell of Stretfford stand undefaced, for that it was alwayes a chapell of ease for the seperacion of the sicke persons from the hole in tyme of plague, and standith in the face of the towne." In the Stratford Charter of 1553, it is certainly spoken of as if it were intended that it should be demolished. The Chapel, with the exception of the chancel, was rebuilt by Sir Hugh Clopton in the reign of Henry the Seventh. The present chancel, as appears from the Guild records, was erected in 1450 and 1451, while the rest of the Chapel, rebuilt towards the end of this century, was still unfinished at the time of Sir Hugh Clopton's death in 1496, so that the exact dates of the erection of all parts of the building are thus accurately known. "And whereas of late I have bargayned with oon Dowland and diverse other masons for the bilding and setting up of the Chapel of the Holy Trinitee within the Towne of Stratford-upon-Avon aforesaide, and the towre of a steple to the same, I will that the saide maisons sufficiently and ably doo and fynysshe the same with good and true werkmanshipp, and they truely to performe the same making the saide werkis as wele of length and brede and hight such as by the advise of mine executours and other diverse of the substantialest and honest men of the same parish shall or canne be thought moost conveniaunt and necessary; and all the foresaid werkis to be doon by myne executors and paied upon my proper goodes and charges; and in like wyse the covering and rofyng of the same chapell with glaising, and all other fornysshmentes therunto necessary to it, to be paide by my said executours as the werkis aforesaide goith fourth," Sir Hugh Clopton's Will, 1496. With the exception of the destruction of the cross over the porch, which was blown down in 1845, and the removal of the pinnacles in consequence of their insecure state in 1846, the exterior of the Guild Chapel is one of the few buildings at Stratford which are yet seen in the same form in which they appeared to Shakespeare. This beautiful little edifice, with its elegant porch and quaint gargoyles, must have been one of the objects most familiar to the poet, and being so near to New Place, it almost becomes identified with his personal history. The

GARGOYLES ON THE PORCH OF THE GUILD CHAPEL.

interior has been sadly altered, the images thrown down, its paintings whitewashed, and the whole in recent years modernized in execrable taste.

Leland appears to have been misinformed when he made the statement that Sir Hugh lived at New Place in the latter part of his life, and that he died there. It seems evident from his having been buried at St. Margaret's in Lothbury, as recorded by Stow, that he died in London, for he expressly stipulates in his will that if Stratford was the place of his death, he should be buried in that town. New Place, as previously mentioned, was not even in Sir Hugh's possession at that period, it having been sold or given by him to one Roger Paget for the life of the latter; so that in fact New Place did not revert to the Cloptons until after the death of Paget. It may be doubted if any members of the Clopton family lived at New Place in the sixteenth century, for they are generally spoken of as residing at Clopton and in no record of that century yet produced is there any evidence they were living in Stratford. In November, 1543, William Clopton let New Place on lease to Dr. Thomas Bentley for the term of fourty years, the Doctor paying a yearly rent of ten pounds for the house including some lands in the neighbourhood. Some time afterwards this lease was surrendered, and a new one granted at the same rental to continue in force during the lives of Dr. Bentley and his wife Anne, or during her widowhood should she survive her husband. Dr. Bentley died in or about the year 1549, leaving New Place *in great ruyne and decay and unrepayryd*. One of the few small fragments of the house of that day now preserved is a piece of ancient brick vaulting, here engraved, which may probably have supported the roof of one of its cellars. Bentley's widow married Richard Charnocke, and the lease by this

event being forfeited, Clopton entered into possession of the premises, a circumstance which occasioned the suit in Chancery the object of which is set forth in the papers which will be found in the Appendix, pp. 124-126. The result is not stated, but there can be little doubt that it terminated in some way in favour of the defendant, William Clopton, who devised his estates at Stratford-on-Avon to his son William by his will dated 4 Jan. 2 Eliz., 1560,—"I will, give and bequeth to William Clopton my sonne all that my mannor of Rion Clyfforde and Bridgetowne withe thappurtenaunces in Ryon Clyfforde and Bridgetowne, with all and singuler my landes, tenementes and hereditamentes, medowes, moores, fedinges, pastures, wooddes, underwooddes, rentes and revercions and services, with all and singuler theire appurtenaunces, situat lyinge and beinge in Ryen Clyfforde and Bridgetowne and Stratford-upon-Aven, to have and to holde the saide mannour, landes, tenementes and all other the premisses, with all and singuler thappurtenaunces, unto the saide William Clopton my sonne, and to the heires of his bodie lawfully begotten." This devise was encumbered with a number of heavy legacies, in consequence of which Clopton was compelled to part with some of the estates, which he did in 1563 to one William Bott, who had previously resided at New Place and in that year became its owner. It may be assumed that the latter was living at New Place in 1564, when his name occurs in the Council-book of Stratford as contributing more than any one else in the town to the relief of the poor. His signature, here annexed, 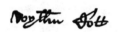 is taken from an autograph to an order signed by the members of the Corporation of Stratford in 1565, in the course of which year it appears that he was engaged in a serious quarrel with that body, and, indeed, there is evidence to show that he was somewhat of a litigious disposition. New Place was conveyed to Bott in 1563 by a deed of feoffment. His transactions with Clopton were mysterious and extensive, but there is no good reason for a supposition that New Place was obtained in other than an honourable manner. Clopton's embarrassments appear to have arisen from his father burdening his estates with legacies of unusual magnitude, and hence arose the necessity for a recourse to a friendly capitalist.

During the time that Bott was in possession of New Place he brought an action of trespass against Richard Sponer, accusing the latter of entering into a close in Chapel Lane belonging to Bott called the *barne yarde nigh le New Place gardyn*, and taking thence by force twelve pieces of squared timber of the estimated value of fourty shillings. This act is stated to have been committed on June 18th, 1565, and the spot referred to was clearly an enclosed space of ground in which stood a barn belonging to New Place, a little way down Chapel Lane next to the garden belonging to that house. This Richard Sponer was a painter living at the time in Chapel Street in the third house from New Place and on the same side of the way, a fact which appears from a lease granted by the Corporation on May 28th, 1563, to "Rychard Sponer of Stratford peynter" of "a tenement wyth appurtenaunces scytuate and beinge in the borrough of Stratford aforseid, in a strete there callyd the Chapell Strete, nowe in the tenure and occupacion of the seid Richard, and also a gardyn and bacsyde adjoynynge to the seid tenemente now lykwyse in the tenure and occupacion of the seid Richard." It appears from an endorsement that the house was the same which was afterwards held by John Tomlins, the garden of which extended to the western side of what was afterwards the Great Garden of New Place. "John Tomlins holdeth one tenemente with thappurtenaunces late in the tenure of Richard Sponer," Rent Roll, January, 1597-8. Now, in all probability, the timber was taken by Sponer from a spot close to his own garden, the division between the premises being in those days either a hedge or mud-wall, not a fence of a nature which would have rendered the achievement a difficult one. Sponer, in his defence, admits taking away six pieces of timber, but asserts that the plaintiff had presented the same to one Francis Bott, who had sold them to the defendant. This statement is declared by William Bott to be false, but it is reiterated by Sponer in the subsequent proceedings. The result of the action is not recorded, but it was settled, probably by compromise, at the close of the year. Several papers respecting this suit have been preserved, but the only one of interest in connexion with the New Place is the following plea which Bott filed against Sponer on September 12th, 1565,—" Willielmus Bott queritur versus Ricardum Sponer de placito transgressionis, et sunt plegii de prosequendo, videlicet Johannes Doo et Ricardus Roo, unde idem Willielmus, per Jacobum Woodward attornatum suum, dicit quod predictus Ricardus, xviij. die Junii, anno regni domine Elizabethe Dei gracia Anglie Francie et Hibernie regine, fidei defensoris, etc., septimo, vi et armis, etc., clausum ipsius Willielmi Bott vocatum *le barne yarde*, jacens et existens in Stretford predicta juxta *le newe place gardyn*, in quodam⁎ venella vocata Dede Lane apud Stretford predictam, infra jurisdiccionem hujus curie, fregit et intravit, et duodecim pecias de meremiis vocatas *xij. peces of tymber squaryd and sawed* precii quadraginta solidorum de bonis cattallis⁎ ipsius Willielmi Bott adtunc et ibidem inventas cepit et asportavit, unde idem Willielmus dicit quod deterioratus est et dampnum habet ad valenciam centum solidorum, et unde producit sectam, etc." The first mention of there being a garden attached to New Place occurs in this document. There could not have been a very large one belonging to the house during the early part of the century, for a portion, if not the whole, of what was afterwards called the Great Garden belonged to the Priory of Pinley up to the year 1544. In deeds of 12 Henry VI. and 21 Henry VI., the Clifford Charity estate is described as adjoining the *land* of the Prioress of Pinley; but in 12 Edward IV., that term is changed into *tenement*,—" inter tenementum Abbathie de Redyng ex parte una et tenementum priorisse de Pynley, nunc in tenura Johannis Gylbert, ex parte altera." From this period until some time after 1544, the probability is that there were a cottage and garden between New Place and the Clifford estate. As to the exact period when the cottage was pulled down, and its site with its garden attached to New Place, it would be in vain now to conjecture.

In July, 1567, the New Place estate was sold by William Bott and others to William Underhill for the sum of £40, being then described as consisting of one messuage and one garden,—" finalis concordia inter Willielmum Underehylle querentem et Willielmum Botte et Elizabetham uxorem ejus et Albanum Hetone deforcientes, de uno mesuagio et uno gardino cum pertinenciis in Stretford super Aven." The house is thus mentioned in a return to a commission issued out of the Exchequer for the survey of the possessions of Ambrose earl of Warwick, made in 1590,— " Willielmus Underhill generosus tenet libere quandam domum vocatum *the newe place* cum pertinentiis pro redditu per annum xij. d. sect. cur." From the circumstance that the owner of New Place, as will be seen afterwards, being connected with Hercules Underhill, the probability is that this William Underhill belonged to the family of the Underhills of Idlicote, and if so, to the father of Sir Hercules Underhill. William Underhill of Idlicote died in July, 1597, a few weeks after the sale of New Place to Shakespeare, and it appears from a nuncupative will, made on his death-bed, that he had owing to him two thousand pounds for which he had securities. It is not impossible that Shakespeare gave a security for part of the purchase-money of New Place by way of mortgage on the estate instead of paying the money, and that this security was handed over by the executors to Hercules Underhill in part payment of a legacy to him of £200. When Shakespeare paid off the security in 1602, the second fine, hereafter named, may have become necessary.

New Place continued in the hands of the Underhill family until the year 1597, when it was purchased by Shakespeare of William Underhill, and was then described as consisting of one messuage, two barns and two gardens, the latter duplications being fruits perhaps of a legal fiction. The following is a copy of the foot of the fine levied on this occasion,—" Inter Willielmum Shakespeare querentem et Willielmum Underhill generosum deforciantem, de uno mesuagio, duobus horreis, et duobus gardinis cum pertinentiis, in Stratford-super-Avon, unde placitum convencionis summonitum fuit inter eos in eadem curia, Scilicet quod predictus Willielmus Underhill recognovit predicta tenementa cum pertinentiis esse jus ipsius Willielmi Shakespeare, ut illa que idem Willielmus habet de dono predicti Willielmi Underhill, et illa remisit et quieta clamavit de se et heredibus suis predicto Willielmo Shakespeare et heredibus suis in perpetuum; et preterea idem Willielmus Underhill concessit pro se et heredibus suis quod ipsi warantizabunt predicto Willielmo Shakespeare et heredibus suis predicta tenementa cum pertinentiis in perpetuum. Et pro hac recognicione, quieta clamancia, waranto, fine et concordia idem Willielmus Shakespeare dedit predicto Willielmo Underhill sexaginta libras sterlingorum," Pasch. 39 Eliz. A facsimile of the exemplification of this fine, the one held by Shakespeare with his title-deeds, is here given. Another fine was levied on New Place in 1602, for the same property is referred to, notwithstanding the addition of the words, *et duobus pomariis*, in the foot of the fine,—" Inter Willielmum Shakespeare generosum querentem et Herculem Underhill generosum deforciantem, de uno mesuagio, duobus horreis, duobus gardinis, et duobus pomariis cum pertinentiis, in Stretford-super-Avon; unde placitum convencionis summonitum fuit inter eos in eadem curia, Scilicet quod predictus Hercules recognovit predicta tenementa cum pertinentiis esse jus ipsius Willielmi, ut illa que idem Willielmus habet de dono predicti Herculis, et illa remisit et quieta clamavit de se et heredibus suis predicto Willielmo et heredibus suis in perpetuum. Et preterea idem Hercules concessit pro se et heredibus suis quod ipsi warantizabunt predicto Willielmo et heredibus suis predicta tenementa cum pertinentiis contra predictum Herculem et heredes suos in perpetuum; et pro hac recognicione, remissione, quieta clamancia, waranto, fine et concordia idem Willielmus dedit predicto Herculi sexaginta libras sterlingorum," Mich. 44 & 45 Eliz. In the absence of the deed which would explain the object of this fine, it can only be conjectured that, after Shakespeare had bought New Place, it was discovered that Hercules Underhill had some contingent interest in the property which was conveyed to the poet by this second transaction.

Theobald, who was acquainted with Sir Hugh Clopton, and furnished by that gentleman with some traditional particulars respecting New Place, writing in 1733, states that when Shakespeare purchased it, he, "having repair'd and modell'd it to his own mind, chang'd the name to New Place, which the mansion-house, since erected on the same spot, at this day retains." Jordan improves upon this by stating that "this house, then a good deal out of repair, was sold to Mr. William

Facsimile of the Fine levied when the Estate of New Place was purchased by Shakespeare in 1597.

Shakespeare, who repaired it in a manner suitably for his reception, and laid out the garden in a handsome manner, where in or about the year 1609 he planted the mulberry-tree, the wood of which is now in such great estimation." The statement that the mulberry-tree was planted in the year 1609 is a mere conjecture, founded on the circumstance of great numbers of that tree having been imported in that year with the view of encouraging the breeding of silk-worms in this country; but the tree itself had been introduced into England long before that period. With respect to Theobald's account of the origin of the name of New Place, although it is known that the house was so called long before Shakespeare's time, considering that he derived his information from Sir Hugh Clopton, credence may be given to it so far as to believe that the poet made very extensive alterations, perhaps nearly rebuilding it. If the house was "in great ruyne and decay" in 1549, it may have been in a very deplorable state when Shakespeare bought it in 1597, and indeed this circumstance may account for the moderate amount of the purchase-money. It was probably altered or rebuilt by him in 1598, for in that year the Corporation, when engaged in repairing "the great stone bridge" over the Avon, "paid to Mr. Shaxspere for on lod of ston, x. *d*," which

stone was perhaps part of the old materials of the house, for there seems no other plausible explanation of his having such an article to dispose of, the subsoil of the land at New Place being gravelly.

The engraving of New Place, as it existed in 1599, executed by A. Birrell from a drawing by John Jordan, published in 1790 as taken "from a drawing in the margin of an ancient survey made by order of Sir George Carew, afterwards Baron Carew of Clopton and Earl of Totness, and found at Clopton near Stratford upon Avon in 1786," is either a modern forgery, or at least no representation of Shakespeare's residence. The best account of the probabilities respecting the true character of this drawing is given in a letter written by R. B. Wheler, dated February, 1810,—"the late John Jordan of Stratford, whose name appears at the corner of the plate, furnished, as he informed me, the drawing, having copied it from the margin of an antient survey made by order of Sir George Carew accidentally discovered by him at Clopton House, and which Sir George Carew married a co-heiress of William Clopton in 1580. This survey, Jordan told me, was of the Clopton family estates; but though New Place was originally built by a former Sir Hugh Clopton, yet it had been sold out of that family a considerable number of years before even Shakespeare became the purchaser and did not devolve to Sir John Clopton till towards the conclusion of the seventeenth century. How then came this house, when actually seventeen years before Sir George's marriage dismembered from the Clopton property and consequently belonging to a different family, introduced upon a survey of the Clopton estates taken by Carew's order? This identical survey Jordan, upon various subsequent searches at Clopton House, never met with again; nor can I, after diligent enquiries, learn what became of it, or even by any collateral evidence that it ever was in existence. Allowing, however, the survey to have been discovered, still I think the drawing on its margin must be ascribed to some other house belonging to that family, and I should be inclined to fix upon the residence of Thomas Hunt opposite Guildhall in Church Street, which formerly belonged to the Cloptons, a house which, antecedently to an alteration made by the late William Hunt, precisely corresponded with Jordan's drawing in the number and exact shape of the windows, the three conical dormants, the chimnies, central projection in front and its comparative dimensions."

In the drawing which Jordan originally sent to Malone, there were wooden pales represented as being in front of the house, and he told that critic that old people talked of remembering such pales before the ancient building of New Place. Jordan added the portico and placed Shakespeare's arms over the doorway on his own responsibility. He told Malone that the date at the top of the survey was 1599, that the names of the various purchasers to whom the property was sold by Joyce Lady Carew and Anne Clopton of Sledwick were written on the map, and that there was in the margin a note or drawing of the manor-house of Alveston represented as then belonging to Nicholas Lane. These statements are inconsistent with facts. Lady Carew never possessed any interest in New Place, and in 1599 the manor of Alveston was in the possession of Sir Edward Greville. The latter was not sold to the Lanes until October, 1603. Ireland, in his Picturesque Views on the Avon, 1795, p. 197, gives a variation of Jordan's pretended drawing of New Place, stating that his copy of the view was taken "from an old drawing of one Robert Treswell's, made in 1599 by order of Sir George Carew, afterwards Baron Carew of Clopton and Earl of Totness; it was found in Clopton House in 1786, and was in the possession of the late Mrs. Patriche, who was the last of the antient family of the Cloptons; the drawing, I am informed, is since lost or destroyed." Mrs. Partheriche, whose name is incorrectly given by Ireland, was the only surviving daughter of Edward, son of the Edward Clopton who owned New Place, and the last of the family. There was, however, at Clopton House a large plan of the family estates delineated by Robert Treswell alias Somersett in April, 1599, which in all probability suggested the pretended discovery of a contemporary drawing of New Place on the margin of such a survey. It is an interesting map of those Clopton estates which were situated on the eastern side of the Avon, and could never have included any representation of a house in Chapel Lane. The slight variation between the supposititious views of New Place published by Malone and Ireland is no good evidence that they were derived from independent sources. Both views were, in fact, furnished by Jordan, as appears from letters of Malone and Ireland to that person still preserved at Stratford. Jordan was a kind of local literary agent to both those writers, and, in the determination to find something new respecting the poet, he does not appear to have had complete regard either to accuracy or truth. It is, indeed, impossible in many cases to accept Jordan's statements unless their probability is strongly supported by other evidences, and it is deeply to be regretted that this should be the case, for Jordan wrote at a period when nearly every word emanating from his pen, had he been truthful, would have been of value. At the same time, it should be observed that he is sometimes right, when all his successors have been wrong, as may be instanced in the account of the rebuilding of New Place which took place about the year 1700.

Shakespeare's Manuscripts.—There is something rather more than a possibility that some of the manuscripts of the great dramatist are still in existence. Malone, writing to the vicar of Stratford-on-Avon in 1788, observes,—"I had *long since* heard a tradition that a parcel of Shakspeare's papers had been carried away by his grand-daughter into Northamptonshire, and such a tradition Mr. Macklin says the old gentleman of the Clopton family mentioned to him." The old gentleman here referred to was Sir Hugh Clopton, and Malone asserts that he told Macklin the story in the year 1742. That the anecdote is correctly reported may be inferred from the circumstance that the fact of Lady Barnard's removal to Abington, co. Northampton, had not been ascertained by research when Malone heard of the tradition, although it was one which obviously might have been known by report to Sir Hugh Clopton, who, as we learn from other evidences, took a warm interest in Shakespearean history. The tradition is in itself a highly probable one. Lady Barnard, Shakespeare's grand-daughter and last lineal descendant, was at the engaging age of eight when the poet was giving instructions for his will, and it clearly appears from the terms of that record that she was one of the testator's favourites. She could scarcely have held his memory otherwise than in affectionate regard, and leaving Stratford for her husband's residence at Abington at some time after her mother's death, New Place thenceforth being tenanted by strangers, had any of Shakespeare's manuscripts then remained in that house it is more than probable that they would have accompanied the plate and other movables to Northamptonshire. This consideration adds greatly to the probability of the tradition, which, if accepted, leads to the conclusion that the manuscripts were in existence at the time of Lady Barnard's decease in 1670, for it is extremely unlikely that she would have voluntarily destroyed papers sufficiently valued by her to have been carefully taken from Stratford-on-Avon a few years previously. Unless, therefore, they were intentionally destroyed by Sir John Barnard or his daughters, a step which was hardly likely to have been taken in a dramatic age long after the persecution of the stage had ceased, they were either dispersed, in which case some of them in all probability would have been seen before now, or they are accidentally concealed in some hidden recess to which they were consigned by Lady Barnard for their greater security. Many of our ancestors, as numerous discoveries testify, had a queer fancy for hiding books and manuscripts in obscure corners behind the wainscot, and it is not unlikely that in the large and elaborately paneled room at Abington Hall, an apartment which has been scarcely or at the most very slightly altered since the days of the Barnards, there may still be concealed inestimable treasures, perhaps the literary correspondence of Shakespeare, with autographs of his published dramas or even of some which have not yet seen the light. It is to be hoped that Lord Overstone, the present owner of that interesting mansion, may be induced to investigate the possibility of such a contingency. Not merely should the spaces behind the extensive old paneling but every nook of the ancient house be explored for the last chance of the discovery of relics which would be cheaply purchased by the wealth of the Indies.

APPENDIX.

I. *Contract between Henslowe and Allen, on the one Part, and Peter Street, Carpenter, on the other Part, for the Erection by the latter of the Fortune Theatre near Golden Lane, January 8th, 1599-1600. The Original of this Document was formerly preserved at Dulwich College, but it is not now known to exist. It is here given from a Copy printed in Malone's Historical Account of the English Stage, 1790, pp. 325-329. There is no doubt of its authenticity.*

This Indenture made the eighte day of Januarye, 1599, and in the two and fortyth yeare of the reigne of our sovereigne ladie Elizabeth, by the grace of God Queene of England, Fraunce and Ireland, defender of the fayth, &c., between Phillipp Henslowe and Edward Allen of the parishe of St. Saviours in Southwark, in the countie of Surry, gentlemen, on thone parte, and Peter Streete, citizen and carpenter of London, on thother parte,—Witnesseth that, whereas the said Phillipp Henslowe and Edward Allen the day of the date hereof have bargained, compounded, and agreed with the said Peter Streete for the erectinge, buildinge, and setting up of a new house and stage for a play-howse, in and uppon a certeine plott or peece of grounde appoynted oute for that purpose, scituate and beinge near Goldinge Lane in the parish of Saint Giles without Cripplegate of London; to be by him the said Peter Streete, or some other sufficient workmen of his providing and appoyntment, and att his propper costes and chardges, for the consideration hereafter in these presents expressed, made, builded, and sett upp, in manner and form following; that is to saie, the frame of the saide howse to be sett square, and to conteine fowerscore foote of lawful assize every waie square withoute, and fiftie five foote of like assize square everye waie within, with a good, suer, and stronge foundacion of pyles, brick, lyme, and sand, both withoute and within, to be wrought one foote of assize at the leiste above the ground; and the saide frame to conteine three stories in heigth, the first or lower storie to conteine twelve foote of lawful assize in heighth, the second storie eleaven foote of lawful assize in heigth, and the third or upper storie to conteine nine foote of lawful assize in height. All which stories shall conteine twelve foote and a half of lawful assize in breadth throughoute, besides a juttey forwards in eyther of the saide two upper stories of tene ynches of lawful assize; with fower convenient divisions for gentlemens roomes, and other sufficient and convenient divisions for twoo-pennie roomes; with necessarie seates to be placed and sett as well in those roomes as throughoute all the rest of the galleries of the said howse; and with suche like steares, conveyances, and divisions, without and within, as are made and contryved in and to the late-erected play-howse on the Bancke, in the said parish of Saint Saviours, called the Globe; with a stadge and tyreinge-howse, to be made, erected and sett upp within the saide frame; with a shadowe or cover over the saide stadge; which stadge shall be placed and sett, as alsoe the stearcases of the said frame, in such sorte as is prefigured in a plott thereof drawen; and which stadge shall conteine in length fortie and three foote of lawfull assize, and in breadth to extende to the middle of the yarde of the said howse; the same stadge to be paled in belowe with good stronge and sufficyent new oken boardes, and likewise the lower storie of the said frame withinsied, and the same lower storie to be alsoe laide over and fenced with stronge yron pyles; and the saide stadge to be in all other proportions contryved and fashioned like unto the stadge of the saide playhouse called the Globe; with convenient windowes and lights glazed to the saide tireynge-howse. And the saide frame, stadge, and stearcases to be covered with tyle, and to have a sufficient gutter of leade, to carrie and convey the water from the coveringe of the said stadge, to fall backwards. And alsoe all the saide frame and the stearcases thereof to be sufficyently enclosed without with lathe, lyme, and haire. And the gentlemens roomes and two-pennie roomes to be seeled with lathe, lyme, and haire; and all the flowers of the saide galleries, stories, and stadge to be boarded with good and sufficient newe deale boardes of the whole thicknes, wheare neede shall be. And the saide howse, and other thinges before mentioned to be made and doen, to be in all other contrivitions, conveyances, fashions, thinge and thinges, effected, finished and doen, according to the manner and fashion of the saide howse called the Globe; saveinge only that all the princypall and maine postes of the saide frame, and stadge forward, shall be square and wrought palaster-wise, with carved proportions called satiers to be placed and sett on the topp of every of the same postes; and saveing alsoe that the saide Peter Streete shall not be charged with anie manner of paynteinge in or aboute the saide frame, howse, or stadge, or anie parte thereof, nor rendering the walles within, nor seelinge anie more or other roomes then the gentlemens roomes, twoo-pennie roomes, and stadge, before mentioned. Nowe thereuppon the saide Peter Streete doth covenante, promise, and graunte for himself, his executors, and administrators, to and with the said Phillip Henslowe and Edward Allen, and either of them, and thexecutors and administrators of them, by these presents, in manner and forme followeinge, that is to say; that he the saide Peter Streete, his executors or assigns, shall and will, at his or their owne propper costes and chardges, well, workman-like, and substantially make, erect, sett upp, and fullie finnishe in and by all thinges, according to the true meaninge of theis presents, with good stronge and substancyall new tymber and other necessarie stuff, all the said frame and other works whatsoever in and uppon the saide plott or parcell of grounde, beinge not by anie authoritie restrayned, and having ingres, egres, and regres to doe the same, before the five and twentyth daye of Julie next comeing after the date hereof; and shall alsoe, att his or their like costes and chardges, provide and find all manner of workmen, tymber, joysts, rafters, boords, dores, bolts, hinges, brick, tyle, lathe, lyme, haire, sande, nailes, lead, iron, glass, workmanshipp and other thinges whatsoever, which shall be needful, convenyent and necessarie for the saide frame and works and everie parte thereof; and shall alsoe make all the saide frame in every poynte for scantlings lardger and bigger in assize then the scantlings of the timber of the saide newe-erected howse called the Globe. And alsoe that he the saide Peter Streete shall furthwith, as well by himselfe as by suche other and soe manie workmen as shall be convenient and necessarie, enter into and uppon the saide buildinges and workes, and shall in reasonable manner procode therein, withoute anie wilfull detraction, untill the same shall be fully effected and finished. In consideration of all which buildings, and of all stuff and workmanshipp thereto belonginge, the said Phillip Henslowe and Edward Allen, and either of them, for themselves, theire and either of theire executors and administrators, doe joyntlie and severallie covenante and graunt to and with the saide Peter Streete, his executors and administrators, by theis presents, that the said Phillipp Henslowe and Edward Allen, or one of them, or the executors, administrators, or assigns of them or one of them, shall and will well and truelie paie or cause to be paide unto the saide Peter Streete, his executors or assignes, att the place aforesaid appoynted for the erectinge of the said frame, the full some of fower hundred and fortie poundes of lawfull money of Englande, in manner and forme followinge; that is to saie, at suche tyme and whenas the tymber woork of the saide frame shall be raysed and sett upp by the saide Peter Streete, his executors or assignes, or within seaven daies then next followinge, twooe hundred and twentie poundes; and att suche time and whenas the said frame-work shall be fullie effected and finished as is aforesaid, or within seaven daies then next followinge, thother twooe hundred and twentie poundes, withoute fraude or coven. Provided allwaies, and it is agreed betwene the said parties, that whatsoever some or somes of money the said Phillip Henslowe or Edward Allen, or either of them, or the executors or assigns of them or either of them, shall lend or deliver unto the saide Peter Streete, his executors or assignes, or anie other by his appoyntment or consent, for or concerninge the saide woork or anie parte thereof, or anie stuff thereto belonginge, before the raiseing and setting upp of the saide frame, shall be reputed, accepted, taken and accoumpted in parte of the first payment aforesaid of the said some of fower hundred and fortie poundes; and all such some and somes of money as they, or anie of them, shall as aforesaid lend or deliver betwene the razeing of the said frame and finishing thereof, and of all the rest of the said works, shall be reputed, accepted, taken and accoumpted in parte of the laste payment aforesaid of the same some of fower hundred and fortie poundes; anie thinge above-said to the contrary notwithstandinge. In witness whereof the parties above-said to theis present indentures interchangeably have sett theire handes and seales. Yeoven the daie and yeare first above-written.

II. *The Docket at the Foot of the King's Bill authorising the Licence to Fletcher, Shakespeare, and others, to exercise the Art of playing Comedies, &c., May, 1603. From the Signet Office Dockets, anno Regni Regis Jacobi primo.*

May, 1603.—A licence from his Majestie to his servaunts, Lawrence Fletcher, William Shakespeare, Richard Burbage, Augustine Phillipps, John Henninges®, Henrie Condell, William Slye, Robert Armin, Richard Cowley, and the rest of their associates, to exercise the art of playing comedies, tragedies, histories, enterludes, moralles, pastoroles, stage playes and such like, in all townes and the Universities when the infection of the plague shall decrease.—vj. s. viij. d.

III. *Licence to Fletcher, Shakespeare, and others, to play Comedies, &c., 17 May, 1603. Bill of Privy Signet; endorsed, "The Players Priviledge."*

By the King.—Right trusty and wel beloved Counsellour, we greete you well, and will and commaund you that, under our Privie Seale in your custody for the time being, you cause our lettres to be directed to the Keeper of our Greate Seale of England, comaunding him that under our said Greate Seale he cause our lettres to be made patentes in forme following. —James, by the grace of God King of England, Scotland, Fraunce and Irland, Defendor of the Faith, &c., to all justices, maiors, sheriffes, constables, hedboroughes, and other our officers and loving subjectes greeting. Know ye that we, of our speciall grace, certaine knowledge and meere motion, have licenced and authorized, and by these presentes doo licence and authorize, these our servantes, Lawrence Fletcher, William Shakespeare, Richard Burbage, Augustine Phillippes, John Henninges®, Henry Condell, William Sly, Robert Armyn, Richard Cowlye and the rest of their associates, freely to use and exercise the arte and facultie of playing comedies, tragedies, histories, enterludes, moralles, pastoralles, stage plaies, and such other, like as they have already studied or heerafter shall use or studie, as well for the recreation of our loving subjectes as for our solace and pleasure when we shall thinke good to see them, during our pleasure. And the said comedies, tragedies, histories, enterludes, morall®, pastoralles, stage plaies and such like, to shew and exercise publiquely to their best commoditie, when the infection of the plague shall decrease, as well within their now usuall howse called the Globe within our countie of Surrey, as also within any towne halles or mouthalles, or other convenient places, within the liberties and freedome of any other cittie, universitie, towne or borough whatsoever within our said realmes and dominions, willing and comaunding you and every of you, as you tender our pleasure, not only to permitt and suffer them heerin without any your lettes, hinderances, or molestacions during our said pleasure, but also to be ayding and assisting to them, yf any wrong be to them offered; and to allowe them such former courtesies as hath bene given to men of their place and qualitie. And also, what further favour you shall shew to these our servantes for our sake, we shall take kindely at your handes. In witnes wherof &c. And these our lettres shall be your sufficient warrant and discharge in this behalf. Given under our Signot at our Mannor of Greenwiche the seavententh day of May in the first yeere of our raigne of England, Fraunce and Irland, and of Scotland the six and thirtieth.— Ex: per Lake.

To our right trusty and wel beloved Counsellour, the Lord Cecill of Esingdon, Keeper of our Privie Seale for the time being.

IV. *Writ of Privy Seal, being the Authority for the Patent under the Great Seal licensing Fletcher, Shakespeare and others, to act Plays. With the Recepi of the Lord Chancellor, 1603.*

Memorandum quod xix.^{mo} die Maij, anno infrascripto, istud breve deliberatum fuit Domino Custodi Magni Sigilli Angliæ apud Westmonasterium exequend:—James by the grace of God Kinge of England, Scotland, Fraunce and Ireland, Defendor of the Faith, &c., To our right trusty and wel beloved Counsellor, Sir Thomas Egerton, Knight, Keeper of our Great Seale of England, greeting. Wee will and commaund you that, under our said Great Seale being in your custody, you cause our lettres patentes to be made forth in forme following,—James by the grace of God Kinge of England, Scotland, Fraunce and Ireland,

Defendor of the Faith, &c., To all justices, maiors, sheriffes, constables, hedborowes and other our officers and loving subjectes, greeting. Knowe yee that wee, of our speciall grace, certeine knowledge and mere motion, have licensed and authorized, and by these present® doe licence and authorize these our servantes, Lawrence Fletcher, William Shakespeare, Richard Burbage, Augustine Phillippes, John Henninges®, Henry Condell, William Sly, Robert Armyn, Richard Cowlye and the rest of their associates, freely to use and exercise the art and facultie of playinge comedies, tragedies, histories, enterludes, moralles, pastoralles, stage plaies and such other like as they have alreadie studied, or hereafter shall use or studye, as well for the recreation of our loving subjectes as for our solace and pleasure when wee shall thinke good to see them during our pleasure; and the said comedies, tragedies, histories, enterludes, morall®, pastorolles, stage playes and such like to shew and exercise publiquely to their best commoditie, when the infection of the plague shall decrease, as well within their now usuall howse called the Globe within our County of Surrey as alsoe within any towne halles, or moutehalles, or other convenient places within the liberties and freedome of any other citie, universitie, towne or borough whatsoever within our said realmes and dominions; willinge and commaunding you, and every of you, as you tender our pleasure, not only to permitt and suffer them herein, without any your lettes, hinderaunces or molestations, during our said pleasure, but alsoe to be aiding and assisting to them if any wronge be to them offered, and to allowe them such former courtesies as hath bene given to men of their place and qualety; and alsoe what further favour you shall shewe to theise our servauntes for our sake wee shall take kindely at your handes. In wittnesse whereof &c. Given under our Privie Seale at our Mannor of Greenewich the eighteenth daie of May in the first yeare of our raigne in England, Fraunce and Ireland, and in Scotland the sixe and thirtieth. Ex: per Mylles.—Rec. 19 Maij, 1603.

V. *Patent under the Great Seal licensing Fletcher, Shakespeare and others, to perform Comedies, &c. 19 May, 1603. From the original Entry on the Patent Rolls, 1 Jac. I. Pars 2. Membr. 4.*

Com: Special: pro Laurencio Fletcher et Willielmo Shackespeare et aliis.—James by the grace of God, &c., to all justices, maiors, sheriffes, constables, hedborowes, and other our officers and lovinge subjectes, greetinge. Knowe yee that wee, of our speciall grace, certeine knowledge and mere motion, have licenced and aucthorized, and by theise presentes doe licence and aucthorize theise our servauntes, Lawrence Fletcher, William Shakespeare, Richard Burbage, Augustyne Phillippes, John Heminges, Henrie Condell, William Sly, Robert Armyn, Richard Cowly, and the rest of theire associates, freely to use and exercise the arte and faculty of playinge commedies, tragedies, histories, enterludes, moralls, pastoralls, stage-plaies, and suche others, like as theie have alreadie studied or hereafter shall use or studie, as well for the recreation of our lovinge subjectes, as for our solace and pleasure when wee shall thincke good to see them duringe our pleasure; and the said commedies, tragedies, histories, enterludes, morrall®, pastoralls, stage-playes, and suche like, to shewe and exercise publiquely to theire best commoditie, when the infection of the plague shall decrease, as well within theire nowe usuall howse called the Globe, within our county of Surrey, as alsoe within anie towne-halls or moutehalls, or other conveniente places within the liberties and freedome of anie other cittie, universitie, towne or boroughe whatsoever within our said realmes and domynions. Willinge and commaunding you and everie of you, as you tender our pleasure, not onlie to permitt and suffer them herein, without anie your lettes, hindrances or molestacions, during our said pleasure, but alsoe to be aiding and assistinge to them yf anie wronge be to them offered, and to allowe them such former curtesies as hath bene given to men of theire place and quallitie; and alsoe what further favour you shall shewe to theise our servauntes for our sake, wee shall take kindlie at your handes. In wytnesse whereof, &c. Witnesse ourselfe at Westminster the nyntenth day of May.—Per Breve de privato sigillo, etc.

VI. *Entry of the preceding Document in an ancient Index to the Patent Rolls.*

Flettcher, Shakespeare, Commiss:—R. xix°. Maij con. commissionem Willielmo® Fletcher, Willielmo Shakspeare et al. to plea commodies et al.

VII. "*A pretty Prancke passed by Ratsey upon certaine Players that he met by chance in an Inne, who denied their owne Lord and Maister, and used another Noblemans Name." This is the Title of the following interesting Chapter in Ratseis Ghost, 1606, here taken from the unique Copy of the original Tract preserved in the Library of Earl Spencer at Althorp, co. Northampton.*

Gamaliell Ratsey and his company travailing up and downe the countrey, as they had often times done before, *per varios casus et tot discrimina rerum*, still hazarding their severall happes as they had severall hopes, came by chance into an inne where that night there harbored a company of players, and Ratsey, framing himselfe to an humor of merriment, caused one or two of the chiefest of them to be sent for up into his chamber, where hee demanded whose men they were, and they answered they served such an honorable personage. I pray you, quoth Ratsey, let me heare your musicke, for I have often gone to plaies more for musicke sake then for action; for some of you, not content to do well, but striving to over-doe and go beyond yourselves, oftentimes, by S. George, mar all; yet your poets take great paines to make your parts fit for your mouthes, though you gape never so wide. Other-some, I must needs confesse, are very wel deserving both for true action and faire deliverie of speech, and yet, I warrant you, the very best have sometimes beene content to goe home at night with fifteene pence share apeece. Others there are whom Fortune hath so wel favored that, what by penny-sparing and long practise of playing, are growne so wealthy that they have expected to be knighted, or at least to be conjunct in authority and to sit with men of great worship on the bench of justice. But if there were none wiser then I am, there should more cats build colledges and more whoores turne honest women then one before the world should be filled with such a wonder. Well, musicke was plaide, and that night passed over with such singing, dauncing and revelling, as if my Lord Prodigall hadde beene there in his ruines of excesse and superfluitie. In the morning, Ratsey made the players taste of his bountie, and so departed. But everie day hee had new inventions to obtaine his purposes, and as often as fashions alter so often did he alter his stratagems, studying as much how to compasse a poore mans purse as players doe to win a full audience. About a weeke after, hee met with the same players, although hee had so disguised himselfe with a false head of hayre and beard that they could take no notice of him, and lying, as they did before, in one inne together, hee was desirous they should play a private play before him, which they did not in the name of the former noblemans servants; for, like camelions, they had changed that colour; but in the name of another, whose indeede they were, although afterwardes, when he heard of their abuse, hee discharged them and tooke away his warrant. For being far off, for their more countenance they would pretend to be protected by such an honourable man, denying their Lord and Maister, and comming within ten or twenty miles of him againe, they would shrowd themselves under their owne lords favour. Ratsey heard their play, and seemed to like that, though he disliked the rest, and verie liberally out with his purse and gave them fortie shillings, with which they held themselves very richly satisfied, for they scarce had twentie shillings audience at any time for a play in the countrey. But Ratsey thought they should not enjoy it long, although he let them beare it about them till the next day in their purses; for the morning beeing come, and they having packt away their luggage and some part of their companie before in a waggon, discharged the house and followed them presently. Ratsey intended not to bee long after, but having learned which way they travailed, hee, being verie wel horsed and mounted upon his blacke gelding, soone overtooke them; and when they saw it was the gentleman that had beene so liberall with them the night before, they beganne to doe him much courtesie and to greete his late kindnesse with many thankes. But that was not the matter which he aymed at. Therefore he roundly tolde them they were deceived in him,—hee was not the man they tooke him for. I am a souldier, sayth he, and one that for meanes hath ventured my fortunes abroade, and now for money am driven to hazard them at home; I am not to bee played upon by players; therefore be short, deliver mee your money; I will turne usurer now; my fortie shillings againe will not serve without interest. They beganne to make many faces, and to cappe and knee, but all would not serve their turne. Hee bade them leave off their cringing and complements and their apish trickes, and dispatch, which they did for feare of the worst, seeing to begge was bootelesse; and having made a desperate tender of their stocke into Ratseyes handes, he bad them play for more, for, sayes hee, it is an idle profession that brings in much profite, and every night where you come your playing beares your charges and somewhat into purse. Besides, you have fidlers fare, meat, drink and mony. If the worst be, it is but pawning your apparell, for as good actors and stalkers as you are have done it, though now they scorne it; but in any case heereafter be not counterfaites, abuse not honorable personages in using their names and countenance without their consent and privitie; and because you are now destitute of a maister, I will give you leave to play under my protection for a senights space, and I charge you doe it, lest when I meet you again, I cut you shorter by the hams and share with you in a sharper manner then I have done at this time. And for you, sirra, saies hee to the chiefest of them, thou hast a good presence upon a stage; methinks thou darkenst thy merite by playing in the country. Get thee to London, for, if one man were dead, they will have much neede of such a one as thou art. There would be none in my opinion fitter then thyselfe to play his parts. My conceipt is such of thee, that I durst venture all the mony in my purse on thy head to play Hamlet with him for a wager. There thou shalt learne to be frugall,—for players were never so thriftie as they are now about London —and to feed upon all men, to let none feede upon thee; to make thy hand a stranger to thy pocket, thy hart slow to performe thy tongues promise; and when thou feelest thy purse well lined, buy thee some place or lordship in the country, that, growing weary of playing, thy mony may there bring thee to dignitie and reputation; then thou needest care for no man, nor not for them that before made thee prowd with speaking their words upon the stage. Sir, I thanke you, quoth the player, for this good counsell; I promise you I will make use of it, for I have heard, indeede, of some that have gone to London very meanly, and have come in time to be exceeding wealthy. And in this presage and propheticall humor of mine, sayes Ratsey, kneele downe,—Rise up, Sir Simon Two Shares and a Halfe; thou art now one of my knights, and the first knight that ever was player in England. The next time I meete thee I must share with thee againe for playing under my warrant, and so for this time adiew. How ill hee brooked this new knighthood, which hee durst not but accept of, or liked his late counsell, which he lost his coine for, is easie to be imagined; but whether he met with them againe, after the senights space that he charged them to play in his name, I have not heard it reported.

VIII. *Transactions between the Actors and Proprietors of Theatres. From an original Paper endorsed, "Instructions touching Salesberry Court Playhouse, 14to Septem., 1639."*
The diffrence betwixt the first Articles and the last.—The houskeepers enjoy not any one benefit in the last which they had not in the first; and they paid only by the first, 1. All repaires of the house; 2. Halfe the gathering places; halfe to the sweepers of the house, the stage keepers, to the poore, and for carying away the soyle.

By the last Articles,—We first allow them a roome or two more then they formerly had; all that was allowed by the former Articles, and halfe the poets wages, which is 10s. a weeke; halfe the lycencing of every new play, which halfe is also xx. s; and one dayes proffitt wholly to themselves every yeare, in consideracion of their want of stooles on the stage, which were taken away by his Majesties comand.

We allow them also that was in noe Articles, —Halfe for lights, both waxe and tallow, which halfe all winter is neare 5s. a day; halfe for coles to all the roomes; halfe for rushes, flowers and strowings on the stage; halfe for all the boyes new gloves at every new play and every revived play not lately plaid.

All the rest of the Articles are some indifferent rules, fitt to be observed for the generall creditt of the house and benefitt of both houskeepers and players.

IX. *A Collection of Papers relating to Shares and Sharers in the Globe and Blackfriars' Theatres*, 1635.
(a) To the Right Honorable Philip Earle of Pembroke and Montgomery, Lord Chamberlaine of His Majesties houshold, Robert Benefield, Heliard Swanston and Thomas Pollard humbly represent these their grievances, ymploring his Lordships noble favor towardes them for their reliefe.

That the petitioners have a long time with much patience expected to bee admitted sharers in the playhouses of the Globe and the Blackfriers, wherby they might reape some better fruit of their labours then hitherto they have done, and bee encouraged to proceed therin with cheerfulnes.

That those few interested in the houses have, without any defalcacion or abatement at all, a full moyety of the whole gaines ariseing therby, excepting the outer dores, and such of the sayd houskeepers as bee actors doe likewise equally share with all the rest of the actors both in th'other moiety, and in the sayd outer dores also.

That out of the actors moiety there is notwithstanding defrayed all wages to hired men, apparell, poetes, lightes and other charges of the houses whatsoever, soe that, betweene the gaynes of the actors, and of those few interessed as houskeepers, there is an unreasonable inequality.

That the house of the Globe was formerly divided into sixteen partes, wherof Mr. Cutbert Burbidge and his sisters had eight, Mrs. Condall four and Mr. Hemings four.

That Mr. Tailor and Mr. Lowen were long since admitted to purchase four partes betwixt them from the rest, vizt., one part from Mr. Hemings, two partes from Mrs. Condall, and halfe a part a peece from Mr. Burbidge and his sister.

That the three partes remaining to Mr. Hemings were afterwardes by Mr. Shankes surreptitiously purchased from him, contrary to the petitioners expectation, who hoped that, when any partes had beene to bee sold, they should have beene admitted to have bought and divided the same amongst themselves for their better livelyhood.

That the petitioners desire not to purchase or diminish any part of Mr. Taylors or Mr. Lowens shares, whose deserveings they must acknowledge to bee well worthy of their gaines, but in regard the petitioners labours, according to their severall wayes and abilityes, are equall to some of the rest, and for that others of the sayd houskeepers are neither actors, nor his Majesties servantes, and yet the petitioners profit and meanes of livelyhood soe much inferior and unequall to theires, as appeares before, they therfore desire that they may bee admitted to purchase for their moneys, at such rates as have beene formerly given, single partes a peece onely from those that have the greatest shares and may best spare them, vizt., that Mr. Burbadge and his sister, haveing three partes and a halfe a peece, may sell them two partes, and reserve two and a halfe a peece to themselves. And that Mr. Shankes, haveing three, may sell them one and reserve two, wherin they hope your Lordship will conceave their desires to bee just and modest; the rather for that the petitioners, not doubting of beeing admitted sharers in the sayd house the Globe, suffered lately the sayd houskeepers, in the name of his Majesties servantes, to sue and obtaine a decree in the Court of Requestes against Sir Mathew Brand for confirmation unto them of a lease paroll for about nine or ten yeeres yet to come, which they could otherwise have prevented untill themselves had beene made parties.

That for the house in the Blackfriers, it beeing divided into eight partes amongst the aforenamed houskeepers, and Mr. Shankes haveing two partes therof, Mr. Lowen, Mr. Taylor and each of the rest haveing but one part a peece, which two partes were by the sayd Mr. Shankes purchased of Mr. Heming, together with those three of the Globe as before, the petitioners desire and hope that your Lordship will conceave it likewise reasonable that the sayd Mr. Shankes may assigne over one of the sayd partes amongst them three, they giveing him such satisfaccion for the same as that hee bee noe looser therby.

Lastly, that your Lordship would to that purpose bee nobly pleased, as their onely gracious refuge and protector, to call all the sayd houskeepers before you, and to use your Lordships power with them to conforme themselves therunto; the rather considering that some of the sayd houskeepers, who have the greatest shares, are neither actors nor his Majesties servantes as aforesayd, and yet reape most or the chiefest benefitt of the sweat of their browes, and live upon the bread of their labours, without takeing any paynes themselves.

For which your petitioners shall have just cause to blesse your Lordship, as however they are dayly bound to doe with the devotions of most humble and obliged beadsmen.

Shares in the Globe
- Burbadge 3½
- Robinson 3½
- Condall 2
- Shankes 3
- Taylor 2
- Lowen 2

of a lease of 9 yeeres from our Lady Day last, 1635, not yet confirmed by Sir Mathew Brand to bee taken to feoffees.

Blackfryers
- Shankes 2
- Burbadge 1
- Robinson 1
- Taylor 1
- Lowen 1
- Condall 1
- Underwood 1

(b) Court at Theoballes, 12 July, 1635.

Haveing considered this petition and the severall answeres and replyes of the parties, the merites of the petitioners, the disproportion of their shares, and the interest of his Majesties service, I have thought fitt and doe accordingly order that the petitioners, Robert Benefield, Eyllœrdt Swanston and Thomas

Pollard bee each of them admitted to the purchase of the shares desired of the severall persons mentioned in the petition for the fower yeeres remayning of the lease of the house in Blackfriers, and for five yeeres in that of the Globe, at the usuall and accustomed rates, and according to the proportion of the time and benefitt they are to injoy. And heerof I desire the houskepers, and all others whome it may concerne, to take notice and to conforme themselves therin accordingly. The which if they or any of them refuse or delay to performe, if they are actors and his Majesties servantes, I doe suspend them from the stage and all the benefitt therof; and if they are onely interessed in the houses, I desire my Lord Privy Seale to take order that they may bee left out of the lease which is to bee made upon the decree in the Court of Requestes.

P. and M.

(c) Robert Benefield, Eyllardt Swanston, and Thomas Pollard doe further humbly represent unto your Lordship.

That the houskepers beeing but six in number, vizt., Mr. Cutbert Burbage, Mrs. Condall, Mr. Shankes, Mr. Taylor, Mr. Lowen and Mr. Robinson (in the right of his wife), have amongst them the full moyety of all the galleries and boxes in both houses, and of the tireing-house dore at the Globe.

That the actors have the other moyety, with the outer dores; but in regard the actors are halfe as many more, vizt., nine in number, their shares fall shorter and are a great deale lesse then the houskepers; and yet, notwithstanding out of those lesser shares the sayd actors defray all charges of the house whatsoever, vizt., wages to hired men and boyes, musicke, lightes, &c., amounting to 900 or 1000 $li.$ per annum or theraboutes, beeing 3 $li.$ a day one day with another; besides the extraordinary charge which the sayd actors are wholly at for apparell and poetes, &c.

Wheras the sayd houskepers out of all their gaines have not till our Lady Day last payd above 65 $li.$ per annum rent for both houses, towardes which they rayse betweene 20 and 30 $li.$ per annum from the tap howses and a tenement and a garden belonging to the premisses, &c., and are at noe other charges whatsoever, excepting the ordinary reparations of the houses.

Soe that upon a medium made of the gaynes of the howskepers and those of the actors one day with another throughout the yeere, the petitioners will make it apparent that when some of the houskepers share 12 $s.$ a day at the Globe, the actors share not above 3 $s.$ And then what those gaine that are both actors and houskepers, and have their shares in both, your Lordship will easily judge, and therby finde the modesty of the petitioners suite, who desire onely to buy for their money one part a peece from such three of the sayd houskepers as are fittest to spare them, both in respect of desert and otherwise, vizt., Mr. Shankes, one part of his three; Mr. Robinson and his wife, one part of their three and a halfe; and Mr. Cutbert Burbidge the like.

And for the house of the Blackfriers, that Mr. Shankes, who now injoyes two partes there, may sell them likewise one, to bee divided amongst them three.

Humbly beseeching your Lordship to consider their long sufferings, and not to permitt the sayd howskeepers any longer to delay them, but to put an end to and settle the sayd busines, that your petitioners may not bee any further troublesome or importunate to your Lordship, but may proceed to doe their duty with cheerfullnes and alacrityo.

Or otherwise in case of their refusall to conforme themselves, that your Lordship would bee pleased to consider whether it bee not reasonable and equitable that the actors in generall may injoy the benefitt of both houses to themselves, paying the sayd howskeepers such a valuable rent for the same as your Lordship shall thinke just and indifferent.— And your petitioners shall continue their dayly prayers for your Lordships prosperity and happines.

(d) The answere of John Shankes to the peticion of Robert Benefield, Eyllardt Swanston and Thomas Pollard, lately exhibited to the Right Honorable Philip, Earle of Pembroke and Montgomery, Lord Chamberlain of his Majesties houshold.

Humbly sheweth,—That about allmost two yeeres since, your suppliant, upon offer to him made by William Hemings, did buy of him one part hee had in the Blackfriers for about six yeeres then to come at the yeerly rent of 6 $li.$ 5 $s.$, and another part hee then had in the Globe for about two yeeres to come, and payd him for the same two partes in ready moneys 156 $li.$, which sayd partes were offered to your suppliant, and were as free then for any other to buy as for your suppliant.

That about eleven months since, the sayd William Hemings, offering to sell unto your suppliant the remaining partes hee then had, viz., one in the Blackfriers, wherin hee had then about five yeeres to come, and two in the Globe, wherin hee had then but one yeere to come, your suppliant likewise bought the same, and payd for them in ready moneys more 350 *li.*, all which moneys soe disbursed by your suppliant amount to 506 *li.*, the greatest part wherof your suppliant was constrained to take up at interest, and your suppliant hath besides disbursed to the sayd William Hemings diverse other small summes of money since hee was in prison.

That your suppliant did neither fraudulently nor surreptitiously defeat any of the petitioners in their hope of buying the sayd partes, neither would the sayd William Hemings have sold the same to any of the petitioners, for that they would not have given him any such price for the same, but would, as now they endeavour to doe, have had the same against his will, and at what rates they pleased.

That your suppliant, beeing an old man in this quality, who in his youth first served your noble father, and after that, the late Queene Elizabeth, then King James, and now his royall Majestye, and haveing in this long time made noe provision for himselfe in his age, nor for his wife, children and grandchild, for his and their better livelyhood, haveing this oportunity, did at deere rates purchase these partes, and hath for a very small time as yet receaved the profites therof, and hath but a short time in them, and is without any hope to renew the same when the termes bee out; hee therfore hopeth hee shall not bee hindred in the injoying the profitt therof, especially whenas the same are thinges very casuall and subject to bee discontinued, and lost by sicknes and diverse other wayes, and to yield noe proffitt at all.

That wheras the petitioners in their complaint say that they have not meanes to subsist, it shall by oath, if need bee, bee made apparent that every one of the three petitioners, for his owne particular hath gotten and receaved this yeere last past of the summe of 180 *li.*, which, as your suppliant conceaveth, is a very sufficient meanes to satisfie and answere their long and patient expectation, and is more by above the one halfe then any of them ever gott, ore were capable of elswhere, besides what Mr. Swanston, one of them who is most violent in this busines, who hath further had and receaved this last yeere above 34 *li.* for the profitt of a third part of one part in the Blackfriers which hee bought for 20 *li.*, and yet hath injoyed the same two or three

PART I.

yeeres allready, and hath still as long time in the same as your suppliant hath in his, who for soe much as Mr. Swanston bought for 20 *li.* your suppliant payd 60 *li.*

That when your suppliant purchased his partes, hee had noe certainty therof more then for one yeere in the Globe, and there was a chargeable suit then depending in the Court of Requestes betweene Sir Mathew Brend, Knight, and the lessees of the Globe and their assignes, for the adding of nine yeeres to their lease in consideration that they and their predecessors had formerly beene at the charge of 1400 *li.* in building of the sayd house upon the burning downe of the former, wherin, if they should miscarry, for as yet they have not the assurance perfected by Sir Mathew Brend, your suppliant shall lay out his money to such a losse, as the petitioners will never bee partners with him therin.

That your suppliant and other the lessees in the Globe and in the Blackfriers are chargeable with the payment of 100 *li.* yeerly rent, besides reparacions, which is dayly very chargeable unto them, all which they must pay and beare, whether they make any proffitt or nott, and soe reckoning their charge in building and fitting the sayd houses, yeerly rent and reparations, noe wise man will adventure his estate in such a course, considering their dealing with whome they have to doe, and the many casualtyes and dayly troubles therwith. That in all the affayres and dealinges in this world betweene man and man, it was and is ever held an inviolable principle that in what thing soever any man hath a lawfull interest and property hee is not to bee compelled to depart with the same against his will, which the complainantes endeavour.

And wheras John Heminges, the father of William Hemings, of whome your suppliant made purchase of the sayd partes, injoyed the same thirty yeeres without any molestacion, beeing the most of the sayd yeeres both player and houskeeper, and after hee gave over playing diverse yeeres; and his sonne, William Hemings, fower yeers after, though hee never had anything to doe with the sayd stage, injoyed the same without any trouble; notwithstanding, the complainantes would violently take from your petitioners the sayd partes, who hath still of his owne purse supplyed the company for the service of his Majesty with boyes, as Thomas Pollard, John Thompson deceased (for whome hee payed 40 *li.*), your suppliant haveing payd his part of 200 *li.* for other boyes since his comming to the company, John

12

Honiman, Thomas Holcome and diverse others, and at this time maintaines three more for the sayd service. Neither lyeth it in the power of your suppliant to satisfie the unreasonable demandes of the complainantes, hee beeing forced to make over the sayd partes, for security of moneys taken up as aforesayd of Robert Morecroft of Lincolne, his wifes uncle, for the purchase of the sayd partes, untill hee hath made payment of the sayd moneys, which hee is not able to doe unlesse hee bee suffered to injoy the sayd partes during the small time of his lease, and is like to bee undone if they are taken from him.

All which beeing considered, your suppliant hopeth that your Lordship will not inforce your suppliant against his will to depart with what is his owne, and what hee hath deerly payd for, unto them that can claime noe lawfull interest therunto. And your suppliant, under your Lordships favour, doth conceave that if the petitioners, by those their violent courses, may obtaine their desires, your Lordship will never bee at quiet for their dayly complaintes, and it will bee such a president to all young men that shall follow heerafter, that they shall allwayes refuse to doe his Majesty service unlesse they may have whatsoever they will, though it bee other mens estates. And soe that which they pretend shall tend to the better gouvernment of the company, and inabling them to doe his Majesty service, the same will bee rather to the destruccion of the company, and disabling of them to doe service to his Majestye; and besides, the benefitt and profitt which the petitioners doe yeerly make without any charge at all is soe good, that they may account themselves to bee well recompenced for their labour and paines, and yet when any partes are to bee sould, they may buy the same if they can gett the bargaine therof, paying for the same as others doe.

The humble suite of your suppliant is that your honour will be pleased that hee may injoy that which hee hath deerly bought and truly payd for, and your suppliant, as in duty hee is bound, shall ever pray for your Lordship.

(e) To the Right Honorable Philip Earle of Pembroke and Montgomery, Lord Chamberlaine of his Majesties houshold.

Right Honorable and our singular good Lord,—Wee your humble Suppliantes, Cutbert Burbage and Winifrid his brothers wife, and William his sonne, doe tender to your honorable consideration for what respectes and good reasons wee ought not in all charity to bee disabled of our livelyhoodes by men soe soone shott up, since it hath beene the custome that they should come to it by farre more antiquity and desert then these can justly attribute to themselves.

And first, humbly shewing to your honor the infinite charges, the manifold law suites, the leases expiration, by the restraintes in sicknes times, and other accidentes, that did cutt from them the best part of the gaines that your honor is informed they have receaved.

The father of us, Cutbert and Richard Burbage, was the first builder of playhowses, and was himselfe in his younger yeeres a player. The Theater hee built with many hundred poundes taken up at interest.

The players that lived in those first times had onely the profitts arising from the dores, but now the players receave all the commings in at the dores to themselves and halfe the galleries from the houskepers. Hee built this house upon leased ground, by which meanes the landlord and hee had a great suite in law, and, by his death, the like troubles fell on us, his sonnes; wee then bethought us of altering from thence, and at like expence built the Globe, with more summes of money taken up at interest, which lay heavy on us many yeeres; and to ourselves wee joyned those deserveing men, Shakspere, Hemings, Condall, Philips and others, partners in the profittes of that they call the House, but makeing the leases for twenty-one yeeres hath beene the destruction of ourselves and others, for they dyeing at the expiration of three or four yeeres of their lease, the subsequent yeeres became dissolved to strangers as by marrying with their widdowes and the like by their children.

Thus, Right Honorable, as concerning the Globe, where wee ourselves are but lessees. Now for the Blackfriers, that is our inheritance; our father purchased it at extreame rates, and made it into a playhouse with great charge and troble; which after was leased out to one Evans that first sett up the boyes commonly called the Queenes Majesties Children of the Chappell. In processe of time, the boyes growing up to bee men, which were Underwood, Field, Ostler, and were taken to strengthen the Kings service; and the more to strengthen the service, the boyes dayly wearing out, it was considered that house would bee as fitt for ourselves, and soe purchased the lease remaining from Evans with our money, and placed men players, which were Hemings,

Condall, Shakspeare, &c. And Richard Burbage, who for thirty-five yeeres paines, cost and labour, made meanes to leave his wife and children some estate, and out of whose estate soe many of other players and their families have beene mayntained, these new men, that were never bred from children in the Kings service, would take away with oathes and menaces that wee shall bee forced and that they will not thanke us for it; soe that it seemes they would not pay us for what they would have or wee can spare, which, more to satisfie your honor then their threatning pride, wee are for ourselves willing to part with a part betweene us, they paying according as ever hath beene the custome and the number of yeeres the lease is made for.

Then, to shew your Honor against these sayinges, that wee eat the fruit of their labours, wee referre it to your Honors judgement to consider their profittes, which wee may safely maintaine, for it appeareth by their owne accomptes for one whole yeere last past, begining from Whitson Munday, 1634, to Whitson Munday, 1635, each of these complainantes gained severally, as hee was a player and noe howskeeper, 180 *li*. Besides Mr. Swanston hath receaved from the Blackfriers this yeere, as hee is there a houskeeper, above 30 *li.*, all which beeing accompted together may very well keepe him from starveing.

Wherfore your honors most humble suppliantes intreates they may not further bee trampled upon then their estates can beare, seeing how deerly it hath beene purchased by the infinite cost and paynes of the family of the Burbages, and the great desert of Richard Burbage for his quality of playing, that his wife should not sterve in hir old age; submitting ourselves to part with one part to them for valuable consideration and let them seeke further satisfaccion elsewhere, that is, of the heires or assignes of Mr. Hemings and Mr. Condall, who had theirs of the Blackfriers of us for nothing; it is onely wee that suffer continually.

Therfore, humbly relyeing upon your Honorable charity in discussing their clamor against us, wee shall, as wee are in duty bound, still pray for the dayly increase of your honors health and happines.

(*f*) John Shankes.—A peticion of John Shankes to my Lord Chamberlaine, shewing that, according to his Lordships order, hee did make a proposition to his fellowes for satisfaccion, upon his assigening of his partes in the severall houses unto them; but they not onely refused to give satisfaccion, but restrained him from the stage; that, therfore, his Lordship would order them to give satisfaccion according to his propositions and computation.

Md. all concerning this and here entred were delivered annexed. } Answered, vizt. I desire Sir H. Herbert and Sir John Finett, and my solliciter Daniell Bedingfield, to take this petition and the severall papers heerunto annexed into their serious considerations, and to speake with the severall parties interested, and therupon and upon the whole matter to sett downe a proportionable and equitable summe of money to bee payd unto Shankes for the two partes which hee is to passe unto Benfield, Swanston and Pollard, and to cause a finall agreement and convayances to be settled accordingly, and to give mee an account of their whole proceedinges in writing. Aug. 1, 1635.

X. *The Story of Felix and Felismena, from the Second Book of the First Part of the Diana of George of Montemayor, translated out of Spanish into English by Bartholomew Yong, of the Middle Temple, Gentleman. fol. London, Printed by Edm. Bollifant,* 1598.

Unfortunate I, reserved by my sinister destinies to greater mishaps, was caried to a grandmother of mine, which place I would I had never seene, since it was an occasion of such a sorrowfull life as never any woman suffered the like. And bicause there is not any thing, faire nymphes, which I am not forced to tell you, as well for the great vertue and desertes which your excellent beauties doe testifie, as also for that my minde doth give me that you shall be no small part and meanes of my comfort, knowe that, as I was in my grandmothers house, and almost seventeene yeeres olde, a certaine yoong gentleman fell in love with me, who dwelt no further from our house then the length of a garden terrasse, so that he might see me every sommers night when I walked in the garden. Whenas therefore ingratefull Felix had beheld in that place the unfortunate Felismena, for this is the name of the wofull woman that tels you her mishaps, he was extremely enamoured of me, or else did cunningly dissemble it, I not knowing then whether of these two I might beleeve; but am now assured that whosoever beleeves lest, or nothing at all, in these affaires, shall be most at ease. Many daies Don Felix spent in endevouring to make me know the paines which he suffered for me, and many more did I spende in making the matter strange, and that he did not suffer them for my sake; and I know not why love delaied the time so long by forcing me to love him, but onely that, when he came indeed, he might enter into my hart at once, and with greater force and violence. When he had, therefore, by sundrie signes, as by tylt and tourneyes, and by prauncing up and downe upon his proude jennet before my windowes, made it manifest that he was in love with me, for at the first I did not so well perceive it, he determined in the end to write a letter unto me; and having practised divers times before with a maide of mine, and at length, with many gifts and faire promises, gotten her good will and furtherance, he gave her the letter to deliver to me. But to see the meanes that Rosina made unto me, for so was she called, the dutifull services and unwoonted circumstances before she did deliver it, the othes that she sware unto me, and the subtle words and serious protestations she used, it was a pleasant thing and woorthie the noting. To whom, neverthelesse, with an angrie countenance I turned againe, saying, If I had not regard of mine owne estate, and what heereafter might be said, I would make this shamelesse face of thine be knowne ever after for a marke of an impudent and bolde minion; but bicause it is the first time, let this suffice that I have saide, and give thee warning to take heede of the second. Me thinkes I see now the craftie wench, how she helde her peace, dissembling very cunningly the sorrow that she conceived by my angrie answer; for she fained a counterfaite smiling, saying, Jesus, Mistresse! I gave it you, bicause you might laugh at it, and not to moove your pacience with it in this sort; for if I had any thought that it woulde have provoked you to anger, I praie God he may shew his wrath as great towards me as ever he did to the daughter of any mother. And with this she added many wordes more, as she could do well enough, to pacifie the fained anger and ill opinion that I conceived of her, and taking her letter with her, she departed from me. This having passed thus, I began to imagine what might ensue thereof, and love, me thought, did put a certaine desire into my minde to see the letter, though modestie and shame forbad me to aske it of my maide, especially for the wordes that had passed betweene us, as you have heard. And so I continued all that day untill night in varietie of many thoughts; but when Rosina came to helpe me to bedde,

God knowes how desirous I was to have her entreat me againe to take the letter, but she woulde never speake unto me about it, nor, as it seemed, did so much as once thinke thereof. Yet to trie, if by giving her some occasion I might prevaile, I saide unto her; And is it so, Rosina, that Don Felix, without any regard to mine honour, dares write unto me? These are things, mistresse, saide she demurely to me againe, that are commonly incident to love, wherfore, I beseech you, pardon me, for if I had thought to have angred you with it, I woulde have first pulled out the bals of mine eies. How cold my hart was at that blow God knowes, yet did I dissemble the matter, and suffer myselfe to remaine that night onely with my desire, and with occasion of little sleepe. And so it was, indeede, for that, me thought, was the longest and most painfull night that ever I passed. But when, with a slower pace then I desired the wished day was come, the discreet and subtle Rosina came into my chamber to helpe me to make me readie, in dooing whereof, of purpose she let the letter closely fall, which, when I perceived,—What is that that fell downe?, said I, let me see it. It is nothing, mistresse, saide she. Come, come, let me see it, saide I; what! moove me not, or else tell me what it is. Good Lord, mistresse, saide she, why will you see it? it is the letter I would have given you yesterday. Nay, that it is not, saide I, wherefore shew it me, that I may see if you lie or no. I had no sooner said so, but she put it into my handes, saying, God never give me good if it be anie other thing; and although I knewe it well indeede, yet I saide,—What, this is not the same, for I know that well enough, but it is one of thy lovers letters; I will read it, to see in what neede he standeth of thy favour. And opening it, I founde it conteined this that followeth;—

"I ever imagined, deere mistresse, that your discretion and wisedome woulde have taken away the feare I had to write unto you, the same knowing well enough, without any letter at all, how much I love you; but the very same hath so cunningly dissembled, that wherein I hoped the onely remedie of my griefes had been, therein consisted my greatest harme. If according to your wisedome you censure my boldnes, I shall not then, I know, enjoy one hower of life; but if you do consider of it according to loves accustomed effects, then will I not exchange my hope for it. Be not offended, I beseech you, good ladie, with my letter, and blame me not for writing unto you, untill you see by experience whether I can leave of to write; and take me besides into the possession of that which is yours, since all is mine doth wholly consist in your hands, the which, with all reverence and dutifull affection, a thousand times I kisse."

When I had now seene my Don Felix his letter, whether it was for reading it at such a time, when by the same he shewed that he loved me more then himselfe, or whether he had disposition and regiment over part of this wearied soule to imprint that love in it whereof he wrote unto me, I began to love him too well,—and, alas, for my harme!, since he was the cause of so much sorrow as I have passed for his sake. Whereupon, asking Rosina forgivenes of what was past, as a thing needfull for that which was to come, and committing the secrecie of my love to her fidelitie, I read the letter once againe, pausing a little at every worde, and a very little, indeede, it was, bicause I concluded so soone with myselfe to do that I did, although in verie truth it lay not otherwise in my power to do. Wherefore, calling for paper and inke, I answered his letter thus;—

"Esteeme not so slightly of mine honour, Don Felix, as with fained words to thinke to enveagle it, or with thy vaine pretenses to offend it any waies. I know wel enough what manner of man thou art, and how great thy desert and presumption is; from whence thy boldnes doth arise, I gesse, and not from the force, which thing thou wouldst faine perswade me, of thy fervent love. And if it be so, as my suspicion suggesteth, thy labor is as vaine as thy imagination presumptuous by thinking to make me do any thing contrarie to that which I owe unto mine honour. Consider, I beseech thee, how seldome things commenced under suttletie and dissimulation have good successe; and that it is not the part of a gentleman to meane them one way and speak them another. Thou praiest me, amongst other things, to admit thee into possession of that that is mine; but I am of so ill an humour in matters of this qualitie, that I trust not things experienced, how much lesse then thy bare wordes; yet, neverthelesse, I make no small account of that which thou hast manifested to me in thy letter; for it is ynough that I am incredulous, though not unthankfull."

This letter did I send, contrarie to that I should have done, bicause it was the occasion of all my harmes and greefes; for after this, he began to waxe more bolde by unfolding his thoughts, and seeking out the meanes to have a parly with me. In the ende, faire nymphes, a few daies being spent in his demaunds and my answers, false love did worke in me after his wonted fashions, every hower seasing more strongly upon my unfortunate soule. The tourneies were now renewed; the musicke by night did never cease; amorous letters and verses were re-continued on both sides; and thus passed I away almost a whole yeere, at the end whereof I felt myselfe so far in his love, that I had no power to retire, nor stay myselfe from disclosing my thoughts unto him, the thing which he desired more then his owne life. But my adverse fortune afterwardes would that of these our mutuall loves, whenas now they were most assured, his father had some intelligence, and whosoever revealed them first, perswaded him so cunningly that his father, fearing least he would have married me out of hand, sent him to the great Princesse Augusta Cæsarinas court, telling him, it was not meete that a yoong gentleman, and of so noble a house as he was, should spende his youth idly at home, where nothing could be learned but examples of vice, whereof the very same idlenes, he said, was the onely mistresse. He went away so pensive that his great greefe would not suffer him to acquaint me with his departure; which when I knew, how sorrowfull I remained she may imagine that hath bene at any time tormented with like passion. To tell you now the life that I led in his absence, my sadnes, sighes, and teares, which every day I powred out of these wearied eies, my toong is far unable; if then my paines were such that I cannot now expresse them, how could I then suffer them? But being in the mids of my mishaps, and in the depth of those woes which the absence of Don Felix caused me to feele, and it seeming to me that my greefe was without remedie, if he were once seene or knowen of the ladies in that court, more beautifull and gracious then myselfe, by occasion whereof, as also by absence, a capitall enemie to love, I might easily be forgotten, I determined to adventure that which I thinke never any woman imagined; which was to apparell myselfe in the habit of a man, and to hye me to the court to see him, in whose sight al my hope and content remained. Which determination I no sooner thought of then I put in practise, love blinding my eies and minde with an inconsiderate regarde of mine owne estate and condition. To the execution of which attempt I wanted no industrie; for, being furnished with the helpe of one of my approved friends, and treasouresse of my secrets, who bought me such apparell as I willed her, and a good horse for my journey, I went not onely out of my countrie, but out of my deere reputation, which, I thinke, I shall never recover againe; and so trotted directly to the court, passing by the way many accidents, which, if time would give me leave to tell them, woulde not make you laugh a little to heare them. Twenty daies I was in going thither, at the end of which, being come to the desired place, I tooke up mine inne in a streete lest® frequented with concurse of people; and the great desire I had to see the destroier of my joy did not suffer me to thinke of any other thing, but how or where I might see him. To inquire of him of mine host I durst not, lest my comming might, perhaps, have bene discovered; and to seeke him foorth I thought it not best, lest some inopinate mishap might have fallen out whereby I might have bene knowen. Wherefore I passed all that day in these perplexities, while night came on, each hower whereof, me thought, was a whole yeere unto me. But midnight being a little past, mine host called at my chamber doore, and tolde me, if I was desirous to heare some brave musicke, I should arise quickly and open a window towards the street. The which I did by and by, and making no noise at all, I heard how Don Felix his page, called Fabius, whom I knew by his voice, saide to others that came with him,— Now it is time, my masters, bicause the lady is in the gallerie over her garden, taking the fresh aire of the coole night. He had no sooner saide so, but they began to winde three cornets and a sackbot with such skill and sweetenesse, that it seemed celestiall musicke; and then began a voice to sing, the sweetest, in my opinion, that ever I heard. And though I was in suspence by hearing Fabius speake, whereby a thousand doubtes and imaginations, repugnant to my rest, occurred in my minde, yet I neglected not to heare what was sung, bicause their operations were not of such force that they were able to hinder the desire, nor distemper the delight that I conceived by hearing it. That therefore which was sung were these verses:—

Sweete mistresse, harken unto me,—
    If it greeves thee to see me die,—
And hearing, though it greeveth thee,
    To heare me yet do not denie.

O grant me then this short content,
    For forc'd I am to thee to flie.

My sighes do not make thee relent,
    Nor teares thy hart do mollifie.

Nothing of mine doth give thee payne,
    Nor thou think'st of no remedie:
Mistresse, how long shall I sustaine
    Such ill as still thou dost applie?

In death there is no helpe, be sure,
    But in thy will, where it doth lie;
For all those illes which death doth cure,
    Alas! they are but light to trie.

My troubles do not trouble thee,
    Nor hope to touch thy soule so nie;
O! from a will that is so free,
    What should I hope when I do crie?

How can I mollifie that brave
    And stonie hart of pittie drie?
Yet mistresse, turne those eies,—that have
    No peeres,—shining like stars in skie;

But turne them not in angrie sort,
    If thou wilt not kill me thereby;
Though yet, in anger or in sport,
    Thou killest onely with thine eie.

After they had first, with a concent of musicke, sung this song, two plaied, the one upon a lute, the other upon a silver sounding harpe, being accompanied with the sweete voice of my Don Felix. The great joy that I felt in hearing him cannot be imagined, for, me thought, I heard him nowe as in that happie and passed time of our loves. But after the deceit of this imagination was discovered, seeing with mine eies, and hearing with mine eares, that this musicke was bestowed upon another, and not on me, God knowes what a bitter death it was unto my soule; and with a greevous sigh, that caried almost my life away with it, I asked mine host if he knew what the ladie was for whose sake the musick was made? He answered me that he could not imagine on whom it was bestowed, bicause in that streete dwelled manie noble and faire ladies. And when I saw he could not satisfie my request, I bent mine eares againe to heare my Don Felix, who now, to the tune of a delicate harpe, whereon he sweetely plaied, began to sing this sonnet following;—

My painefull yeeres impartiall Love was spending
    In vaine and booteles hopes my life appaying,
    And cruell Fortune to the world bewraying
Strange samples of my teares that have no ending.
Time, everie thing to truth at last commending,
    Leaves of my steps such markes that now betraying,
    And all deceitfull trusts shall be decaying,
And none have cause to plaine of his offending.

> Shee, whom I lov'd to my obliged power,
> That in her sweetest love to me discovers
> Which never yet I knew (those heavenly pleasures),
> And I do saie, exclaiming every bower,
> Do not you see what makes you wise, O lovers?
> Love, Fortune, Time, and my faire mystresse treasures.

The sonnet being ended, they paused awhile, playing on fower lutes togither, and on a paire of virginals, with such heavenly melodie that the whole worlde, I thinke, could not affoord sweeter musick to the eare nor delight to any minde, not subject to the panges of such predominant greefe and sorrow as mine was. But then fower voices, passing well tuned and set togither, began to sing this song following;—

> That sweetest harme I doe not blame,
> First caused by thy fairest eies,
> But greeve, bicause too late I came
> To know my fault, and to be wise.
>
> I never knew a worser kinde of life,
> To live in feare, from boldnesse still to cease:
> Nor, woorse then this, to live in such a strife,
> Whether of both to speake, or holde my peace?
>
> And so the harme I doe not blame,
> Caused by thee or thy faire eies;
> But that to see how late I came
> To knowe my fault, and to be wise.
>
> I ever more did feare that I should knowe
> Some secret things, and doubtfull in their kinde,
> Bicause the surest things doe ever goe
> Most contrarie unto my wish and minde.
>
> And yet by knowing of the same
> There is no hurt; but it denies
> My remedie, since late I came
> To knowe my fault, and to be wise.

When this song was ended, they began to sound divers sorts of instruments, and voices most excellently agreeing togither, and with such sweetnes that they could not chuse but delight any very much who were not so farre from it as I. About dawning of the day the musicke ended, and I did what I could to espie out my Don Felix, but the darknes of the night was mine enimie therein. And seeing now that they were gone, I went to bed againe, where I bewailed my great mishap, knowing that he, whom most of al I loved, had so unwoorthily forgotten me, whereof his musicke was too manifest a witnes. And when it was time, I arose, and without any other consideration, went straight to the Princesse her pallace, where, I thoght, I might see that which I so greatly desired, determining to call my selfe Valerius, if any, perhaps, did aske my name. Comming therefore to a faire broad court before the pallace gate, I viewed the windowes and galleries, where I sawe such store of blazing beauties and gallant ladies that I am not able now to recount, nor then to do any more but woonder at their graces, their gorgeous attyre, their jewels, their brave fashions of apparell, and ornaments wherewith they were so richly set out. Up and downe this place, before the windowes, roade many lords and brave gentlemen in rich and sumptuous habits, and mounted upon proud jennets, every one casting his eie to that part where his thoughts were secretly placed. God knowes how greatly I desired to see Don Felix there, and that his injurious love had beene in that famous pallace; bicause I might then have beene assured that he shoulde never have got any other guerdon of his sutes and services, but onely to see and to be seene, and sometimes to speake to his mistresse, whom he must serve before a thousand eies, bicause the privilege of that place doth not give him any further leave. But it was my ill fortune that he had setled his love in that place where I might not be assured of this poore helpe. Thus, as I was standing neere to the pallace gate, I espied Fabius, Don Felix his page, comming in great haste to the pallace, where, speaking a word or two with a porter that kept the second entrie, he returned the same waie he came. I gessed his errant was to knowe whether it were fit time for Don Felix to come to dispatch certaine busines that his father had in the court, and that he could not choose but come thither out of hand. And being in this supposed joy which his sight did promise me, I sawe him comming along with a great traine of followers attending on his person, all of them being bravely apparelled in a liverie of watchet silke, garded with yellow velvet, and stitched on either side with threedes of twisted silver, wearing likewise blew, yellow, and white feathers in their hats. But my lorde Don Felix had on a paire of ash colour hose, embrodered and drawen foorth with watchet tissue; his dublet was of white satten, embrodered with knots of golde, and likewise an embrodered jerkin of the same coloured velvet; and his short cape cloke was of blacke velvet, edged with gold lace, and hung full of buttons of pearle and gold, and lined with razed watchet satten; by his side he ware, at a paire of embrodered hangers, a rapier and dagger with engraven hilts and pommell of beaten golde. On his head a hat beset full of golden stars, in the mids of everie which a rich orient pearle was enchased, and his feather was likewise blew, yellow, and white.

Mounted he came upon a faire dapple graie jennet, with a rich furniture of blew embrodered with golde and seede pearle. When I sawe him in this rich equipage, I was so amazed at his sight that how extremely my sences were ravished with sudden joye I am not able, faire nymphes, to tell you. Truth it is that I could not but shed some teares for joy and greefe, which his sight did make me feele, but, fearing to be noted by the standers by, for that time I dried them up. But as Don Felix, being now come to the pallace gate, was dismounted, and gone up a paire of staires into the chamber of presence, I went to his men, where they were attending his returne; and seeing Fabius, whom I had seene before amongst them, I tooke him aside and saide unto him,—My friend, I pray you tell me what lord this is which did but even now alight from his jennet, for, me thinkes, he is very like one whom I have seene before in an other farre countrey. Fabius then answered me thus;—Art thou such a novice in the court that thou knowest not Don Felix? I tell thee, there is not any lord, knight, or gentleman better knowne in it then he. No doubt of that, saide I, but I will tell thee what a novice I am, and how small a time I have beene in the court, for yesterday was the first that ever I came to it. Naie, then, I cannot blame thee, saide Fabius, if thou knowest him not. Knowe, then, that this gentleman is called Don Felix, borne in Vandalia, and hath his chiefest house in the ancient cittie of Soldina, and is remaining in this court about certaine affaires of his fathers and his owne. But, I pray you, tell me, said I, why he gives his liveries of these colours? If the cause were not so manifest, I woulde conceale it, saide Fabius, but since there is not any that knowes it not, and canst not come to any in this court who cannot tell thee the reason why, I thinke by telling thee it I do no more then in courtesie I am bound to do. Thou must therefore understand that he loves and serves a ladie heere in this citie named Celia, and therefore weares and gives for his liverie an azure blew, which is the colour of the skie, and white and yellow, which are the colours of his lady and mistresse. When I heard these words, imagine, faire nymphes, in what a plight I was; but, dissembling my mishap and griefe, I answered him;—This ladie, certes, is greatly beholding to him, bicause he thinkes not enough, by wearing her colours, to shew how willing he is to serve her, unlesse also he beare her name in his liverie; whereupon I gesse she cannot be but very faire and amiable. She is no lesse indeede, saide Fabius, although the other whom he loved and served in our owne countrey in beautie farre excelled this, and loved and favoured him more then ever this did; but this mischievous absence doth violate and dissolve those things which men thinke to be most strong and firme. At these wordes, faire nymphes, was I faine to come to some composition with my teares, which, if I had not stopped from issuing foorth, Fabius could not have chosen but suspected, by the alteration of my countenance, that all was not well with me. And then the page did aske me what countrey-man I was, my name, and of what calling and condition I was; whom I answered, that my countrey where I was borne was Vandalia, my name Valerius, and till that time served no master. Then by this reckoning, saide he, we are both countrey-men, and may be both fellowes in one house if thou wilt; for Don Felix my master commanded me long since to seeke him out a page. Therefore, if thou wilt serve him, say so. As for meate, drinke, and apparell, and a couple of shillings to play away, thou shalt never want; besides pretie wenches, which are not daintie in our streete, as faire and amorous as queenes, of which there is not anie that will not die for the love of so proper a youth as thou art. And to tell thee in secret, because, perhaps, we may be fellowes, I know where an old cannons maide is, a gallant fine girle, whom if thou canst but finde in thy hart to love and serve as I do, thou shalt never want at her hands fine hand-kerchers, peeces of bacon, and now and then wine of S. Martyn. When I heard this, I could not choose but laugh to see how naturally the unhappie page played his part by depainting foorth their properties in their lively colours. And because I thought nothing more commodious for my rest, and for the enjoying of my desire, then to follow Fabius his counsell, I answered him thus;—In truth, I determined to serve none; but now, since fortune hath offered me so good a service, and at such a time, when I am constrained to take this course of life, I shall not do amisse if I frame myselfe to the service of some lord or gentleman in this court, but especially of your master, because he seemes to be a woorthy gentleman, and such an one that makes more reckoning of his servants then an other. Ha, thou knowest him not as well as I, said Fabius; for I promise thee, by the faith of a gentleman,—for I am one indeede, for my father comes of the Cachopines of Laredo,—that my master Don Felix is the best natured gentleman that ever thou knewest in thy life, and one who useth his pages better then any other. And were it not for those troublesome loves, which makes us runne up and downe more, and sleepe lesse, then we woulde, there were not such a master in the whole worlde againe. In the end, faire nymphes, Fabius spake to his master, Don Felix, as soone as he was come foorth, in my behalfe, who commanded me the same night to come to him at his lodging. Thither I went, and he entertained me for his page, making the most of me in the worlde; where, being but a fewe daies with him, I sawe the messages, letters, and gifts that were brought and caried on both sides,—greevous wounds, alas! and corsives to my dying hart,—which made my soule to flie sometimes out of my body, and every hower in hazard to leese my forced patience before every one. But after one moneth was past, Don Felix began to like so well of me that he disclosed his whole love unto me from the beginning unto the present estate and forwardnes that it was then in, committing the charge thereof to my secrecie and helpe; telling me that he was favoured of her at the beginning, and that afterwards she waxed wearie of her loving and accustomed entertainment, the cause whereof was a secret report, whosoever it was that buzzed it into her eares, of the love that he did beare to a lady in his owne countrey, and that his present love unto her was but to entertaine the time while his busines in the court were dispatched. And there is no doubt, saide Don Felix unto me, but that, indeede, I did once commence that love that she laies to my charge; but God knowes if now there be any thing in the world that I love and esteeme more deere and precious then her. When I heard him say so, you may imagine, faire nymphes, what a mortall dagger pierced my wounded heart. But with dissembling the matter the best I coulde, I answered him thus; —It were better, sir, me thinkes, that the gentlewoman should complaine with cause, and that it were so indeed; for if the other ladie whom you served before did not deserve to be forgotten of you, you do her, under correction, my lord, the greatest wrong in the world. The love, said Don Felix againe, which I beare to my Celia will not let me understand it so; but I have done her, me thinkes, the greater injurie, having placed my love first in an other and not in her. Of these wrongs, saide I to myselfe, I know who beares the woorst away! And disloyall he, pulling a letter out of his bosome, which he had received the same hower from his mistresse, reade it unto me, thinking that he did me a great favour thereby, the contents whereof were these;—

Celias letter to Don Felix.—"Never any thing that I suspected, touching thy love, hath beene so farre from the truth, that hath not given me occasion to beleeve more often mine owne imagination then thy innocencie; wherein, if I do thee any wrong, referre it but to the censure of thine owne follie. For well thou mightest have denied, or not declared thy passed love, without giving me occasion to condemne thee by thine owne confession. Thou saiest, I was the cause that made thee forget thy former love. Comfort thyselfe, for there shall not want another to make thee forget thy second. And assure thyselfe of this, lord Don Felix, that there is not any thing more unbeseeming a gentleman then to finde an occasion in a gentlewoman to leese himselfe for her love. I will saie no more, but that in an ill, where there is no remedie, the best is not to seeke out any."

After he had made an end of reading the letter, he said unto me,—What thinkest thou, Valerius, of these words? With pardon, be it spoken, my Lord, that your deedes are shewed by them. Go to, said Don Felix, and speake no more of that. Sir, saide I, they must like me wel, if they like you, because none can judge better of their words that love well then they themselves. But that which I thinke of the letter is, that this gentlewoman would have beene the first, and that fortune had entreated her in such sort, that all others might have envied her estate. But what wouldest thou counsell me?, saide Don Felix. If thy griefe doth suffer any counsell, saide I, that thy thoughts be divided ⊛ into this second passion, since there is so much due to the first. Don Felix answered me againe, sighing, and knocking me gently on the shoulder, saying, How wise art thou, Valerius, and what good counsell dost thou give me if I could follow it. Let us now go in to dinner, for when I have dined, I will have thee carie me a letter to my lady Celia, and then thou shalt see if any other love is not woorthy to be forgotten in lieu of thinking onely of her. These were wordes that greeved Felismena to the hart, but bicause she had him before her eies, whom she loved more then her-selfe, the content that she had by onely seeing him was a sufficient remedie of the paine that the greatest of these stings did make her feele. After Don Felix had dined, he called me unto him, and giving me a speciall charge what I should do, because he had imparted his griefe unto me and put his hope and remedie in my hands, he willed me to carie a letter to Celia, which he had alreadie written, and, reading it first unto me, it said thus;—

Don Felix his Letter to Celia.—"The thought, that seekes an occasion to forget the thing which it doth love and desire, suffers itselfe so easily to be knowne, that, without troubling the minde much, it may be quickly discerned. And thinke not, faire ladie, that I seeke a remedie to excuse you of that wherewith it pleased you to use me, since I never came to be so much in credit with you that in lesser things I woulde do it. I have confessed unto you that indeede I once loved well, because that true love, without dissimulation, doth not suffer any thing to be hid, and you, deere ladie, make that an occasion to forget me which should be rather a motive to love me better. I cannot perswade me that you make so small an account of yourselfe, to thinke that I can forget you for any thing that is or hath ever been, but rather imagine that you write cleane contrarie to that which you have tried by my zealous love and faith towards you. Touching all those things that, in prejudice of my good will towards you, it pleaseth you to imagine, my innocent thoughts assure me to the contrarie, which shall suffice to be ill recompenced besides being so ill thought of as they are."

After Don Felix had read this letter unto me, he asked me if the answer was correspondent to those words that his ladie Celia had sent him in hers, and if there was any thing therein that might be amended; whereunto I answered thus;—I thinke, sir, it is needlesse to amende this letter, or to make the gentlewoman amendes to whom it is sent, but her whom you do injurie so much with it. Which under your lordships pardon I speake, bicause I am so much affected to the first love in all my life that there is not any thing that can make me alter my minde. Thou hast the greatest reason in the world, said Don Felix, if I coulde perswade myselfe to leave of that, which I have begun. But what wilt thou have me do, since absence hath frozen the former love, and the continuall presence of a peerelesse beautie rekindled another more hot and fervent in me? Thus may she thinke herselfe, saide I againe, unjustly deceived, whom first you loved, because that love which is subject to the power of absence cannot be termed love, and none can perswade me that it hath beene love. These words did I dissemble the best I could, because I felt so sensible griefe to see myselfe forgotten of him who had so great reason to love me, and whom I did love so much, that I did more then any would have thought to make myselfe still unknowen. But taking the letter and mine errant with me, I went to Celias house, imagining by the way the wofull estate whereunto my haplesse love had brought me; since I was forced to make warre against mine owne selfe, and to be the intercessour of a thing so contrarie to mine owne content. But comming to Celias house, and finding a page standing at the dore, I asked him if I might speake with his ladie; who being informed of me from whence I came, tolde Celia how I would speake with her, commending therewithall my beautie and person unto her, and telling her besides that Don Felix had but lately entertained me into his service; which made Celia saie unto him,—What, doth Don Felix so soone disclose his secret loves to a page but newly entertained?—he hath, belike, some great occasion that mooves him to do it; bid him com in, and let us know what he would have. In I came, and to the place where the enimie of my life was, and, with great reverence kissing her hands, I delivered Don Felix his letter unto her. Celia tooke it, and casting her eies upon me, I might perceive how my sight had made a sudden alteration in her countenance, for she was so farre besides herselfe that for a good while she was not able to speake a worde, but, remembring herselfe at last, she saide unto me,—What good fortune hath beene so favourable to Don Felix to bring thee to this court to make thee his page? Even that, faire ladie, saide I, which is better then ever I imagined, bicause it hath beene an occasion to make me behold such singular beautie and perfections as now I see cleerely before mine eies. And if the paines, the teares, the sighes, and the continuall disquiets that my lord Don Felix hath suffred have greeved me heeretofore, now that I have seene the source from whence they flow, and the cause of all his ill, the pittie that I had on him is now wholly converted into a certaine kinde of envie. But if it be true, faire lady, that my comming is welcome unto you, I beseech you by that which you owe to the great love which he beares you, that your answer may import no lesse unto him. There is not anie thing, saide Celia, that I would not do for thee, though I were determined not to love him at all who for my sake hath forsaken another; for it is no small point of wisedome for me to learne by other womens harmes to be more wise and warie in mine owne. Beleeve not, good lady, saide I, that there is any thing in the worlde that can make Don Felix forget you; and if he hath cast off another for your sake, woonder not thereat, when your beautie and wisedome is so great, and the others so small, that there is no reason to thinke that he will, though he hath woorthelie forsaken her for your sake, or ever can forget you for any woman else in the worlde. Doest thou then know Felismena, said Celia, the lady whom thy master did once love and serve in his owne countrey? I know her, saide I, although not so well as it was needfull for me to have prevented so many mishaps,—and this I spake softly to myselfe; for my fathers house was neere to hers; but seeing your great beautie adorned with such perfections and wisedome, Don Felix can not be blamed, if he hath forgotten his first love onely to embrace and honour yours. To this did Celia answer, merily and smiling, Thou hast learned quickly of thy master to sooth. Not so, faire ladie, saide I, but to serve you woulde I faine learne; for flatterie cannot be where, in the judgement of all, there are so manifest signes and proofes of this due commendation. Celia began in good earnest to aske me what manner of woman Felismena was, whom I answered that, touching her beautie, some thought her to be very faire; but I was never of that opinion, bicause she hath many daies since wanted the chiefest thing that is requisite for it. What is that? said Celia. Content of minde, saide I, bicause perfect beautie can never be where the same is not adjoyned to it. Thou hast the greatest reason in the world, said she, but I have seene some ladies whose lively hewe sadnes hath not one whit abated, and others whose beautie anger hath encreased, which is a strange thing me thinkes. Haplesse is that beauty, said I, that hath sorrow and anger the preservers and mistresses of it, but I cannot skill of these impertinent things; and yet that woman that must needes be molested with continuall paine and trouble, with greefe and care of minde and with other passions, to make her looke well, cannot be reckoned among the number of faire women, and for mine owne part I do not account her so. Wherein thou hast great reason, said she, as in all things else that thou hast saide thou hast shewed thyselfe wise and discreete. Which I have deerely bought, said I againe; but I beseech you, gracious lady, to answer this letter, because my lord Don Felix may also have some contentment by receiving this first well emploied service at my hands. I am content, saide Celia, but first thou must tell me if Felismena in matters of discretion be wise and well advised? There was never any woman, saide I againe, more wise then she, bicause she hath beene long since beaten to it by her great mishaps; but she did never advise herselfe well, for if she had, as she was accounted wise, she had never come to have bene so contrarie to herselfe. Thou speakest so wisely in all thy answeres, saide Celia, that there is not any that woulde not take great delight to heare them;—which are not viands, said I, for such a daintie taste, nor reasons for so ingenious and fine a conceit, faire lady, as you have, but boldly affirming that by the same I meane no harme at all. There is not any thing, saide Celia, whereunto thy wit cannot attaine, but because thou shalt not spende thy time so ill in praising me as thy master doth in praying me, I will reade thy letter, and tell thee what thou shalt say unto him from me. Whereupon unfolding it, she began to read it to herselfe, to whose countenance and gestures in reading of the same, which are oftentimes outwarde signes of the inwarde disposition and meaning of the hart, I gave a watchfull eie. And when she had read it, she said unto me,—Tell thy master that he that can so well by wordes expresse what he meanes cannot choose but meane as well as he saith; and comming neerer unto me, she saide softly in mine eare,—And this for the love of thee, Valerius, and not so much for Don Felix thy master his sake, for I see how much thou lovest and tenderest his estate. And from thence, alas, saide I to myselfe, did all my woes arise. Whereupon kissing her hands for the great curtesie and favour she shewed me, I hied me to Don Felix with this answer, which was no small joy to him to heare it, and another death to me to report it, saying manie times to myselfe, when I did either bring him home some joyfull tydings or carrie letters or tokens to her,—O thrise unfortunate Felismena, that with thine owne weapons art constrained to wounde thy ever-dying hart, and to heape up favours for him who made so small account of thine. And so did I passe away my life with so many torments of minde that, if by the sight of my Don Felix they had not beene tempered, it coulde not have otherwise beene but that I must needes have lost it. More then two monethes togither did Celia hide from me the fervent love she bare me, although not in such sort but that by certaine apparant signes I came to the knowledge thereof, which was no small lighting and ease of that griefe which incessantly haunted my wearied spirites; for as I thought it a strong occasion and the onely meane to make her utterly forget Don Felix, so likewise I imagined that, perhaps, it might befall to him as it hath done to many, that the force of ingratitude and contempt of his love might have utterly abolished such thoughtes out of his hart. But, alas, it happened not so to my Don Felix; for the more he perceived that his ladie forgot him, the more was his minde troubled with greater cares and greefe, which made him leade the most sorowfull life that might be, whereof the least part did not fall to my lot. For remedie of whose sighes and pitious lamentations, poore Felismena, even by maine force, did get favours from Celia, scoring them up, whensoever she sent them by me, in the catalogue of my infinite mishaps,—for if by chaunce he sent her anie thing by any of his other servants, it was so slenderly accepted that he thought it best to send none unto her but myselfe, perceiving what inconvenience did ensue thereof. But God knowes how many teares my messages cost me, and so many they were that in Celias presence I ceased not to powre them foorth, earnestly beseeching her with praiers and petitions not to entreat him so ill, who loved her so much, bicause I woulde binde Don Felix to me by the greatest bonde as never man in like was bounde to any woman. My teares greeved Celia to the hart, as well for that I shed them in her presence, as also for that she sawe, if I meant to love her, I woulde not, for requitall of hers to me, have sollicited her with such diligence, nor pleaded with such pittie, to get favours for another. And thus I lived in the greatest confusion that might be, amids a thousand anxieties of minde, for I imagined with myselfe that if I made not a shew that I loved her as she did me, I did put it in hazard lest Celia, for despite of my simplicitie or contempt, woulde have loved Don Felix more then before, and by loving him that mine coulde not have any good successe; and if I fained myselfe, on the other side, to be in love with her, it might have beene an occasion to have made her reject my lord Don Felix; so that with the thought of his love neglected, and with the force of her contempt, he might have lost his content, and after that, his life, the least of which two mischiefes to prevent I woulde have given a thousand lives, if I had them. Manie daies passed away in this sort, wherein I served him as a thirde betweene both, to the great cost of my contentment, at the end whereof the successe of his love went on woorse and woorse, bicause the love that Celia did beare me was so great that the extreme force of her passion made her leese some part of that compassion she should have had of herselfe. And on a day after that I had caried and recaried many messages and tokens betweene them, somtimes faining some myselfe from her unto him, because I could not see him whom I loved so deerly so sad and pensive, with many supplications and earnest praiers I besought lady Celia with pittie to regard the painfull life that Don Felix passed for her sake, and to consider that by not favouring him, she was repugnant to that which she owed to herselfe; which thing I entreated, bicause I sawe him in such a case that there was no other thing to be expected of him but death, by reason of the continuall and great paine which his greevous thoughts made him feele. But she, with swelling teares in her eies, and with many sighes, answered me thus ;—Unfortunate and accursed Celia, that nowe in the end dost know how thou livest deceived with a false opinion of thy great simplicitie, ungratefull Valerius, and of thy small discretion. I did not beleeve till now that thou didst crave favours of me for thy master, but onely for thyselfe, and to enjoy my sight all that time that thou diddest spende in suing to me for them. But now I see thou dost aske them in earnest, and that thou art so content to see me use him well, that thou canst not, without doubt, love me at all. O how ill dost thou acquite the love I beare thee, and that which, for thy sake, I do nowe forsake! O that time might revenge me of thy proude and foolish minde, since love hath not beene the meanes to do it. For I cannot thinke that Fortune will be so contrarie unto me but that she will punish thee for contemning that great good which she meant to bestow on thee. And tell thy lord Don Felix that if he will see me alive, that he see me not at all: and thou, vile traitour, cruell enemie to my rest, com no more, I charge thee, before these wearied eies, since their teares were never of force to make thee knowe how much thou art bound unto them; —and with this she suddenly flang out of my sight with so many teares, that mine were not of force to staie her; for in the greatest haste in the worlde she got her into her chamber, where, locking the dore after her, it availed me not to call and crie unto her, requesting her with amorous and sweete words to open me the dore, and to take such satisfaction on me as it pleased her; nor to tell her many other things, whereby I declared unto her the small reason she had to be so angrie with me, and to shut me out. But with a strange kinde of furie she saide unto me, Come no more, ungratefull and proud Valerius, in my sight, and speake no more unto me, for thou art not able to make satisfaction for such great disdaine, and I will have no other remedie for the harme which thou hast done me, but death itselfe, the which with mine owne hands I will take in satisfaction of that which thou deservest; which words when I heard, I staied no longer, but with a heavie cheere came to my Don Felix his lodging, and, with more sadnes then I was able to dissemble, tolde him that I could not speake with Celia, because she was visited of certaine gentlewomen her kinsewomen. But the next day in the morning it was bruted over all the citie that a certaine trance had taken her that night, wherein she gave up the ghost, which stroke all the court with no smal woonder. But that, which Don Felix felt by her sudden death, and how neere it greeved his very soule, as I am not able to tell, so cannot humane intendement conceive it, for the complaints he made, the teares, the burning sighes, and hart-breake sobbes, were without all measure and number. But I saie nothing of myselfe, when on the one side the unluckie death of Celia touched my soule very neere, the teares of Don Felix on the other did cut my hart in two with greefe; and yet this was nothing to that intollerable paine which afterwardes I felt; for Don Felix heard no sooner of her death, but the same night he was missing in his house, that none of his servants nor any bodie else could tell any newes of him. Whereupon you may perceive, faire nymphes, what cruell torments I did then feele; then did I wish a thousand times for death to prevent all those woes and myseries which afterwards befell unto me; for Fortune, it seemed, was but wearie of those which she had but till then given me. But as all the care and diligence which I emploied in seeking out my Don Felix was but in vaine, so I resolved with myselfe to take this habite upon me as you see, wherein it is more then two yeeres since I have wandred up and downe, seeking him in manie countryes; but my Fortune hath denied me to finde him out, although I am not a little now bounde unto her by conducting me hither at this time, wherein I did you this small peece of service. Which, faire nymphes, beleeve me, I account, next after his life in whom I have put all my hope, the greatest content that might have fallen unto me.

XI. *A Sequel to the Tale of Felix and Felismena, from the Seventh Book of the First Part of the Diana of George of Montemayor, translated into English by Yong,* 1598.

The Shepherdesse having made an ende of her sharpe answer, and Felismena beginning to arbitrate the matter between them, they heard a great noise in the other side of the meadow like to the sounde of blowes and smiting of swordes upon harneies, as if some armed men had fought togither, so that all of them with great haste ranne to the place where they heard the noise to see what the matter was; and being come somewhat neere they saw in a little iland, which the river with a round turning had made, three knights fighting against one, and although he defended himselfe valiantly by shewing his approoved strength and courage, yet the three knights gave him so much to do that he was faine to helpe himselfe by all the force and pollicie he could. They fought on foote, for their horses were tied to little trees that grew thereabouts; and now by this time the knight that fought all alone and defended himselfe had laide one of them at his feete with a blowe of his good sword which ended his life; but the other two that were very strong and valiant redoubled their force and blowes so thicke on him, that he looked for no other thing then death. The shepherdesse Filismena, seeing the knight in so great danger, and if she did not speedily helpe him that he could not escape with life, was not afraide to put hers in jeopardy by doing that which in such a case she thought she was bound to performe; wherefore, putting a sharpe headed arrowe into her bowe, shee saide unto them,—Keepe out, knights, for it is not beseeming men that make account of this name and honour to take advantage of their enimies with so great oddes; and, ayming at the sight of one of their helmets, she burst it with such force that the arrow running into his eies came out of the other side of his head, so that he fell downe dead to the ground. When the distressed knight sawe two of his enimies dead, he ran upon the third with such force as if he had but then begun the combat, but Felismena helped him out of that trouble by putting another arrow into her bow, the which transpiercing his armour she left under his left pap and so justly smot his hart that this knight also followed his two companions. When the shepherds and the knight beheld what Felismena had done, and how at two shootes she had killed two such valiant knights, they were all in great woonder. The knight, therefore, taking off his helmet and comming unto her, saide,—How am I able, faire shepherdesse, to requite so great a benefite and good turne as I have received at thy hands this day, but by acknowledging this debt for ever in my gratefull minde. When Felismena beheld the knights face and knew him, her sences were so troubled that, being in such a traunce, she could scarce speake, but comming to herselfe againe, she answered him,—Ah! my Don Felix, this is not the first debt wherein thou art bound unto me, and I cannot beleeve that thou wilt acknowledge this as thou saiest, no more then thou hast done greater then this before. Beholde, to what a time and ende my fortune and thy forgetnesse⊕ hath brought me, that she that was woont to be served of thee in the citie with tilt and tourneyes, and honoured with many other things whereby thou didst deceive me, or I suffered myselfe to be deceived, doth nowe wander uppe and downe exiled from her native countrey and libertie for using thus thine owne. If this brings thee not into the knowledge of that which thou owest me, remember how one whole yeere I served thee as thy page in the Princesse Cesarinas Court, and how I was a solicitor against myselfe without discovering myselfe or my thoughts unto thee, but onley to procure thy remedie and to helpe the greefe which thine made thee feele. How many times did I get thee favours from thy mistresse Celia to the great cost of my teares and greefes? all which account but small, Don Felix, in respect of those dangers, had they beene unsufficient, wherein I would have spent my life for redresse of thy paines which thy injurious love affoorded thee; and unlesse thou art weary of the great love that I have borne thee, consider and weigh with thyselfe the strange effects which the force of love hath caused me to passe. I went out of my native countrey and came to serve thee, to lament the ill that thou did'st suffer, to take upon me the injuries and disgraces that I received therein, and to give thee any content, I cared not to lead the most bitter and painefull life that ever woman lived. In the habite of a tender and daintie ladie I loved thee more then thou canst imagine, and in the habite of a base page I served thee, a thing more contrarie to my rest and reputation then I meane now to reherse; and yet now in the habite of a poore and simple shepherdesse I came to do thee this small service. What remaines then more for me to doe but to sacrifice my life to thy lovelesse soule, if with the same yet I could give thee more content; and if in lieu therof thou wouldest but remember how much I have loved and do yet love thee, here hast thou thy sword in thy hand; let none, therefore, but thyselfe revenge the offence that I have done thee. When the knight heard Felismenas words, and knew them all to be as true as he was disloyall, his hart by this strange and sudden accident recovered some force againe to see what great injurie he had done her, so that the thought thereof, and the plenteous effusion of blood that issued out of his woundes, made him like a dead man fall downe in a swoone at faire Felismenas feete, who with great care and no lesse feare laying his head in her lap, with showers of teares that rained from her eies upon the knights pale visage, began thus to lament,—What meanes this cruell Fortune? Is the periode of my life come just with the last ende of my Don Felix his daies? Ah! my Don Felix, the cause of all my paine, if the plenteous teares which for thy sake I have shed are not sufficient, and these which I now distill upon thy lovely cheekes too fewe to make thee come to thyselfe againe, what remedie shall this miserable soule have to prevent that this bitter joy by seeing thee turne not into occasion of utter despaire? Ah! my Don Felix, awake, my love; if thou dost but sleepe or beest in a traunce, although I would not woonder if thou dost not, since never anything that I could do prevailed with thee to frame my least content. And in these and other lamentations was faire Felismena plunged, whom the Portugall Shepherdesses with their teares and poore supplies endevored to incourage, when on the sudden they saw a faire nymph comming over the stony causey that lead the way into the ilande, with a golden bottel in one hand and a silver one in the other, whom Felismena knowing, by and by saide unto her,—Ah! Doria, could any come at this time to succour me but thou, faire nymph? Come hither then, and thou shalt see the cause of al my troubles, the substance of my sighs and the object of my thoughts, lying in the greatest danger of death that may be. In like occurrents, saide Doria, vertue and a good hart must take place. Recall it then, faire Felismena, and revive thy daunted spirits; trouble not thyselfe any more, for nowe is the ende of thy sorrowes and the beginning of thy contentment come. And speaking these wordes, she besprinkled his face with a certaine odoriferous water which she brought in the silver bottle, whereby he came to his memorie againe, and then saide unto him,—If thou wilt recover thy life, Sir Knight, and give it her that hath passed such an ill one for thy sake, drinke of the water in this bottle; the which Don Felix taking in his hande, drunke a good draught, and resting upon it a little, founde himselfe so whole of his wounds which the three knights had given him, and of that which the love of Celia had made in his brest, that now he felt the paine no more which either of them had caused in him then if he had never had them. And in this sort he began to rekindle the old love that he bare to Felismena, the which he thought was never more zealous then now; whereupon sitting downe upon the greene grasse, hee tooke his lady and shepherdesse by the hands, and kissing them manie times, saide thus unto her,—How small account would I make of my life, my deerest Felismena, for cancelling that great bond wherein with more then life I am for ever bound unto thee; for since I enjoy it by thy means, I thinke it no more then right to restore thee that which is thine owne. With what eies can I behold thy peerelesse beauty, which though unadvisedly I knew not to be such, yet how dare I for that which I owe thee cast them in any other part? What wordes are sufficient to excuse the faults that I have committed against thy faith and firmest love and loyaltie? Wretched and accursed for ever shall I be, if thy condition and clemencie be not enclined to my favour and pardon, for no satisfaction can suffice for so great an offence, nor reason to excuse me for that which thou hast to forget me. Truth it is that I loved Celia well and forgot thee, but not in such sort that thy wisedome and beautie did ever slide out of my minde; and the best is that I knowe not wherein to put this fault that may be so justly attributed to me, for if I will impute it to the yoong age that I was then in, since I had it to love thee I shoulde not have wanted it to have beene firme in the faith that I owed thee. If to Celias beautie it is cleere that thine did farre excell hers and all the worlds besides; if to the change of time this shoulde have beene the touchstone which should have shewed the force and vertue of my firmenes; if to injurious and trayterous absence it serves as little for my excuse, since the desire of seeing thee should not have been absent from supporting thy image in my memorie; behold, then, Felismena, what assured trust I put in thy goodnes, that without any other meanes I dare put before thee the small reason thou hast to pardone me. But what shall I doe to purchase pardon at thy gracious hands, or, after thou hast pardoned me, to beleeve that thou art satisfied, for one thing greeves me more then any thing else in the world, and this it is; that though the love which thou hast borne me and wherewith thou dost yet blesse me is an occasion perhaps to make thee forgive me and forget so many faults, yet I shall never lift up mine eies to behold thee but that everie injurie which I have done thee will be worse then a mortal incision in my guiltie hart. The shepherdesse Felismena, who saw Don Felix so penitent for his passed misdeedes, and so affectionately returned to his first thoughts, with many teares told him that she did pardon him bicause the love that she had ever borne him would suffer her to do no lesse, which if she had not thought to do she would never have taken so great paines and so many wearie journeyes to seeke him out, and many other things, wherewith Don Felix was confirmed in his former love. Whereupon the faire nymph Doria came then to the knight, and after many loving words and courteous offers in the Ladie Felicias behalfe passed betweene them, she requested him and faire Felismena to goe with her to Dianas Temple, where the sage ladie with great desire to see them was attending their comming. Don Felix agreed thereunto, and taking their leave of the Portugall shepherdesses, who wondered not a little to see what had happened, and of the woefull shepherd Danteus, mounting upon the horses of the dead knights that were slaine in the late combate they went on their waie. And as they were going, Felismena told Don Felix with great joy what she had past since she had last seene him, which made him to marvell verie much, and especially at the death of the three savages, and at the palace of the sage ladie Felicia, and successe of the shepherds and shepherdesses, and at everie thing else contained in this booke. And Don Felix wondred not a little to understand how his Ladie Felismena had served him so many daies as his page, and that he was so far gon out of his wits and memorie that he knew her not all that while; and his joy on the other side to see that his ladie loved him so well was so great that by no meanes he could hide it. Thus, therefore, riding on their way, they came to Dianas Temple, where the sage Felicia was looking for their comming, and likewise the shepherd Arsileus and Belisa, Sylvanus and Selvagia, who were now come thither not many daies before. They were welcommed on everie side and with great joy intertained, but faire Felismena especially, who for hir rare vertues and singular beautie was greatly honored of them all. There they were all married with great joy, feasts and triumphes, which were made by all the goodly nymphes and by the sage and noble Ladie Felicia, the which Syrenus with his comming augmented not a little.

XII. *"How Fiddlers fiddled away Tarltons Apparell." An anecdote from Tarlton's Jests, 1638, the earliest edition now known, the one said to have been printed in 1611 having that date incorrectly given in manuscript.*

It chanced that one Fancy and Nancy, two musicians in London, used often with their boyes to visit Tarlton when he dwelt in Gracious-street, at the signe of the Saba, a taverne, he being one of their best friends or benefactors, by reason of old acquaintance, to requite which they came one summers morning to play him the Hunt's up with such musicke as they had. Tarlton, to requite them, would open his chamber doore, and for their paines would give them muskadine; which a cony-catcher noting, and seeing Tarlton came forth in his shirt and nightgowne to drinke with these musicians, the while this nimble fellow stept in and tooke Tarltons apparell which every day he wore, thinking that, if he were espied, to turne it to a jest; but it past for currant, and he goes his wayes. Not long after, Tarlton returned to his chamber, and looked for his cloaths, but they were safe enough from him. The next day this was noised abroad, and one in mockage threw him in this theame, he playing then at the Curtaine.—

Tarlton, I will tell thee a jest
Which after turned to earnest.
One there was, as I heard say,
Who in his shirt heard musicke play,
While all his clothes were stolne away.

Tarlton smiling at this, answered on the sudden thus :—

That's certaine, sir, it is no lie,
That same one in truth was I.
When that the theefe shall pine and lacke,
Then shall I have cloathes to my backe :
And I, together with my fellowes,
May see them ride to Tiborne gallowes.

XIII. *A Short Discourse of the English Stage, by Richard Flecknoe; printed at the end of his Love's Kingdom. 12mo. Lond. 1664.*

Playes, which so flourisht amongst the Greeks, and afterwards amongst the Romans, were almost wholly abolished when their empire was first converted to Christianity, and their theaters together with their temples for the most part demolished as reliques of paganisme, some few onely reserved and dedicate to the service of the true God, as they had been to their false gods before; from which time to the last age they acted nothing here but playes of the Holy Scripture or saints lives, and that without any certain theaters or set companies till about the beginning of queen Elizabeths reign they began here to assemble into companies and set up theaters, first in the city, as in the inn-yards of the Cross-Keyes and Bull in Grace and Bishopsgate street at this day is to be seen, till that fanatick spirit which then began with the stage, and after ended with the throne, banisht them thence into the suburbs, as after they did the kingdom, in the beginning of our Civil Wars; in which time playes were so little incompatible with Religion, and the theater with the Church, as on week-dayes after vespers both the Children of the Chappel and St. Pauls acted playes, the one in White-Friers the other behinde the Convocation-house in Pauls, till people growing more precise, and playes more licentious, the theatre of Pauls was quite supprest and that of the Children of the Chappel converted to the use of the Children of the Revels. In this time were poets and actors in their greatest flourish, Johnson, Shakespear, with Beaumont and Fletcher, their poets, and Field and Burbidge their actors. For playes Shakespear was one of the first who inverted the dramatick stile from dull history to quick comedy, upon whom Johnson refin'd; as Beaumont and Fletcher first writ in the heroick way, upon whom Suckling and others endeavoured to refine. Agen, one saying wittily of his Aglaura that 'twas full of fine flowers, but they seem'd rather stuck then growing there; as another, of Shakespear's writings, that 'twas a fine garden but it wanted weeding. There are few of our English playes, excepting onely some few of Johnsons, without some faults or other, and if the French have fewer then our English, 'tis because they confine themselves to narrower limits and consequently have less liberty to erre. The chief faults of ours are our huddling too much matter together, and making them too long and intricate; we imagining we never have intrigue enough till we lose ourselves and auditors, who shu'd be led in a maze but not a mist, and through turning and winding wayes but so still as they may finde their way at last. A good play shu'd be like a good stuff, closely and evenly wrought without any breakes, thrums or loose ends in 'um, or like a good picture well painted and designed, the plot or contrivement the design, the writing the coloris, and counterplot the shaddowings with other embellishments; or finally it shu'd be like a well contriv'd garden cast into its walks and counterwalks betwixt an alley and a wilderness, neither too plain nor too confus'd. Of all arts that of the dramatick poet is the most difficult and most subject to censure, for in all others they write onely of some particular subject, as the mathematician of mathematicks or philosopher of philosophy, but in that the poet must write of every thing, and every one undertakes to judge of it. A dramatick poet is to the stage as a pilot to the ship, and to the actors as an architect to the builders or master to his schollars; he is to be a good moral philosopher, but yet more learned in men then books. He is to be a wise as well as a witty man, and a good man as well as a good poet; and I'de allow him to be so far a good fellow too, to take a chearful cup to whet his wits, so he take not so much to dull 'um and whet 'um quite away. To compare our English dramatick poets together without taxing them, Shakespear excelled in a natural vein, Fletcher in wit, and Johnson in gravity and ponderousness of style, whose onely fault was he was too elaborate, and had he mixt less erudition with his playes they had been more pleasant and delightful then they are; comparing him with Shakespear, you shall see the difference betwixt nature and art, and with Fletcher the difference betwixt wit and judgement, wit being an exuberant thing like Nilus, never more commendable then when it overflowes, but judgement a stayed and reposed thing alwayes containing itself within its bounds and limits. Beaumont and Fletcher were excellent in their kinde, but they often err'd against decorum, seldom representing a valiant man without somewhat of the braggadoccio, nor an honourable woman without somewhat of Dol Common in her, to say nothing of their irreverent representing kings persons on the stage, who shu'd never be represented but with reverence. Besides, Fletcher was the first who introduc't that witty obscenity in his playes, which, like poison infused in pleasant liquor, is alwayes the more dangerous the more delightful. And here to speak a word or two of wit, it is the spirit and quintessence of speech extracted out of the substance of the thing we speak of, having nothing of the superfice or dross of words, as clenches, quibbles, gingles and such like trifles have; it is that in pleasant and facetious discourse as eloquence is in grave and serious, not learnt by art and precept but nature and company. 'Tis in vain to say any more of it, for if I could tell you what it were, it would not be what it is, being somewhat above expression and such a volatil thing as 'tis altogether as volatil to describe. It was the happiness of the actors of those times to have such poets as these to instruct them and write for them, and no less of those poets to have such docile and excellent actors to act their playes as a Field and Burbidge, of whom we may say that he was a delightful Proteus, so wholly transforming himself into his part, and putting off himself with his cloathes, as he never not so much as in the tyring-house assum'd himself again until the play was done; there being as much difference betwixt him and one of our common actors as between a ballad singer who onely mouths it and an excellent singer who knows all his graces, and can artfully vary and modulate his voice even to know how much breath he is to give to every syllable. He had all the parts of an excellent orator, animating his words with speaking and speech with action, his auditors being never more delighted then when he spake, nor more sorry then when he held his peace, yet even then he was an excellent actor still, never falling in his part when he had done speaking, but with his looks and gesture maintaining it still unto the heighth, he imagining *age quod agis* onely spoke to him; so as those who call him a player do him wrong, no man being less idle then he whose whole life is nothing else but action, with only this difference from other mens, that as what is but a play to them is his business, so their business is but a play to him. Now for the difference betwixt our theaters and those of former times, they were but plain and simple, with no other scenes nor decorations of the stage but onely old tapestry and the stage strew'd with rushes, with their habits accordingly, whereas ours now for cost and ornament are arriv'd to the heighth of magnificence; but that which makes our stage the better makes our playes the worse, perhaps they striving now to make them more for sight then hearing, whence that solid joy of the interior is lost, and that benefit which men formerly receiv'd from playes from which they seldom or never went away but far better and wiser then they came; the stage being a harmless and innocent recreation where the minde is recreated and delighted, and that *ludus literarum* or school of good language and behaviour that makes youth soonest man, and man soonest good and vertuous, by joyning example to precept and the pleasure of seeing to that of hearing. Its chiefest end is to render folly ridiculous, vice odious, and vertue and noblenesse so amiable and lovely as every one shu'd be delighted and enamoured with it, from which when it deflects as *corruptio optimi pessima* of the best it becomes the worst of recreations. And this His Majesty well understood when, after his happy Restauration, he took such care to purge it from all vice and obscenity, and would to God he had found all bodies and humours as apt and easie to be purg'd and reform'd as that. For scenes and machines, they are no new invention, our masks and some of our playes in former times, though not so ordinary, having had as good or rather better then any we have now. They are excellent helps of imagination, most grateful deceptions of the sight, and graceful and becoming ornaments of the stage, transporting you easily without lassitude from one place to another, or rather by a kinde of delightful magick whilst you sit still does bring the place to you. Of this curious art the Italians this latter age are the greatest masters, the French good proficients, and we in England onely schollars and learners yet, having proceeded no further then to bare painting, and not arriv'd to the stupendious wonders of your great ingeniers, especially not knowing yet how to place our lights for the more advantage and illuminating of the scenes.

XIV. *Patent under the Great Seal licensing the Servants of Anne, Queen of James the First, to act Plays*, 15 *April*, 1609. *From the Patent Rolls*, 7 *Jac. I., Pars* 39.

James, by the grace of God, &c. To all justices, mayors, sheriffes, baylieffes, constables, headborrowes, and other our officers and lovinge subjectes, greetinge. Knowe yee that wee, of our especiall grace, certayne knowledge and meere mocion, have lycenced and authorised, and by these presentes doe lycence and aucthorize, Thomas Greene, Christofer Beeston, Thomas Haywood, Richard Pirkyns, Richard⁽ᵃ⁾ Pallant, Thomas Swinnerton, John Duke, Robert Lee, James Haulte and Roberte Beeston, servantes to our moste deerely beloved wiefe, Queene Anne, and the reste of theire associates, to use and exercise the arte and facultye of playinge comedies, tragedies, historyes, enterludes, moralles, pastoralles, stage playes and suche other, like as they have already studied, or heareafter shall use or studye, as well for the recreacion of our lovinge subjectes as for our solace and pleasure, when wee shall thinke good to see them, duringe our pleasure. And the saide comedies, tragedies, histories, enterludes, moralles, pastoralles, stage playes and suche like, to shewe and exercise publiquely and openly to theire beste commoditye, as well within theire nowe usuall houses called the Redd Bull in Clarkenwell and the Curtayne in Hallowell, as alsoe within anye towne halles, mouthalles, and other conveniente places within the libertye and freedome of any other citty, universitye, towne or boroughe whatsoever within our realmes and domynions. Willinge and commaundinge you and every of you, as you tender our pleasure, not only to permitt and suffer them herein, without anye your lettes, hinderances or molestacions, duringe our said pleasure, but alsoe to be aydinge assistinge⁽ᵃ⁾ unto them, yf anye wronge be to them offered, and to allowe them suche former curtesies as hath byn given to men of theire place and qualitye; and alsoe what favoure you shall shewe to them for our sake wee shall take kyndly at your handes. Provided alwaies, and our will and pleasure is, that all aucthoritye, power, priviledges and profyttes whatsoever belonginge and properly apertayninge to Master⁽ᵃ⁾ of Revelles in respecte of his office, and everye clause, article or graunte contayned within the Lettres Patentes or Commission which have byn heretofore graunted or directed by the late Queene Elizabeth, our deere sister, or by ourselves, to our wel beloved servantes, Edmond Tylney, Master of the Office of our saide Revelles, or to Sir George Bucke, Knighte, or to eyther of them, in possession or revercion, shal be, remayne and abyde entyer and full in effecte, force, estate and vertue, as⁽ᵃ⁾ ample sorte as if this our Commission had never byn made. In Witnes wherof, &c. Witnes ourselfe at Westminster, the fifteenth daye of Aprill.—Per breve de Privato Sigillo, &c.

XV. *An Order of the Lords of the Privy Council "for the Restrainte of the imoderate Use and Companye of Playehowses and Players," June 22nd, 1600. From the original Register of the Privy Council. There is another Transcript of this Order preserved in the Archives of the City of London. In the latter Copy the word "too" is in the Place of "so" in l. 40 of the next Column. This is the only Variation worthy of Notice.*

Whereas divers complaintes have bin heretofore made unto the Lordes and others of her Majesties Privye Counsell of the manyfolde abuses and disorders that have growen and do contynue by occasion of many houses erected and employed in and about the cittie of London for common stage-playes, and now verie latelie by reason of some complainte exhibited by sundry persons againste the buyldinge of the like house in or neare Golding-lane by one Edward Allen, a servant of the right honorable the Lord Admyrall, the matter as well in generaltie touchinge all the saide houses for stage-playes and the use of playinge, as in particular concerninge the saide house now in hand to be buylte in or neare Golding-lane, hath bin broughte into question and consultacion amonge their Lordships; forasmuch as it is manifestly knowen and graunted that the multitude of the saide houses and the mysgovernment of them hath bin and is dayly occasion of the ydle, ryotous and dissolute living of great nombers of people, that, leavinge all such honest and painefull course of life as they should followe, doe meete and assemble there, and of many particular abuses and disorders that doe thereupon ensue; and yet, nevertheles, it is considered that the use and exercise of such playes, not beinge evill in ytself, may with a good order and moderacion be suffered in a well-governed state, and that her Majestie, beinge pleased at somtymes to take delight and recreation in the sight and hearinge of them, some order is fitt to be taken for the allowance and mayntenaunce of such persons as are thought meetest in that kinde to yealde her Majestie recreation and delighte, and consequently of the houses that must serve for publike playinge to keepe them in exercise. To the ende, therefore, that both the greate abuses of the playes and playinge-houses may be redressed, and yet the aforesaide use and moderation of them retayned, the Lordes and the reste of her Majesties Privie Counsell, with one and full consent, have ordered in manner and forme as followeth,—

Firste,—that there shal be aboute the Cittie two houses and no more allowed to serve for the use of the common stage-playes, of the which houses one shal be in Surrey in that place which is commonly called the Banckeside or theraboutes, and the other in Middlesex. And forasmuch as their Lordships have bin enformed by Edmund Tylney Esqr., her Majesties servante and Master of the Revells, that the house nowe in hand to be builte by the saide Edward Allen is not intended to encrease the number of the playhouses, but to be insteede of another, namely the Curtayne, which is ether to be ruyned and plucked downe or to be put to some other good use, as also that the scytuation thereof is meete and convenient for that purpose, it is likewise ordered that the saide house of Allen shal be allowed to be one of the two houses and namely for the house to be allowed in Middlesex for the company of players belonging to the Lord Admirall, so as the house called the Curtaine be, as it is pretended, either ruynated or applyed to some other good use. And for the other house allowed to be on Surrey side, whereas their Lordships are pleased to permitt to the company of players that shall play there to make their owne choice which they will have of divers houses that are there, choosing one of them and no more, and the said company of plaiers, being the servantes of the Lord Chamberlain, that are to play there, have made choise of the house called the Globe, it is ordered that the saide house and none other shal be there allowed; and especially it is forbidden that any stage-playes shal be played, as sometymes they have bin, in any common inne for publique assembly in or neare aboute the Cittie.

Secondly,—forasmuch as these stage-plaies, by the multitude of houses and company of players, have bin so frequent, not servinge for recreation but invitinge and callinge the people dayly from their trade and worke to myspend their tyme, it is likewise ordered that the two severall companies of players assigned unto the two houses allowed may play each of them in their severall house twice a weeke and no oftener, and especially they shall refrayne to play on the Sabbath-day upon paine of imprysonment and further penaltie; and that they shall forbeare altogether in the tyme of Lent, and likewise at such tyme and tymes as any extraordinary sicknes or infection of disease shall appeare to be in or about the cittie.

Thirdly,—because these orders wil be of little force and effecte unlesse they be duely putt in execution by those unto whome it appertayneth to see them executed, it is ordered that severall copies of these orders shal be sent to the Lord Maior of London and to the Justices of the Peace of the counties of Middlesex and Surrey, and that lettres shal be written unto them from their Lordships straightly charginge them to see to the execucion of the same, as well by commyttinge to prison any owners of play-houses and players as shall disobey and resist these orders as by any other good and lawfull meanes that in their discretion they shall finde expedient, and to certifie their Lordships from tyme to tyme as they shall see cause of their proceedinges heerein.

XVI. *The Letter from the Lords of the Privy Council to the Justices of the Peace for the County of Surrey, June 22nd, 1600, referred to in the preceding Order. From the original Register of the Privy Council.*

By occasion of some complaintes that of late have bin made unto us of the multitude of houses servinge for common stage-playes in and aboute the Citty of London, and of the greate abuses and disorders growen by the overmuch haunte and resorte of many licentious people unto those houses and places, we have entred into consideracion of some fitt course to be taken for redresse of the saide disorders by suppressinge dyvers of those houses, and by some restrainte of the imoderate use of the plaies, for which cause wee have sett downe certaine orders to be duely henceforth observed and kept, a copy whereof we sende yow here inclosed, and have sent the like to the Lord Maior of London and to the Justices of the Peace of Middlesex; but as wee have done our partes in prescribinge the orders, so, unlesse yow perfourme yours in lookinge to the due execution of them, we shall loose our labor, and the wante of redresse must be imputed unto yow and others unto whome it apperteyneth; and, therefore, wee doe hereby authorize and require you to see the saide orders to be putt in execucion and to be continued, as yow do wish the amendement of the aforesaide abuses and will remove the blame thereof from yourselves.

XVII. *Notices of the Popularity of the Drama in London in the year 1587, contained in a Letter from a Soldier, a zealous Protestant, to Sir Francis Walsingham, January the 25th, 1586-7. From the Original in the British Museum, MS. Harl. 286.*

The daylie abuse of stage playes is such an offence to the godly and so great a hinderance to the gospell as the Papistes doe exceedingly rejoyce at the blemyshe theareof and not without cause, for every day in the weeke the playeres billes are sett upp in sondry places of the cittie, some in the name of her Majesties menne, some the Earle of Leic:, some the E. of Oxfordes, the Lo. Admyralles, and dyvers others, so that when the belles tole to the lectoures, the trumpettes sounde to the stages, wheareat the wicked faction of Romo lawgheth for joy, while the godly weepe for sorrowe. Woe is me, the play howses are pestered when the churches are naked. At the one it is not possible to gett a place; at the other, voyde seates are plentie. The profaning of the Sabaoth is redressed, but as badde a custome entertayned, and yet still our longe suffering God forbayrith to punisshe. Yt is a wofull sight to see two hundred proude players jett in theire silkes, wheare fyve hundred pore people sterve in the streetes; but yf needes this misschief must be tollorated, whereat, no doubt, the Highest frownith, yet for Godes sake, sir, lett every stage in London pay a weekely pention to the pore, that *ex hoc malo proveniat aliquod bonum;* but yt weare rather to be wisshed that playes might be used as Appollo did his lawghinges, *semel in anno.*

XVIII. *Deed of Feoffment from Sir William More of Loseley, co. Surrey, to James Burbage, 4 February,* 1596, *conveying to the Latter that Portion of a large House in the Blackfriars which was shortly afterwards converted by him into a Theatre.*

This indenture made the fourth daye of Februarie in the eighte and thirtyth yeare of the raigne of our Soveraigne lady Elizabeth, by the grace of God Queene of Englande, Fraunce and Irelande, Defendor of the Fayth, &c., betwene Sir William More of Loseley in the County of Surrey, Knight, of thone partye, and James Burbage of Hollowell in the Countye of Middlesex, gentleman, of thother partye, Witnesseth that the said Sir William More, for and in consideracyon of the some of sixe hundreth poundes of lawfull money of England to him by the said James Burbage at and before thensealinge of theis presentes truelye payd, whereof and wherewith he the said Sir William More dothe acknowledge and confesse himselfe fully satysfied and paid, and thereof and of every parte thereof doth cleirely acquite and discharge the said James Burbage, his heyres, executors and administrators, and every of them, by theis presentes hath bargayned, sold, alyened, enfeoffed and confirmed, and by theis presentes doth fully and cleirelye bargaine, sell, alyen, enfeoffe and confirme to the said James Burbage, his heires and assignes, for ever, all those seaven greate upper romes as they are nowe devided, beinge all uppon one flower and sometyme beinge one greate and entire rome, with the roufe over the same covered with lead, together also with all the lead that doth cover the same seaven greate upper roemes, and also all the stone stayres leading upp unto the leades or roufe over the said seaven greate upper romes out of the said seaven greate upper romes, and also all the greate stone walles and other walles which doe enclose, devid and belonge to, the same seaven greate upper romes, and also all that greate payre of wyndinge stayres, with the stayre case thereunto belongeing, which leadeth upp unto the same seaven greate upper romes out of the greate yarde there which doth lye nexte unto the Pype Office, which said seaven greate upper romes were late in the teanure or occupacyon of William de Lawne, Doctor of Phisick, or of his assignes, and are scituate, lyeinge and beinge, within the precincte of the late Blackfryers Preachers nere Ludgate in London; together also with all the waynescott, glasse, dores, lockes, keyes and boltes to the same seaven greate upper romes and other the premisses by theis presentes bargayned and sold incident or apperteyning, or beinge fixed or fastened thereunto; togeather also with the easemente and commoditie of a vaulte beinge under some parte of the sayde seaven greate upper romes, or under the entrye or voyde rome lyeing betwen those seaven greate upper romes and the sayde Pipe Office, by a stole and tonnell to be made into the same vault in and out of the greate stone wall in the ynner side thereof next and adjoyneinge to the said entry or voide rome, beinge towardes the south; and alsoe all those romes and lodginges, with the kitchin thereunto adjoyning, called the Midle Romes or Midle Stories, late beinge in the tenure or occupacion of Rocco Bonnetto, and nowe being in the tenure or occupacyon of Thomas Bruskett, gentleman, or of his assignes, conteyninge in length fyftie twoo foote of assize more or lesse, and in bredith thirtie seaven foote of assize more or lesse, lyeing and beinge directlye under parte of those of the sayd seaven greate upper romes which lye westwardes; which said Mydle Romes or Mydle Stories doe extende in length southwardes to a parte of the house of Sir George Cary, Knight; and also all the stone walles and other walles which doe enclose, devide and belonge to, the same Midle Romes or Midle Stories, together alsoe with the dore and entrey which doe lye nexte unto the gate entring into the house of the said Sir George Cary, and used to and from the said Midle Romes or Midle Stories out of a lane or waye leadinge unto the house of the sayd Sir George Cary, with free waye, ingres, egres and regres, into and from the said Midle Romes or Midle Stories in, by and through, the waies nowe used to the said house of the said Sir George Cary; and also all those twoo vaultes or sellers late being in thoccupacyon of the said Rocco Bonnetto, lyeinge under parte of the said Midle Romes or Midle Stories at the north end thereof, as they are nowe devided, and are nowe in the teanure or occupacion of the said Thomas Bruskett and of John Favor, and are adjoyneing to the twoo lytle yardes nowe in thoccupacyons of Peter Johnson and of the sayd John Favor, together also with the stayres leading into the same vaultes or cellers out of the foresaid kitchen in thoccupacyon of the said Thomas Bruskett; and also all those two upper romes or chambers with a lyttle butterey at the north end of the said seaven greate upper romes and on the weste side thereof, nowe being in thoccupacyon of Charles Bradshawe, together with the voyd rome, waye and passage, nowe thereunto used from the said seaven greate upper romes; and also all those twoo romes or loftes nowe in thoccupacion of Edward Merry, thone of them lyeing and being above or over the said two upper romes or chambers in thoccupacion of the said Charles Bradshawe, and on thest and north parte thereof, and having a chimney in it, and thother of them lieinge over parte of the foresaid entrey or voyde rome next the foresaid Pipe Office, together with the stayres leading from the foresaid romes in thoccupacion of the foresaid Charles Bradshawe upp unto the foresaid two romes in thoccupacyon of the said Edward Merry; and also all that lytle rome now used to laye woode and coles in, being aboute the midle of the said stayers westwardes, which said litle rome laste mencyoned is over the foresaid buttrey nowe in thoccupacyon of the sayd Charles Bradshawe, and is now in thoccupacyon of the said Charles Bradshawe; and also all that rome or garrett lyeing and being over the said twoo romes or loftes laste before mencyoned in thoccupacyon of the said Edward Merry, together with the dore, entrye, void grounde, waye and passage and stayres leading or used to, with or from, the said romes in thoccupacyon of the said Edward Merry up unto the said rome or garrett over the said twoo romes in thoccupacyon of the said Edward Merrie; and also all those twoo lower romes, now in thoccupacyon of the said Peter Johnson, lying directlye under parte of the said seaven greate upper romes; and also all those twoo other lower romes or chambers nowe being also in the tenure or occupacion of the said Peter Johnson, being under the foresaid romes or chambers in thoccupacyon of the said Charles Bradshawe; and also the dore, entry, waye, voyd grounde and passage leading and used to and from the said greate yard next the said Pipe Office into and from the said fouer lower romes or chambers; and also all that litle yard adjoyneing to the said lower romes as the same is nowe enclosed with a bricke wall, and nowe beinge in thoccupacyon of the said Peter Johnson, which said foure lower romes or chambers and litle yard doe lye betwene the said greate yard nexte the sayd Pipe Office on the north parte, and an entery leading into the messuage which Margaret Pooley, widdow, holdeth for terme of her lyefe, nowe in the occupacyon of the said John Favor, on the west parte, and a wall devidinge the said yard now in the occupacyon of the said Peter Johnson and the yard nowe in thoccupacion of the said John Favor on the south parte; and also the stayres and staire case leadinge from the said litle yard nowe in thoccupacyon of the sayde Peter Johnson up unto the foresaid chambers or romes nowe in thoccupacyon of the said Charles Bradshawe; and alsoe all that litle yard or peice of void grounde, with the bricke wall thereunto belongeing, lyeinge and beinge nexte the Queenes highewaye leadinge unto the ryver of Thamis, wherein an old privy nowe standeth, as the same is nowe enclosed with the same bricke wall and with a pale next adjoyneinge to the house of the said Sir William More, nowe in thoccupacyon of the right honorable the Lord Cobham, on the east parte, and the streete leadinge to the Thamys there on the west parte, and the said yarde nexte the said Pipe Office on the south parte, and the house of the saide Lorde Cobham on the north parte,—All which premisses before in theis presentes mencyoned to be hereby bargayned and sold are scituate, lyeinge and beinge, within the saide prescincte of the said late Blackfryers Preachers; together also with all libertyes, priveledges, lightes, watercourses, easementes, commodities and appurtenaunces to the foresaid romes, lodginges and other the premisses before in theis presentes mencyoned to be hereby bargained and sold belongeing or in any wyse apperteyninge.

And also the sayd Sir William More, for the consyderacyon aforesayd, hath bargayned, sold, alyened, enfeoffed and confirmed, and by theis presentes doth bargayne, sell, alyen, enfeoffe and confirme unto the said James Burbage, his heires and assignes for ever, free and quiett ingres, egres and regres, to and from the streete or waye leadeing from Ludgate unto the Thamys over, uppon and thoroughe, the same greate yarde next the said Pipe Office by the wayes nowe thereunto used into and from the sayde seaven greate upper romes, and all other the premisses before in and by theis presentes mencyoned to be bargayned and sold, and to and from every or any parte or parcell thereof, together alsoe with free libertye for the said James Burbage, his heires and assignes, to laye and discharge his and their wood, cole and all other carriages, necessaries and provisions in the same greate yarde laste before mencyoned for conveniente tyme, untill the same maye be taken and carried awaie from thence unto the premisses before by theis presentes mencyoned to be bargayned and sold, and so from tyme to tyme and at all tymes hereaffter the sayd James Burbage, his heyres and assignes, leavinge convenyent waies and passages to goe and come in, uppon and throughe, the said greate yarde from tyme to tyme to and from the said Pipe Office, and to and from the garden and other houses and romes of the said Sir William More not hereby bargayned and sold, out of the streete leadeinge to the said ryver of Thamys, so that the said wood, cole, carriages and provisyons so layed and discharged in the said yarde last mencyoned by the said James, his heyres or assignes, be removed and avoided out of and from the said yarde within three dayes next after it shalbe broughte thither, without fraude or further delaye. And further, the said Sir William More, for the consideracion aforesaid, doth by theis presentes graunte, bargayne and sell, unto the said James Burbage, his heyres and assignes, for ever, the revercyon and revercyons, remainder and remainders, of all and singuler the premisses before by theis presentes mencyoned to be heareby bargained and sold, and every parte and parcell thereof, excepte and reserved unto the said Sir William More, his heyres and assignes, one rome or stole as the same is now made in and out of the foresaide wall nexte the said entrey adjoyneinge to the said Pipe Office into the foresaid vault. All which said seaven greate upper romes, and all other the premisses with thappurtenaunces above by theis presentes mencyoned to be bargayned and sold, amonge others Sir Thomas Cawarden, knighte, deceased, late had to him, his heyres and assignes, for ever, of the guifte and graunte of the late Kinge of famous memorie Edwarde the Sixte, late Kinge of England, as in and by his letters Patentes under the Greate Seale of Englande, beareinge date at Westminster the twelveth daye of Marche, in the fourth yeare of his raigne, more at lardge appeareth; and all which said premisses above by theis presentes mencyoned to be bargayned and sold, the said Sir Thomas Cawarden, in and by his last will and testamente in writing, beareing, date in the daye of St. Barthilmew the apostle in the yeare of our Lord God, 1559, amonges other thinges dyd will and declare his intente to be that his executors, with the consente of his overseers, should have full power and aucthoritye to bargaine sell and alyen for the performance of his said last will and testamente; and also in and by the same his said laste will and testamente dyd ordeyne and make Dame Elizabeth his then wyef and the said Sir William More, by the name of William More of Loseley, in the County of Surrey, esquier, executors of his said last will and testamente, and Thomas Blagrave and Thomas Hawe overseers of the same, as in and by his said last will and testament more at large appereth; and all which premisses above mencyoned to be hereby bargayned and sold, amonges others, the said Dame Elizabeth Cawarden and William More, executors of the said laste will and testament, by and with thassent, consent, agreement and advise, of the said Thomas Hawe and Thomas Blagrave, overseers of the said last will, in accomplyshment thereof dyd bargayne and sell unto John Byrche, gentleman, John Awsten and Richard Chapman, and their heyres for ever, as in and by their deed indented of bargaine and sale thereof made, beareing date the twentith day of December in the second yere of the raigne of our said soveraigne lady the Queenes Majestie that nowe is, and enrolled in her Majesties High Courte of Chauncerie more at lardg appeareth; and all which said premisses with thappurtenaunces above mencioned to be hereby bargayned and sold amonges others, the said John Birche, John Awsten and Richard Chapman, did by their deed indented of bargaine and sale, beareing date the twoo and twentith daie of December in the said second yere of the raigne of our said Soveraigne lady the Queenes Majestye that nowe is, bargaine and sell to the said Dame Elizabeth Cawarden and Sir William More and their heires for ever, as in and by the same deed indented of bargaine and sale last above recited, and also enrolled in her Majesties said Highe Courte of Chancery, more at lardge also appeareth; which said Dame Elizabeth is longe sithence deceased, by reason whereof all and singuler the same premisses in and by theis presentes mencyoned to be hereby bargayned and sold, are accrued and come unto the said Sir William More and his heires by righte of survivorshippe. To have and to hold all the said romes, lodginges, cellers, vaultes, stayres, yardes, waies, and all and singuler other the premisses, with all and singuler their appurtenaunces before in theis presentes mencyoned to be hereby bargained and sold, excepte before excepted, to the said James Burbage his heires and assignes for ever, to the onelye use and behoofe of the said James Burbage his heires and assignes for evermore. And the said Sir William More doth covenaunte and graunte for himselfe, his heires, executors and administrators, to and with the said James Burbage, his heires and assignes, by theis presentes, that he, the said Sir William More, is and standeth at the tyme of thensealinge and deliverye of theis presentes lawfully and absolutelye seysed of the sayd romes, lodginges, yardes, and of all and singuler other the premisses in and by these presentes mencyoned to be bargayned and sold in his demeasne as of fee simple, and that the sayd romes, lodginges, cellers, vaultes, stayres, yardes, and all and singuler other the premisses before in and by these presentes mencyoned to be hereby bargayned and sold, excepte before excepted, the daye of the date heareof are and at all tymes, and from tyme to tyme for ever heareafter, shall stande, contynue and remayne to the said James Burbage, his heyres and assignes, for ever, cleirely acquited, exonerated and discharged, or els by the said Sir William More, his heyres or assignes, uppon reasonable requeste thereof to him or them made by the sayd James Burbage, his heyres or assignes, sufficyently saved or kepte harmeles of and from all former bargaynes, sales, guiftes, grauntes, joynctures, dowers, leases, estates, anuytyes, rentes-chardge, arrerages of rentes, statutes merchaunte, and of the staple recognizaunces, judgmentes, execucyons, yssues, fees, fynes, amercyamentes, and of and from all other chardges, tytles, troubles and incomberances whatsoever had, made, comitted or done by the sayd Sir William More and by the foresaid Sir Thomas Cawarden, knighte, deceased, or by eyther of them, or by any other person or persons, by, with or under, their or any of their estate, righte, tytle, assente, consente, acte, meanes or procuremente. And alsoe that he, the sayde James Burbage, his heyres and assignes, shall or maye from henceforthe for ever peacebly and quietlye have, hold, occupye, possesse, enjoye and keepe, all the sayd romes, lodginges, cellers, yardes, and all and singuler other the premisses, with the appurtenaunces, before by these presentes mencyoned to be hereby bargayned and sould, and every parte and parcell thereof, excepte above excepted, without any lett, troble, vexacyon, eviccyon, recoverye, interupcyon or contradiccion of the sayd Sir William More, his heyres or assignes, or of any of them, and without any lawfull lett, troble, vexacyon, eviccion, recoverye or interrupcyon of any other person or persons whatsoever lawefullye haveinge or claymeinge, or which heareafter shall lawefully have or clayme, any estate, righte, tytle or interest in or to the said romes, lodginges, and all other the premisses before by these presentes mencyoned to be bargayned and sold, or in or to any parte or parcell thereof, by, from or under, the sayd Sir William More and Sir Thomas Cawarden, or any of them, or their or either of their estate, righte, tytle or interest. And the said Sir William More dothe alsoe covenaunte and graunte, for himselfe, his heyres, executors and assignes, to and with the said James Burbage, his heyres and assignes, by these presentes, that he the said Sir William More and his heyres shall and will from tyme to tyme, duringe the space and terme of three yeres next ensueinge after the date heareof, at or uppon reasonable requeste thereof to him or them or any of them to be made by the sayd James Burbage, his heyres or assignes or any of them, well and truelye doe knowledge, execute, cause and suffer to be made, done and executed, all and every such further acte and actes, thinge and thinges, devise and devises, assuraunce and assuraunces in the lawe whatsoever for the further and more better assurance, suertye and more suer makeinge, of the sayd romes, lodginges and all other the premisses with the appurtenaunces before in these presentes mencyoned to be hereby bargayned and sold unto the sayd James Burbage, his heyres and assignes for ever, to thonlye use and behoofe of the sayd James Burbage his heyres and assignes for evermore, be it by deed or deedes indented or inrolled, or not inrolled, thinrollment of theis presentes, fyne, feoffement, recoverye with single or double voucher, releas, confirmacion or otherwise, with warrantie onelye of the sayd Sir William More and his heyres againste him the sayd Sir William More and his heires, or all or as many of theis wayes or meanes or any other, as by the said James Burbage, his heyres or assignes or any of them, or by his or their or any of their learned Counsell in the lawe, shal be reasonably advised or devised and required, at thonely costes and chardges in the lawe of the sayd James Burbage, his heyres or assignes, so as the same assurance or assuraunces in forme aforesaid, to be had and made by the sayd Sir William More or his heyres, to the said James Burbage his heyres or assigns, doe not comprehend in them or any of them any furder or greater warrantie then onely againste the said Sir William More and his heyres, and the heyres of the sayd Sir Thomas Cawarden; and so as the sayd Sir William More and his heyres, or any of them, be not compelled to travell in person any furder then to the Cittyes of London and Westminster, or any of them, for the makeing, knowledging or executeinge, of the sayd assurances in forme aforesaid to be had or made. And furthermore the sayd Sir William More doth by theis presentes aucthorize, nominate and appointe, George Austen, gentleman, and Henrye Smyth, merchantaylor, to be his lawefull deputyes and attorneys joynctly and severallye for him and in his name to enter into all the sayd romes, lodginges, cellers, and other the premisses before in theis presentes mencyoned to be hereby bargayned and sold, and into every parte thereof, and peaceable possession and seazen thereof for him and in his name to take, and after such possessyon and seazon thereof so had and taken, to delyver possessyon and seazon thereof, and of every parte thereof, unto the sayd James Burbage, his heires and assignes, accordinge to the purporte, effecte, true intente and meaninge of theis presentes; and all and whatsoever his said attorneys, or either of them, shall by vertue of theis presentes doe or cause to be done in his name in execucion of the premisses, he the sayd Sir William More and his heyres shall and will ratifye, confirme and allowe, by theis presentes. In witnes whereof the partyes firste above named to theis indentures sonderlye have sett their seales the daye and yeare firste above written.

XIX. *A Petition to the Privy Council from the Inhabitants of the Blackfriars, November, 1596, against the Theatre which was then about to be established by Burbage in that Locality. From the State Papers, Domest. Eliz. cclx.* 116. *This Manuscript is not the original Petition, but an undated Copy of it made in or about the year* 1631, *as is ascertained by a Comparison of the Handwriting with that in Transcripts of other Documents in the State Papers, Domestic Charles I.,* ccv. 32. *The Date of the Original is shown by the next Article.*

To the right honorable the Lords and others of her Majesties most honorable Privy Councell,—Humbly shewing and beseeching your honors the inhabitants of the precinct of the Blackfryers, London, that whereas one Burbage hath lately bought certaine roomes in the same precinct neere adjoyning unto the dwelling houses of the right honorable the Lord Chamberlaine and the Lord of Hunsdon, which romes the said Burbage is now altering and meaneth very shortly to convert and turne the same into a comon playhouse, which will grow to be a very great annoyance and trouble, not only to all the noblemen and gentlemen thereabout inhabiting but allso a generall inconvenience to all the inhabitants of the same precinct, both by reason of the great resort and gathering togeather of all manner of vagrant and lewde persons that, under cullor of resorting to the playes, will come thither and worke all manner of mischeefe, and allso to the greate pestring and filling up of the same precinct, yf it should please God to send any visitation of sicknesse as heretofore hath been, for that the same precinct is allready growne very populous, and besides that the same playhouse is so neere the Church that the noyse of the drummes and trumpetts will greatly disturbe and hinder both the ministers and parishioners in tyme of devine service and sermons; in tender consideracion wherof, as allso for that there hath not at any tyme heretofore been used any comon playhouse within the same precinct, but that now all players being banished by the Lord Mayor from playing within the Cittie by reason of the great inconveniences and ill rule that followeth them, they now thincke to plant themselves in liberties; that therfore it would please your honors to take order that the same roomes may be converted to some other use, and that no playhouse may be used or kept there; and your suppliants as most bounden shall and will dayly pray for your Lordships in all honor and happines long to live.

Elizabeth Russell, dowager.
G. Hunsdon.
Henry Bowes.
Thomas Browne.
John Crooke.
Will. Meredith.
John Robbinson.
Thomas Homes.
Ric. Feild.
Will. Watts.
Henry Boice.
Edward Ley.
Stephen Egerton.
Richard Lee.
. . . . Smith.
William Paddy.
William de Lavine.
Francis Hinson.
John Edwards.
Andrew Lyons.
Thomas Nayle.
Owen Lochard.
John Clarke.
Will. Bispham.
Robert Baheire.
Ezechiell Major.
Harman Buckholt.
John Le Mere.
John Dollin.
Ascanio de Renialmire.
John Wharton.

XX. *An Order by the Corporation of the City of London, dated January* 21st, 1618-9, *for the Suppression of the Blackfriars Theatre. From the original Entry recording the Proceedings of that Day in a Manuscript preserved in the City Archives.*

Item, this day was exhibited to this Court a peticion by the constables and other officers and inhabitantes within the precinct of Blackfryers, London, therein declaring that in November, 1596, divers honorable persons and others, then inhabiting in the said precinct, made knowne to the Lordes and others of the Privy Councell what inconveniences were likely to fall upon them by a common playhowse then preparing to be erected there, and that their honors then forbad the use of the said howse for playes, and in June, 1600, made certaine orders by which, for many weightie reasons therein expressed, it is limitted there should be only two playhowses tolerated, whereof the one to be on the Banckside, and the other in or neare Golding Lane, exempting thereby the Blackfryers; and that a lettre was then directed from their Lordships to the Lord Maior and Justices, strictly requiringe of them to see those orders putt in execucion and so to be continued. And nowe, forasmuch as the said inhabitantes of the Blackfryers have in their said peticion complayned to this court that, contrarie to the said Lordes orders, the owner of the said playehowse within the Blackfryers under the name of a private howse hath converted the same to a publique playhowse, unto which there is daily so great resort of people, and soe great multitudes of coaches, whereof many are hackney coaches bringing people of all sortes that sometimes all their streetes cannot conteyne them, that they endanger one the other, breake downe stalles, throw downe mens goodes from their shopps, hinder the passage of the inhabitantes there to and from their howses, lett the bringing in of their necessary provisions, that the tradesmen and shoppkeepers cannot utter their wares, nor the passengers goe to the common water staires without danger of their lives and lyms, whereby manye times quarrells and effusion of blood hath followed, and the minister and people disturbed at the administracion of the Sacrament of Baptisme and publique prayers in the afteernoones; whereupon, and after reading the said order and lettre of the Lordes shewed forth in this Court by the foresaid inhabitauntes, and consideracion thereof taken, this Court doth thinke fitt and soe order that the said playhowse be suppressed, and that the players shall from henceforth forbeare and desist from playing in that howse in respect of the manifold abuses and disorders complayned of as aforesaid.

XXI. *A Royal Warrant to the Master of the Revels granting him special Powers in Matters connected with the Revels and the Drama, December,* 1581. *From the original Entry on the Patent Rolls.*

Elizabeth by the Grace of God, &c., to all manner our justices, maiors, sheriffes, bayliffes, constables and all other our officers, ministers, true liege men and subjectes, and to every of them greetinge. We lett you witt that we have authorised, licensed and commaunded, and by these presentes do aucthorise, licence and commaunde our wel beloved Edmunde Tylney esquire, Maister of our Revells, as well to take and retaine for us and in our name at all tymes from hensforth, and in all places within this our realme of England, as well within francheses and liberties as without, at competent wages, as well all suche and as many painters, imbroderers, taylors, cappers, haberdashers, joyners, carvers, glasiers, armorers, basket makers, skinners, sadlers, waggen makers, plaisterers, fethermakers, as all other propertie makers and conninge artificers and laborers whatsoever, as our said servant or his assigne, bearers hereof, shall thinke necessarie and requisite for the speedie workinge and fynisheinge of any exploite, workmanshippe or peece of service that shall at any tyme hereafter belonge to our saide office of the Revells; as also to take at price reasonable in all places within our said realme of England, as well within francheses and liberties as without, any kinde or kindes of stuffe, ware or marchandise, woode or coale or other fewell, tymber, wainscott, boarde, lathe, nailes, bricke, tile, leade, iron, wier and all other necessaries for our said workes of the said office of our Revells as he the said Edmunde or his assigne shall thinke behoofefull and expedient from tyme to tyme for our said service in the said office of the Revells, together with all carriages for the same both by land and by water, as the case shall require. And furthermore we have by these presentes aucthorised and commaunded the saide Edmunde Tylney that in case any person or persons, whatsoever they be, will obstinatelie disobey and refuse from hensforth to accomplishe and obey our commaundement and pleasure in that behalfe, or withdrawe themselves from any of our said workes, upon warninge to them or any of them given by the saide Edmunde Tylney, or by his sufficient deputie in that behalfe to be named, appointed for their diligent attendance and workmanship upon the said workes or devises, as to their naturall dutie and alleigeance apperteineth, that then it shal be lawfull unto the same Edmund Tilney, or his deputie for the tyme beinge, to attache the partie or parties so offendinge, and him or them to commyt to warde, there to remaine without baile or maineprise untill suche tyme as the saide Edmunde or his deputie shall thinke the tyme of his or their imprisonment to be punishement sufficient for his or their saide offences in that behalfe; and that done, to enlarge him or them so beinge imprisoned at their full libertie without any losse, penaltie, forfaiture or other damage in that behalfe to be susteined or borne by the saide Edmunde Tilney or his saide deputie. And also if any person or persons, beinge taken into our said workes of the said office of our Revells, beinge arrested comminge or goinge to or from our saide workes of our said office of our Revells at the sute of any person or persons, then the said Edmunde Tilney by vertue and aucthoritie hereof to enlarge him or them as by our speciall proteccion duringe the tyme of our said workes. And also if any person or persons, beinge reteyned in our said workes of our said office of Revells, have taken any manner of taske worke, beinge bound to finishe the same by a certen day, shall not runne into any manner of forfeiture or penaltie for breakinge of his day, so that he or they ymmediatly after the fynishinge of our said workes indevor him or themselves to fynishe the saide taske worke. And furthermore also we have and doe by these presentes aucthorise and commaunde our said servant, Edmunde Tilney, Maister of our said Revells, by himselfe or his sufficient deputie or deputies, to warne, commaunde and appointe in all places within this our realme of England, as well within francheses and liberties as without, all and every plaier or plaiers, with their playmakers, either belonginge to any nobleman or otherwise bearinge the name or names of usinge the facultie of playmakers or plaiers of comedies, tragedies, enterludes or what other showes soever, from tyme to tyme and at all tymes to appeare before him with all suche plaies, tragedies, comedies or showes as they shall have in readines or meane to sett forth, and them to presente and recite before our said servant or his sufficient deputie, whom wee ordeyne, appointe and aucthorise by these presentes of all suche showes, plaies, plaiers and playmakers, together with their playinge places, to order and reforme, auctorise and put downe, as shal be thought meete or unmeete unto himselfe, or his said deputie in that behalfe. And also, likewise, we have by these presentes aucthorised and commaunded the said Edmunde Tylney that, in case if any of them, whatsoever they bee, will obstinatelie refuse, upon warninge unto them given by the said Edmunde or his sufficient deputie, to accomplishe and obey our commaundement in this behalfe, then it shal be lawful to the saide Edmunde or his sufficient deputie to attache the partie or parties so offendinge, and him or them to commytt to warde, to remaine without bayle or mayneprise untill suche tyme as the same Edmunde Tylney or his sufficient deputie shall thinke the tyme of his or theire ymprisonment to be punnishement sufficient for his or their said offences in that behalfe, and, that done, to inlarge him or them so beinge imprisoned at their plaine libertie without any losse, penaltie, forfeiture or other daunger in this behalfe to be susteyned or borne by the said Edmunde Tylney or his deputie, any acte, statute, ordynance, or provision heretofore had or made to the contrarie hereof in any wise notwithstandinge. Wherefore we will and commaunde you and every of you that unto the said Edmunde Tylney or his sufficient deputie, bearer hereof, in the due execucion of this our aucthoritie and commaundement ye be aydinge, supportinge and assistinge from tyme to tyme, as the case shall require, as you and every of you tender our pleasure, and will answer to the contrarie at your uttermost perills. In witnesse whereof, &c. Witnes ourselfe at Westminster the xxiiij.th day of December in the xxiiij.th yere of our raigne.

XXII. *A Letter from the Lords of the Council to the Lord Mayor of London and the Magistrates of Surrey and Middlesex desiring them to sanction Performances at the Globe, Fortune and Curtain Theatres, April,* 1604. *From a contemporary Transcript preserved at Dulwich College.*

After our hartie . . . . . Wheras the Kings Majesties Plaiers have given . . . . . highnes good service in ther quallitie of playinge, and for as much lickwise as they are at all times to be emploied in that service, whensoever they shal be commaunded, we thinke it therfore fitt, the time of Lent being now past, that your Lordship doe permitt and suffer the three Companies of Plaiers to the King, Queene and Prince, publicklie to exercise ther plaies in ther severall and usuall howses for that purpose and noe other; viz., the Globe scituate in Maiden Lane on the Banckside in the Countie of Surrey, the Fortune in Goldinge Lane, and the Curtaine in Hollywelle in the Cowntie of Midlesex, without any lett or interruppion in respect of any former Lettres of Prohibition heertofore written by us to your Lordship, except ther shall happen weeklie to die of the plague above the number of thirtie within the Cittie of London and the Liberties therof, att which time wee thinke itt fitt they shall cease and forbeare any further publicklie to playe untill the sicknes be againe decreaced to the saide number; and so we bid your Lordship hartilie farewell. From the Court at Whitehalle, the ix.th of Aprill, 1604.

Your very loving Frends,
Nottingham.

To our verie good L. the Lord Suffolk.
Maior of the Cittie of Lon- Gill. Shrowsberie.
don, and to the Justices of Ed. Worster.
the Peace of the Counties of W. Knowles.
Middlesex and Surrey. J. Stanhopp.

XXIII. "*The Remonstrance of Nathan Field,*" *addressed to the Rev. Mr. Sutton, Preacher at St. Mary Overy's, Southwark,* 1616, *against his Denunciations of the Stage. From a contemporary Transcript inscribed,* "Feild the Players Letter to Mr. Sutton, Preacher att St. Mary Overs., 1616," *MS. State Papers, Domestic James I., lxxxix.* 105.

Beare wittnes with me, O my Conscience, and reward me, O Lord, according to the truth of my lipps, how I love the Sanctuary of my God and worship towardes his holy alter; how I have, according to my poore talent, indeavoured to study Christ and make sure my eleccion; how I reverence the feete of those that bring glad tidings of the Gospell, and that I beare in my soule the badge of a Christian practise to live the lief of the faithfull, wish to dye the death of the righteous, and hope to meete my Saviour in the cloudes. If yow merveyle, sir, why I beginne with a protestacion soe zelous and sacred, or why I salute yow in a phrase soe confused and wrapped, I beseech yow understand that yow have bene of late pleased, and that many tymes from the Holy Hill of Sion, the pulpitt, a place sanctified and dedicated for the winning not discouraging of soules, to send forth many those bitter breathinges, those uncharitable and unlimitted curses of condemnacions, against that poore calling it hath pleased the Lord to place me in, that my spiritt is moved; the fire is kindled and I must speake; and the rather because yow have not spared in the extraordinary violence of your passion particularly to point att me and some other of my quallity, and directly to our faces in the publique assembly to pronounce us dampned, as thoughe yow ment to send us alive to hell in the sight of many wittnesses. Christ never sought the strayed sheepe in that manner; he never cursed it with acclamacion or sent a barking dogg to fetch it home, but gently brought it uppon his owne shoulders. The widdowe never serched for her lost groate with spleene and impatience, but gently swept her house and founde it. If it be sinfull to lay stumbling blockes in the way of the blind, if it be cruelty to bruse the broken reede, if children are to be fedd with milke and not strong meate, let God and his working tell yow whether yow have not sinned in hindering the simplenes of our soules from the suckicis⁕ of your better doctrine by laying in their wayes your extravagant and unnecessary passions; whether yow have not bene cruell to inflame those hartes with choller that brought into the Church knees and mindes of sorrow and submission, and whether yow have not bene a preposterous nurse to poyson us with desperacion insteede of feeding us with instruccion. Surely, sir, your iron is soe entred into my soule, yow have soe laboured to quench the spiritt, to hinder the Sacrament and banish me from myne owne parishe Church, that my conscyence cannot be quiett within me untill I have defended it by putting yow in mind of your uncharitable dealing with your poore parishioners, whose purses participate in your contribucion and whose labour yow are contented to eate, howsoever yow despise the man that gaynes it or the wayes he gettes it, like those unthankfull ones that will refreshe themselves with the grape and yet breake and abuse the branches. And pardon me, sir, if that for defence of my profession in patience and humblenes of spiritt I expostulate a little with yow, wherein I desire yow to conceave that I enter not the list of contencion, but only take holde of the hornes of the altar in myne owne defence, and seeke to wipe of those deepe, deadly and monstrous blemishes yow have cast uppon me, such as, indeed, made us blush, all Christian eares to glow and all honest hartes to admire att. Yow waded very low with hatred against us when yow ransacked hell to finde the register wherein our soules are written dampned, and I make noe question, soe confident am I of my parte in the death and passion of Christ, who suffred for all mens sinnes not excepting the player, thoughe in his tyme there were some, that, if yow had with charity cast your eyes to heaven, yow might more easily have found our names written in the booke of lief; and herein is my faith the stronger, because in Godes whole volume—which I have studied as my best parte—I find not any trade of lief except conjurers, sorcerers and witches, *ipso facto*, damned; nay, not expressely spoken against, but only the abuses and bad uses of them, and in that point I defend not ours, nor should have disagreed with yow if yow had only strooke att the corrupt branches and not laid your axe to the roote of the tree. Doe yow conclude it dambnable because, in the olde world or after in the tyme of the patriarckes, judges, kinges and prophettes, there were noe players?—why, sir, there was a tyme there was noe smith in Israel. Are all smithes therefore damned?—a sinfull conclucion! Doe yow conclude it damnable because that, in the tyme of Christ and his Apostles, it was not peculiarly justified and commended to after ages? Why neither Christ nor they by their Letters Pattentes incorporated either the mercer, draper, gouldsmith or a hundred trades and misteries that att this day are lawfull, and would be very sorry to heare the sentence of damnacion pronounced against them, and simply because they are of such a trade, and yet there are faultes in all professions, for all have sinne, may be freely spoken against. Doe yow conclude them damned because that in the raigne of tyrant Cæsar they suffred banishment, which he did because he had worse thoughtes and more divelishe desseires to imploy himself. But our Cæsar, our David, that cann vouchsafe amongst his grave exercises some tyme to tune himnes, and harken unto harmelesse matters of delight, our Josua that professeth, howsoever other nacions doe, he and his houshould will serve the Lord, holdes it noe execrable matter to tollerate them; and how ungodly a speech it is in a publik pulpitt to say that he maynteynes those whome God hath damned, I appeale to the censure of all faithfull subjectes, nay, all Christian people; or doe yow conclude them damned because the woman yow sited, perhaps out of Legenda Auria®, that comming to a playe was possessed with an evill spiritt, and tolde by the divell that he could have had noe power of her but that he took her uppon his owne ground, which yow strayne to be the playhouse; I pray, sir, what became of all thother audience?—they were all uppon the same ground—were they all possessed? Truly, sir, in my religion it is daungerous to harken to the divell, dambnable to beleeve him and to produce his testimony to proove the poore members of Christ dampned. God deliver me from an argument soe polluted, or an imaginacion soe abominable; but could yow have inferred that uppon this silly woman, for uppon such weaknes the divell trieth his conclucions, the finger of the Holy Ghost had come as unto Baltasar and written "thou art possest for seeing a play," I would with Jeromy have imployed rivers of teares to wash away the name of a player, and with Jeromy have kneeled untill my knees had bene as huffes to repent soe faltie a profession. But, God willing, noe instance grounded uppon the divell, father of lies, shall make me ashamed of it which a state soe Christian and soe provident are pleased to spare, and none repines att but some few whose curiosity overwayeth their charity, but rather the better conceited because the divell dislikes it, holding it for a generall maxime that the sclanders of the wicked are approbacions unto the godly.

XXIV. *A Letter from the Lords of the Council to the Lord Mayor of London in reply to a Complaint made by the Latter of the Number of Playhouses, 31 December, 1601. From the Privy Council Register.*

Wee have receaved a lettre from yow renewing a complaint of the great abuse and disorder within and about the cittie of London by reason of the multitude of play-howses, and the inordinate resort and concourse of dissolute and idle people daielie unto publique stage-plaies; for the which information, as wee do commende your Lordship because it betokeneth your care and desire to reforme the disorders of the Cittie, so wee must lett yow know that wee did muche rather expect to understand that our order sett downe and prescribed about a yeare and a half since for reformation of the said disorders upon the like complaint at that tyme had bin duelie executed, then to finde the same disorders and abuses so muche encreased as they are. The blame whereof, as wee cannot but impute in great part to the Justices of the Peace or some of them in the counties of Middlesex and Surrey, who had speciall direction and charge from us to see our said Order executed for the confines of the Cittie, wherein the most part of those play-howses are scituate, so wee do wishe that it might appeare unto us that any thing hath bin endeavoured by the predecessors of yow the Lord Maior, and by yow, the Aldermen, for the redresse of the said enormities and for observation and execution of our said Order within the Cittie. Wee do therefore once againe renew hereby our direction unto yow, as wee have donne by our lettres to the justices of Middlesex and Surrey, concerninge the observation of our former Order, which wee do praie and require yow to cause duelie and dilligentlie to be put in execution for all poyntes thereof, and especiallie for the expresse and streight prohibition of any more playhowses then those two that are mentioned and allowed in the said Order, charging and streightlie commanding all suche persons as are the owners of any the howses used for stage-plaies within the Cittie not to permitt any more publique plaies to be used, exercised or shewed, from henceforth in their said howses, and to take bondes of them, if yow shall finde it needeful, for the perfourmaunce thereof; or if they shall refuse to enter into bonde or to observe our said Order, then to committ them to prison untill they shall conforme themselves thereunto. And so praying yow, as yourself do make the complaint and finde the enormitie, so to applie your best endeavour to the remedie of the abuse, wee bidd, &c.

XXV. *A Letter from the Lords of the Council to the Magistrates of Surrey and Middlesex severely censuring them for not having enforced the Order of June, 1600, and desiring them to amend their negligence without delay. From the Privy Council Register, 31 December, 1601.*

Two lettres of one tenour to the Justices of Middlesex and Surrey. It is in vaine for us to take knowledg of great abuses and disorders complayned of and to give order for redresse, if our directions finde no better execution and observation then it seemeth they do, and wee must needes impute the fault and blame thereof to yow or some of yow, the Justices of the Peace, that are put in trust to see them executed and perfourmed; whereof wee may give yow a plaine instance in the great abuse contynued or rather encreased in the multitude of plaie-howses and stage-plaies in and about the cittie of London. For whereas about a yeare and a half since, upon knowledge taken of the great enormities and disorders by the overmuch frequentinge of plaies wee did carefullie sett downe and prescribe an order to be observed concerninge the number of play-howses and the use and exercise of stage-plaies, with lymytacion of tymes and places for the same, namely, that there should be but two howses allowed for that use, one in Middlesex called the Fortune and the other in Surrey called the Globe, and the same with observacion of certaine daies and times, as in the said order is particularly expressed, in such sorte as a moderate practice of them for honest recreation might be contynued and yet the inordinate concourse of dissolute and idle people be restrayned; wee do now understande that our said order hath bin so farr from taking dew effect as, insteede of restrainte and redresse of the former disorders, the multitude of playhowses is much encreased, and that no daie passeth over without many stage-plaies in one place or other within and about the Cittie publiquelie made; the default of perfourmance of which our said order we must in greate parte the rather impute to the Justices of the Peace, because at the same tyme wee gave earnest direction unto yow to see it streightly executed and to certifie us of the execution, and yet we have neither understoode of any redresse made by yow, nor receaved any certificate at all of your proceedinges therein, which default or omission wee do now pray and require you forthwith to amende, and to cause our said former order to be putt duely in execution; and especiallie to call before you the owners of all the other play-howses, excepting the two howses in Middlesex and Surrey aforementioned, and to take good and sufficient bondes of them not to exercise, use or practise, nor to suffer from henceforth to be exercised, used or practized, any stage-playinge in their howses, and, if they shall refuse to enter into such bondes, then to comitt them to prison untill they shall conforme themselves. And so &c.

XXVI. *Depositions of Witnesses respecting an Affray at Norwich in the year 1583, in which some of the Queen's Players, then acting at the Red Lion Inn, were involved. From a contemporary Transcript.*

Decimo-quinto die Junij, 1583, the examynacion of Henrye Browne, taken before Mr. Roberte Sucklyng, maior, &c., Thomas Sotherton and Thomas Pecke, justices, &c. This examynate sayeth that he this examynate, beinge at the play this afternone, word was brought into the play that one of her Majesties servauntes was abused at the gate, whereupon this examynate with others went owt, and one in a blew cote cast stones at Bentley, and brocke his heade, beinge one of her Majesties servantes, whereupon this examynate sayed,—Villan, wilt thow murder the quenes man?—and the fellowe called this examynate villan agayne, and thereupon this examynate stroke hym with his sworde, and hyt hym on the legg. Note,—this blowe was geven at Bloomes back gate betwne⊕ the Red Lyon and Mr. Davycs howse. Henrye Browne being further examyned the sevententh day of June, 1583, before Mr. Thomas Gleane, maior⊕, Mr. Robert Sucklinge, Mr. Thomas Sotherton, Mr. Thomas Peck, Mr. Thomas Layer, Mr. Symone Bowde, and Mr. Christofer Layer, justices, &c., sayeth as followethe,—beinge examined how manye of the players went from of the stage on Satturdaye to stryke the man wyche was slayne, he sayeth there were but two of the players wich went, viz., Bentley and one other in a black dublyt called Synger, and Tareton⊕ also was going, but he was stayed by the way, and being examyned whoe dyd stryke the man wiche was killed besydes this examynate, hee sayethe the other man wyche went owte with Bentley strake the man with an armyngesworde one blowe uppon the shoulder, and followed the fellow wiche fled from the WhyteHorse gate in St. Stephens unto Mr. Roberte Davyes howse. Henrye Browne, further examyned the sayed day and yere, saeth that after that he this examynate had stricken the man, Synger dyd stricke the man, and this examynate sayed to hyme,—Give hym noe more,—for he dowted he had ynoughe already, and wen they came frome the man agayn, Synger sayed to this examynate,—Be of good chere, for yf all this matter bee layed on the, thowe shalt have what frendshipe we can procure thee;—and he further sayeth, before he dyd strycke the man he dyd see Bentley thrust at hym twice with his naked raper; the one thrust was about thee knee, but hee knoweth not where the other thrust was.—The examynacion of William Kylbye of Pockthorpe, worsted wever, taken the sevententh daye of June, 1583, before the sayd maior and justices. Fyrst, this examynate sayeth that on Satturnday last in the after noone he was at a play in the yard at the Red Lyon in St. Stephans, and hee dyd see three of the players ronne of the staige with there swordes in there handes, being in the scaberdes, and hard a noyse of skufflinge at the Lyon gate, whereupon this examynate went out of the gate to se what the matter was, and he dyd see a man at Mr. Robert Davyes howse leaninge agaynst a stone bledinge, wiche, as this examynate dyd then here say, was hurt in the skufflinge, wiche was at the Lyon gate, and one Edmunde Kerrie towld this examynate that two of the players dyd ronne after the man withe there wepons drawn, and Kerrie tooke one of the players in his armes, and woold have stayed hym, but one ran at hym with his sworde, and he, feering some daunger to hymselfe, lett thother goe, and fled hymselfe. Being demaunded whether they were in there play or noe, he sayeth they had begonne the play, and one of them ran owt in his playing apparell, but he knoweth not the names of the players.—Thomas Holland of Norwiche, caryer, examyned the sayd day and yere, sayeth that on Satturdaye last in the afternoone, he, beinge without the Red Lyon gate, dyd see one of the Quenes players in his playinge apparell in the gate-howse stricke a man uppon the heade withe the hyltes of his sworde, and brake his heade, but what his name was whose heade was broken he knoweth not, but, as he hard, he was called Mr. Wynsdon; and the sayde Wynsdon and a man in a blew cote went from the gate and stode over the way, and the people standing at the gate dyd stay the quenes servaunte, and desyred hym to be content, whereupon he, havinge his raper drawen out of the skaberd, dyd put yt up, and sayde he had doone, and withdrawing hymselfe a lyttle frome the peple, ran over the way towardes Wynsdon and hym that had the blewe cote, and they ran away, but the player overtooke hym that had the blewe cote at the Cockey, nere Mr. Davyes howse, with his raper drawn, and thrust at hym that had the blew cote into the legg, whereat hee that had the blew cote cryed,—Oh! you have mayned me,—and at the Cockey tooke up a stone and therwe⊕ at the quenes servaunt, but whether he dyd hurt hym or not he knoweth not; but then came one Browne, Sir William Pastons servaunt, and strake a blaw⊕ at hym that had the blew cote with his sworde drawen, but whether he dyd hurt hym or not he knoweth not. Then agaynst Mr. Davyes corner one in a black dublet with an arminge-sworde drawnen⊕ straike at hym in the blew cote uppon the shoulder, whereupon he that had the blew cote fell downe, and then they all three wiche pursued hym that had the blew cote came backe agayne, and Browne sayde to the other two,—hee is sped, I warrant hym;—and the other two men sayed,—what-

soever thou hast doen, woe will bere the out. —Edmunde Brown of Norwiche, draper, examyned the sayd day and yere, sayeth that on Satturday last he was at the playe at the Redd Lyon, and while the players were in playeng, one Wynsdon would have intred in at the gate, but wold not have payed untyll he had been within, and thereupon the gate-keper and hee stryvynge, Tarleton came out of the stayge, and would have thrust hym out at the gate, but in the meane tyme one Bentley, he wich played the Duke, came of the stage, and with his hiltes of his sworde he strooke Wynsdon upon the heade, and offered hym another strype, but Tarleton defended yt, whereupon Wynsdon fled out of the gate, and Bentley pursued hym; and then he in the blacke dublet wich kept the gate ran up into the stayge, and brought an armynge-sworde, and as he was goinge out at the gate, he drew the sworde, and ran out at the gate, and this examynate went owte to se the matter, and in the strete almoste at Mr. Robert Davyes howse he dyd se the men⊕ in the blacke dublett stricke twoe blowes uppon the showder⊕ of the man in a blewe cote, but this examynate, searchinge the man, dyd see his cote cut but not his fleshe in that place, but he sayeth that he that had the blewe cote had received his deathes wounde before blacke⊕ dublet strooke hym, but whoe gave hym hys deathes wounde he knoweth not; and he sayeth the wounde whereof he supposeth the man dyeth was a thrust above his knee.—Edmunde Knee of Yelverton in the countye of Norfolk, yoman, examyned the sayde day and yere, before the said maior and justices, sayeth that on Satturnday last he was at the play at the Red Lyon in St. Stephens, and there was one Mr. Wynsdon who wold have come in at the gate agaynst the will of the gate-keper, and, in thrusting, spilt the monye out of the gate-kepers hand, as this examynate dyd here reported, but this examynate sayeth that he dyd see the monye when yt laye uppon the grounde, and was in gathering up, whereupon one Bentley, whoe played the Duke in the play, havinge a raper in his hand, beinge upon the stage, and understanding of the stryffe at the gate, went of the staige, and one Tarleton, another of the players, went of the staige also, and one in a blacke dublett and another in a tawnye cote, but Wynsdon ran out of the gate into the strete toward Mr. Robert Davyes, and Bentley pursued hym with his raper drawen, but Tarelton would have stayed Bentley; and when he was withoute the gate Tarelton stayed, but the man in the blacke dublyt and he in the tawnye cote ran after Bentley, but betwen the Lyon back gate and Mr. Davyes backe gate he dyd se a man in a blewe cote cast stones, but he dyd not see the stones hyt anye man, but he dyd se Bentlyes head blead, and he dyd also se bothe the man in the black dublett and hym in the tawnye cote stricke with there naked swordes, and the man in the tawnye cote dyd stricke at his legg, but whether he dyd hurte the man in the blew cote or noe he knoweth not, because this examynate stode so far of as he could not well deserne yt. Beinge asked what men they were in the blacke dublett and tawnye cote, hee sayeth he knoweth not his name in the blacke dublett, but he in the tawnye cote is Mr. Pastons man, whose name is Henry Browne. Alsoe this examynate dyd heare say that Browne comeng from the hurt man should saye that he had sped hym, and he wiche told hym this is Thomas Osborne of Kyrbye Bydon gent.—Elizabeth the wyff of Robert Davy of Norwiche, grosser, examyned the sayed yere and daye, sayeth that on Satturnday in the afternone there was a man hurt and wounded at her gate, whome for pyttye sake shee tooke in to comforte hym, and there cam in a woman whoe, as yt was sayed, was fermor to the manns master, and shee called hym George, and the sayde George sayed he would fayne speake with his master, and the woman desyred this examynate to see well to hym and his charges should be answered; and one Mr. Wynsden anon after cam in, and he denyeth hym to be his maister, but sayed he had been his servaunte aboute xv. or xvj. yeres past; and the sayed George sayed it was not he, but yt was his other master; and after a whyle one of the other Wynsdons came to hym, and he allsoe sayed he was not hys servaunte, but he had been hym® aboute three or iiijᵒʳ dayes. Shee sayeth he had two woundes or prickes, but shee knoweth not whoe dyd hurt hym.—Margerye, the wyff of Thomas Bloome, examyned the sayed daye and yere, sayeth that on Satturnday in the afternoone she founde a man in a blewe cote ly bleedinge at Mr. Atkyns back gate, and shee went to hym, and stopped hys wounde with her fyngar, and then sent for a surgeon, and after hee spake and called for his maister, wich was one Wynsdon; she sayeth that she asked hym whoe dyd hurt hym, and he sayd a fellowe in a red cote, and she saieth that he had two woundes or prickes, but she dyd see noe man hurt hym, but sayeth when hee sayed yt was a red cote that dyd hurt hym, she thought it had been one of the quenes servauntes, but none of them had one there cotes at that tyme.—Nicholas Thurston examyned before the sayed maior and justices; that beinge at the play on Satturnday, and seinge one of the players wich played the Duke goe of the staige, he followed after, and in the strete nighe the Cockey by Mr. Robert Davyes howse this examinate, standinge by Mr. Bowdes back gate, he dyd se the sayed player pricke at the man wich was slane, but whether he dyd hurt hym or noe he knoweth not.—Thomas Holland confesseth that one of the quenes men runninge out of there playe, for that there was a quarreling at the gate, the Quenes man drew his raper at one that stode a lyttle from the gate, wiche he percevinge run awaye, and the quenes man following hym, thrust hym into the legg, and the fellowe sayed,—O! thou hast mayned mee;—but recovering hymselfe agayne, threw a stone at the quenes man, and hyt hym, and after that the quenes man run after hym, and thrust at hym, and Henry Browne following, stroke hym on the legg, and turned backe agayne, and sayed to the quenes man,—I have sped hym;—and the quenes man sayed,—Well don, boy! we will beare the out in yt;—and one other in a blacke dublytt dyd stricke at hym before that on the backe, but he this examynate knoweth not hym that stroke hym on the backe.—Edmunde Browne confesseth that hee see one in a blacke dublytt strycke the man in the blew cote on the shoulder, but the fellowe fell not downe, and this examynate sayed to hym,—you have done ill to cut the man;—and he sayed,—no, I have not cut hym.—George Jackson of Norwiche, beere-bruer, sworne and examyned the xvij.th day of June, 1583, before Mr. Robert Davye and Mr. Lawrenc Wood, coroners of the cittye of Norwiche, sayethe and deposeth that on Satturnday last, being the xv.th day of this instant June, he went toward the Red Lyon in St. Stephans, and he dyd se a man runninge hastylye owt of the Lyon gate, and another man in a blacke dublytt dyd rune owte of the same gate after hym with a sworde or raper drawen in his hand, and running styll after the partye aboute the Cockey by Mr. Davyes howse, because he could not overtake the partye, he pricked his weapon out of his hand at the party, but he dyd not hurt hym; he sayeth he knoweth neyther of the sayd partyes. After hym came one of the players in his players apperell with a players berd uppon his face, with a sworde or a raper in his hand drawen, as far as the backe gate of Thomas Bloome, and there a straunge man in a blew cote, as he remembreth, fell at wordes, and the sayde man fled frome the player, and he ran after hym and stroke hym with his sworde, but whether he dyd hurt hym or noe he knoweth not; but thereupon he that had the blew cote, when he had got almoste to the Cockey, toke up a stone, and threwe at the player, and the player dyd gyve two or three thrustes with his sword at the man, and hit hym, but whether he drew blode or noe he knoweth not, but he that had the blewe cote ran from hym untyll he came almoste at Mr. Davyes corner, the player still pursuinge hym, and one Brown alsoe with his drawen sworde ran after the sayd man, and Brown strake a blowe at the legg of hym that had the sayd blew cote, and further he cannot saye.—William Drake of Norwiche, grosser, sworne and examyned the sayd day and yere, sayethe that his brother Stephane Drake, being at the play on Satturday last, dyd tell this examynate that there was a man slayne, and this examynate asked hym how yt came to passe, and he sayed that a man in a white hat misused the players, and was thrust out at the dores, and dyd owt-run the players; and the man wiche was slayne dyd quarrell with the players and threw stones at hym⊕, and, as hee thought, the player was dazeled, for he could not stricke hym, whereupon one of Mr. Pastons servauntes sayed,—wilt thou misuse the quenes men?—and therewith ran after the man, and strake hym as he ran from hym, whereupon the people cryed out to Browne, Mr. Pastons man, saying,—houghe hym not;—then he turned his blowe to a thruste, and gave hym that thrust and one other with his naked sworde, and this examynate sayeth that his brother sayed he never sawe man bleed so muche as hee dyd after Mr. Pastons man had pricked hym; he sayeth his brother dyd not know Browne, nor whose servaunte he was, but three or fower of Mr. Pastons servauntes comynge by this examynates howse, his brother sayed that he wych kylled the man had suche a cognoscence, and further he sayeth not.—Symon Sumpter of Norwiche, baker, sworne and examyned the sayed day and yere, sayeth that Stephan Drake dyd tell hym all the matter in suche sorte as William Drake hath above declared.—Thomas Crowe of Horton confesseth that one in a tawny cote and a cognoscence on his sleve stroke at hym that is deade, and hit hym on the knee, and after that blud followed, and after that one of the quens men hit hym on the back, and thrust hym twyce or thryce under the syde, and thereupon the fellow cryed,—O! Lorde,

I am mayned!—Stephen Drake sayeth that one in a tawney cote thruste hym that is deade into the legg with his sworde, and that his legg bledd presentlye uppon the same thruste, and that the fellowe in the tawny cote, myndinge to stricke at hym, lyftinge up his sworde to fetche the blowe, some cryed to hym,—Oh! houghe hym not;—and with that he drew backe his sworde, and dyd not stricke hym, but thrust hym into the legg.—These two were sworne and examyned before the coroners at the tym of the takinge of the inquysycion uppon the vew of the dead bodye.

XXVII. *Satirical Verses upon a great Frequenter of the Curtain Theatre, from Marston's Scovrge of Villanie, 1598, reprinted V. L. The same Lines, a few literal Errors being corrected, are in the second Edition of that Work, 1599.*

Luſcus what's playd today? faith now I know
I ſet thy lips abroach, from whence doth flow
Naught but pure *Iuliat* and *Romio*.
Say, who acts beſt? *Druſus*, or *Roſcio*?
Now I haue him, that nere of ought did ſpeake
But when of playes or Plaiers he did treate.
H'ath made a common-place booke out of plaies,
And ſpeakes in print, at leaſt what ere he ſayes
Is warranted by Curtaine *plaudeties*,
If ere you heard him courting *Leſbias* eyes;
Say (Curteous Sir) ſpeakes he not mouingly
From out ſome new pathetique Tragedie?
He writes, he ieſts, he courts, what not,
And all from out his huge long ſcraped ſtock
Of well penn'd playes.

XXVIII. *"A Prologue at the Globe to his Comedy call'd the Doubtfull Heire, which should have been presented at the Black-Friers," from Shirley's Poems, 1646. There is another Copy of it, with a few Variations, in the second Edition of the Doubtful Heir, 1652.*

Gentlemen, I am onely sent to say,
Our Author did not calculate his play
For this meridian; the Bank-side he knowes
Is far more skilful at the ebbes and flowes
Of water then of wit; he did not mean
For the elevation of your poles this scene,—
No shews, no frisk, and, what you most delight in,
Grave understanders, here's no target fighting;
Upon the stage all work for cutlers barrd,
No bawd'ry nor no ballads, this goes hard;
The wit is clean, and what affects you not,
Without impossibilities the plot;
No clown, no squibs, no divell's in't; oh, now,
You squirrels that want nuts, what will ye do?
Pray do not crack the benches, and we may
Hereafter fit your palats with a play.

But you that can contract yourselves, and sit
As you were now in the Blackfriers pit,
And will not deaf us with lewd noise or tongues,
Because we have no heart to break our lungs,
Will pardon our vast scene, and not disgrace
This play, meant for your persons not the place.

XXIX. *Will of John Davenant, of Oxford, Vintner, proved on October 21st, 1622. From the recorded Copy in the Registry of the Prerogative Court of Canterbury.*

It hathe pleased God to afflict me these four moneths rather with a paine then a sickenes, which I ackowledge a gentle correction for my former sinnes in having soe faire a time to repent, my paines rather daily encreasing then otherwise. And for soe much as many wise men are suddenly overtaken by death, by procrastinateing of their matters concerning the settling of their estates, I thincke it fitt, though mine be of noe great value, considering the many children I have, and the mother dead which would guide them, as well for the quietnes of my owne mind when I shall depart this life as to settle a future amity and love among them, that there may be noe strife in the division of those blessainges which God hath lent me, to set downe my mind in the nature of my laste will and testament, both for the disposeing of the same, as also how I would have them order themselves after my decease till it shall please God to order and direct them to other courses. First, I committ my soule to Almighty God, hopeinge by my Redeemer Christ Jesus to have remission of my sinnes; my body I committ to the earth to be buryed in the parish of St. Martins in Oxford as nere my wife as the place will give leave where shee lyeth. For my funeralls and obsequies, if I dye in the yeare of my marolty*, I desire should be in comely manner, neither affecting pompe nor to much sparing, leaveing the same to my executors discretion, whom I name to be as followeth, hartily desiring these five following whom I name to be my overseers to take paines not only in that but alsoe in any other matter of advice to my children concerning the settling of their estates, which five are these, Alderman Harris, Alderman Wright, Mr. John Bird, Mr. Wm. Gryce, Mr. Tho: Davis. Item, I will that my debts be paid by my executors which I owe either by bond, bill or booke, which I have made within the compasse of this two yeares. Item, I give and bequeath to my three daughters, Elizabeth, Jane, and Alice, two hundred pound a-peece to be payd out of my estate within one yeare after my buriall.

Item, I give to my four sonnes one hundred fiftie pound a-peece to be payd them within a yeare after my buriall. Item, I give to my sonne Nicholas my house at the White Beare in Dettford, which is lett to Mr. Haines, Schoolemaster of Marchant Tailers Schoole. Item, I give to my sonne Robert my seale-ring. Item, my will is that my houshold stuffe and plate be sold to the best value within the compasse of a yeare, excepting such necessaryes as my executors and overseers shall thinck fitt for the furnishing of my house, to goe towardes the payment of my childrens portions. Item, my will is that my house shall be kept still as a taverne, and supplied with wines continually, for the bringing up and entertainment of my children, untill such time as Thomas Hallom, my servant, comes out of his yeares, and the yearly profitt thereof, necessary expenses of rent, reparacion and housekeeping being deducted, to retorne at the time of his comeing forth of his yeares to my seaven children in equall portions, together with the stocke in the seller and the debtes, or to the survivors, if any happen to dye in the meane tyme. And that this may be the better effected according to my will and intent, I will that my servant Thomas have the managing thereof duringe his apprentishipp, and that he shall give a true account of his dealing unto my executors and overseers four times in the yeare; alsoe that George be kept here still in the house till his yeares come forth, at which time my will is that he be made free of the Marchant Tailers in London, and have five pound given him when he comes out of his yeares. And to the intent that this my devise of keeping my house as a taverne for the better releefe of my children may take the better effect, according to my meaning, in consideracion that my three daughters, being maidens, can hardly rule a thing of such consequence, my will is that my sister Hatton, if it stand with her good liking, may come with her youngest sonne, and lye and table at my house with my children till Thomas Hallom comes out of his yeares, for the better comfort and countenancing of my three daughters, and to have her said dyett free, and five pound a yeare in money, knowing her to have bin alwaies to me and my wife loving, just and kind. Alsoe my will is that twoe of my youngest daughters doe keepe the barre by turnes, and sett doune every night under her hand the dayes taking in the veiwe of Thomas Hallom, my servant, and that this booke be orderly kept for soe long time as they shall thus sustaine the house as a taverne, that, if need be, for avoiding of deceite and distrust there may be a calculation made of the receites and disbursementes. Now if any of my daughters marry with the consent of my overseers, that her porcion bee presently paid her, and shee that remaineth longest in the house either to have her porcion when Thomas Hollome comes out of his yeares, or if he and shee can fancy one another, my will is that they marry together, and her porcion to be divided by itselfe towardes the maintenance of the trade; and the one halfe of my two youngest sonnes stockes shal be in his the said Thomas his handes, payeinge or allowing after twenty nobles per hundred, giving my said two sonnes or my overseers security sufficient for the same to be paid at their cominge to twenty-one yeares of age, the other halfe to be putt forth for their best profitt by the advise of my overseers; my will is also that my sonne William, being now arrived to sixteen yeares of age, shall be put to prentice to some good marchant of London or other tradesman by the consent and advise of my overseers, and that there be forty pound given with him to his master, whereof 20*li*. to be payd out of his owne stocke, and 20*li*. out of my goodes, and double apparrell, and that this be done within the compasse of three moneths after my death, for avoyding of inconvenience in my howse for mastershippe when I am gone. My will is alsoe concerning the remainder of the yeares in my lease of my house, the taverne, that if Thomas and any of my daughters doe marry together, that he and she shall enjoy the remainder of the yeares, be it five or six more or lesse, after he comes out of his yeares, paying to my sonn Robert over and above the rent to Mr. Huffe yearely soe much as they two shall agree uppon, my overseers beinge umpires betwixt them, whereof the cheefest in this office I wish to be my friend Mr. Grice; provided alwaies my meaning is that neither the gallery nor chambers, or that floore nor cockelofts over, nor kitchin, nor lorther nor little sellar, be any part of the thing demised, but those to remaine to the use of my sonn Robert, if he should leave the universitie, to entertaine his sisters if they should marry, &c., yet both to have passage into the wood-yard, garden and house of office. My will is alsoe that my sonne Robert shall not make nor meddle with selling or trusting of wyne, nor with any thing in the house, but have entertenament as a brother for meale tydes and the like, or to take phisicke in sicknes, or if he should call for wyne and the like with his friendes and acquaintance, that he presently pay for it or bee sett downe upon his name to answeare the same out of his part, my meaning being that the government shall consist in my three daughters and in my servant Thomas, whom I have alwaies found faithfull unto me; and to reward his vertue the better and to putt him into more encouragement, I give him twenty pound to be payd him when he comes out of his yeares. Alsoe, my will is that my sonn Robert for his better allowance in the university have quarterly paid him fifty shillinges and twenty shillinges to buy him necessaryes out of the provenew of the profitt of wyne, till Thomas comes out of his yeares, besides the allowance of the interest of his stocke; and in the meane tyme, if I dye before he goes out Bachelor, his reasonable apparell and expences of that degree to be payd out of my goodes, provided alwaies if it be done with the advice of Mr. Turr. My will is that Nicholas be kept at schoole at Bourton till he be fifteen yeares old, and his board and apparell be payd for out of the profitt of selling of the wyne; and for John my will is he be kept halfe an yeare at schoole if my overseers thinke good, and his brothers and sisters, and after put to prentice and have thirty pound given with him, x.*li*. out of his owne stocke and twenty pound out of the profitt of selling of wyne. Alsoe my will is that within twenty-four houres after my funerall, the wynes of all sortes and condicions be filled up, and reckon how many tunnes of Gascoyne wine there is, which I would have rated at twenty-five pound per tunne, and how many butts and pipes of sweet wynes there are, which I would have rated at twentie pound per peece, both which drawne into a summe are to be sett downe in a booke. Alsoe the next day after, a schedule of the debtes which are oweing me in the debt-booke, the sperate by themselves and the desperate by themselves them alsoe sett downe, the ordinary plate to drincke in the taverne to be wayed and valued, the bondes and billes in my study to be lookt over and sett downe, in all which use the opinion of Mr. Gryce; accompt with any marchant that I deale withall betimes, and aske my debtes with as much speede as may be. Lastly, take an inventory of all the utensells in my house, and let them be praysed; in that use the advise of my overseers; and what money shal be in caishe more then shal be needfull for the present to pay my debtes or buy wyne with, let it be putt foorth to the best advantage.

Proved in 1622 by Robert and Jane, two of the children of the testator.

XXX. *Bill and Answer in a Chancery Suit respecting a Lease of New Place, which was granted by William Clopton to Dr. Bentley in 1545. From the Miscellaneous Chancery Proceedings in the Record Office.*

To the right reverende father in Godde Thomas Bysshoppe of Elye and Lorde Chauncellour of Englande,—In most humble wyse shewethe and complaynethe unto your honorable lordeshippe, your daylie oratrix Anne Bentley, wydowe, late the wyffe of Thomas Bentley, doctour of physick, deceased, that whereas one Wylliam Clopton of Clopton in the countye of Warwicke esquier was laufullye seased in his demeane as of fee of and in one capytall messuage or mannour place in Stratforde-uppon-haven in the said countye of Warwyck called the Newe Place, and also of and in two yardes lande lyeng in the fellde of Ryen Clyfforde in the said countye of Warwicke whiche late wer unto⊛ Sir George Throckmerton knight, wyth diverse closes, landes, lesues and pastures to the said two yardes lande belonginge, and also of and in one close in Yngen in the said countye of Warwycke called Malnot-hyll⊛ Close, and also of and in one lesue or pasture in Yngen aforsaid in the parysshe of Byshoppes Hampton called the Frame Close; and the said Wylliam, so beinge of the said landes tenementes and other the premysses seased, did by his suffycyent deede indented in the lawe demyse graunt and to farme lett unto the said Thomas Bentley and to your said oratrix the said mannour place, landes, tenementes and other the premysses, to have and to hollde the said mannour place and other the premysses aforsaid unto the said Thomas Bentley and to your said oratrix for the terme of certen yeres yet endewringe, yeldinge and payeng therefore yerelye to the said Wylliam Clopton and to his heyres and assignes tenn poundes of laufull money of Inglande at the feastes of the Annuncyacion of Our Ladye and Saint Mychaell the Archaungell by even porcions; by force of whiche demyse and lease the said Thomas and your said oratrixe unto the said landes tenementes and other the premysses did enter and wer thereof possessed accordinglye, and the same did quyetlye and⊛ injoye for the space of fowre yeres then next folowinge, and the rentes reserved for the same as ys aforsaid haythe well and trewlye payed hytherto unto the said Wylliam Clopton; and after the said Thomas Bentley dyed, and your said oratrixe did hollde her in the premysses by tytle of survyvour, and the same haythe ever sins the deathe of the said Thomas Bentley her husbonde occupyed and injoyed and payed the rentes dewe for the same; so yt is, right honorable lorde, that the said dede indented of lease aforsaid ys by casualltye comen unto the handes possession and custodye of the said Wylliam Clopton, whiche said Wylliam Clopton by colour of having of the said indenture of lease haythe dyverse and sundrye tymes sins the deathe of the said Thomas Bentley, her late husband, entred and interrupted the quyet possessyon of your said oratrix, myndynge and intending therebye to expulse your said oratrixe from the possession of the same, to the utter impoveryssheement of your said oratrixe and contrarie to all right and conscience; and forasmoche as your said oratrixe knowethe not the certentye of the said indenture, nor the certen date nor nomber of yeres in the same conteyned, nor whether yt is in bagge or boxe sealed, or chest locked, your said oratrixe ys therefore withowt remedye for the said indenture by the Kinges commen lawe, and lyke to be expulsed and put owt of the possession of the premysses, except sum speadye order be therein taken by your good lordeshippe as to equytie and justyce shall apperteyne. In consideracion whereof yt maye please your good lordshippe, the premysses considered, to dyrect the Kinges most gracious wrytt of injunccion unto the said Wylliam Clopton, injoyning hym by the same no further at any tyme hereafter to interrupt or dysquyett your said oratrixe of her laufull possessyon in the said premysses, but that she maye laufullye injoye the same according to the demyse and graunt therof to her made; and that he maye be further commaunded by the same personallye to appeare before the Kinge our soveraigne Lorde in his honorable courte of the Chauncerye at a certen daye, and under a certen payn therein to be conteyned, then and thear to answer the premysses and to abyde suche fynall order therein as to your good Lordeshippe shalbe thought to stande wyth right and conscyence. And your said oratrixe shall daylie praye to Godde for the preservacion of your good Lordeshippe in honour longe to endewer.

The Aunswers of William Clopton unto the Byll of Complaynt of Ane Bentlye.—The said defendant saythe that the said Bill of Complaynte is untruly feynyd and surmysyd only to put the said defendant to most wrongefull vexacion, costs and charges, without any maner of good or reasonable cause, and for answere further saythe that true it is that he, the said deffendant, was and is seasyd in his demane as of fee of one cappitall mesuage or manor place at Stratford-upon-Haven in the countie of Warwicke callyd the New Place, and allso of and in two yerd land lyynge in the maner and feyldes of Ryen Clyfford in the said countie, with dyvers closes, land, leasures and pastures to the said two yerde land belonginge; and also was and is possessyd for terme of certeyn yeres yet enduryng of and in one close lyyng and beynge in a place callyd Yngon in the paryshe of Bysshopes Hamton in the said countie of Warr: callyd Walnothill Close, and also of and in one leasure or pasture in Yngon aforsaid callyd the Frame Close; and the said defendant, so beyng seasyd and possessyd of the premysses, dyd by his dead indentyd, beryng date the xx.ti day of November in the xxxv.th yere of the raigne of our sovereigne Lord of famous memory Kynge Henry the eight, demyse graunte and to ferme lett unto the said Thomas Bentley and to the said Ane his wyff now playntyfe, the said manour place and all other the premysses, to have and to hold the said manour place and other the premysses to the said Thomas Bentley and to the said Anne his wyffe frome the feaste of thanuncyacyon of Our Lady then next folowynge to the end and terme of fortie yeres, yieldyng and payynge therefore yerly durynge the said terme unto the said William Clopton his heyres and assignes the rent of ten pounndes of lawfull money of England at ij. festes in the yere, that is to say, at the feastes of Saynt Mychell tharchaungell and thannuncyacyon of Our Lady by even porcyons, in maner and forme as ys expressyd in the said bill of compleynt and as by the same indenture dothe and may more pleynly appere; in the whiche indenturs amonges other thynges ys also expressyd and conteynyd dyvers and soundrye covenauntes, grauntes, artycles, agrementes and condycyones of the parte and behalf of the said Thomas Bentley and the saide Anne, theyre executours and assygnes, to be performed after suche maner and forme and to lyke effecte and purpose as hereafter folowythe, that is to say, firste, that the said Thomas Bentlye and Anne and theire assignes, durynge the said terme of xl.ti yeres, and as often as neyd shoulde requyre within the said terme, should well and suffycyently uphold, kepe, repaire and mayntayne as well the saide manour place in Stratford, as allso the moundes of all the leasures and closes by the said indentur demysyd and lett to ferme, in all maner of reparacyons, and so sufficyently in repayre should leave all the premysses at the end of the said terme; and allso that the said Thomas and Anne and their assignes durynge the same terme should stand and obey all suche ordynaunces as should be made and devysed by the court holden within the Lordshipe off Ryen Clyfford, and that they shoulde nether sell nor cut doune any thornys growyng in or upon the heathe theyre callyd Burgetoune Hethe without lycence of the said William Clopton his heyres and assygnes; and also that yf the saide rente of ten poundes or any parte or parcell of hyt should happen to be behynde in parte or in all after ony of the said days or feastes of paymentes therof in the whiche hyt ought to be payyd as ys aforsaid by the space of syxe weykes, that then yt should be lawfull for the said William Clopton hys heyres or assignes to reenter into all and syngular the premysses with thappertenaunces, and the same to have hold and enjoye as in his fyrst estate, interest, right and tytyll, eny thynge expressyd or declaryde in the said indenture in any wysse notwithstandynge; and hyt ys allso further expressyd and declaryd in the same indenture that yf any artycle or graunte comprysyd in the said indenture of the parte and behalf of the said Thomas and Anne be not well and truly observyd, performyd, kept and fullfyllyd on that behalf accordynge to the tenour purport and effecte of the same indenture before rehersyd, that then the said indentur to be voyd and of none effecte, as by the said indenture playnly it may and shall appere; and the said defendant saythe that he ys redy to averre and prove in this honorable courte that nather the said Thomas and Anne nor any of them have kepte their suffycyent reparacyons in the said manour place accordynge to theire said covenaunte, nor have not obeyyd the ordenaunces of the said courte of Ryen Clyfford ordeynyd and maide for the reparacyones of the said manour howsse, nor have not payed their said rente within the tymes lymyttyd by the said indenture, by reason wherof and for dyvers other causes, whiche the said defendant ys able suffycyently to prove in this honorable courte, the said indentur of leasse heretofore rehersed was and ys by the lawsse of this realme became clerely frustrate voyd and of none effecte, and in lyke maner the demyse and leasse contenyd in the same; and bycause the said Thomas and Anne dyd well perceyve and understonde by the relacion to them maid of the premysses by the said defendant and of the said forfetures in what case they stod for and concernynge their said interest and terme of yeres by the reason for not performynge of the covenauntes, grauntes, artycles, agrementes and condycyones before rehersed, frely and wyllyngly in the presens of dyvers credable persons at Stratford aforsaid dyd surrender and gyve upe all their whole right interest terme and tytle that they the said Thomas and Anne had or owght to have in the same manour place and all other the premysses by vertue and force of the said leas unto the handes and possessyon of the said William Clopton to thentent he myȝt do therwith as he should thynke most meet and convenyent, by reason of the whiche surrender and of the said forfeture the said defendant enteryd into the premysses as lawfull yt was for hym to doo; and after the said William Clopton defendant, upon certen reasonable consideraciones and requestes to hym movyd, dyd graunte to and with the sayd Thomas Bentlye and Anne that he the said Thomas and Anne durynge theyre lyves, yf the sayd Anne dyd lyve sole and a wydowe contynually durynge her naturall lyf after the decesse of the said Thomas, should have holde and enjoye the said capitall mesuage or burgage with thappertenaunces, and all the landes closes and pastures comprysyd and specefyyd in the sayd indenture, yeldynge and payinge therfore yerly to the said William Clopton his heyres and assignes the said yerely rente of tene poundes, and upon lyke covenauntes and paymentes were and ben conteynyd and expressyd in the said indentures before rehersed concernynge the said former demyse or lease; sythen whiche second lease so mad by the said William Clopton as ys aforesaid, the said Thomas Bentlye ys deceassed out of this present lyf, and hath lefte the said manour place in great ruyne and decay and unrepayryd, and yt dothe styll remayne unrepayryd ever sythen the deathe of the same Thomas to the greate damage and los of the defendant; and also the said Anne now of late ys maryed unto one Rychard Charnocke, so that the second leas by reason of the same seconde mariage and of the said decay is also voyed and of none effecte. In consyderacion of all the whiche matters the said William Clopton now of late eftesones enteryd into the sayd ferme and other the premysses, and interruptyd the possessyon of the same compleynaunte as well and lawfull was and is for him to doe with; and that the said defendaunt dyd enter or interrupte the possessyon of the said compleynaunt by the reason of the casuall comyng to his handes of any suche indenture as ys expressyd in the said byll of complaint ys moste untruly surmysed by the same byll, or that any suche dede indentyd as casually or otherwyse come to the handes of the said defendante, or that any other thyng materyall conteynyd in the said byll not beynge before by this answere confessyd and avoydyd denyyd or traversyd ys true, all the whiche matteres the said defendant ys redy to averr and prove as this honorable Courte shall award, and praythe that the sayd injunccion may be dyssolvyd and further to be demyssyd of this honorable courte with hys reasonable costes and charges by hym most wrongfully borne and susteyned in that behalf.

XXXI. *Bill of Complaint brought by John Shakespeare, the Poet's Father, against Lambert in the Court of Queen's Bench, 1589, respecting an Estate at Wilmecote near Stratford-on-Avon. From the Coram Rege Rolls, Term. Mich. 31-32 Eliz. This Document contains the only positive Notice of the great Dramatist between the years 1585 and 1592 which has yet been discovered.*

WARR:—Memorandum quod alias, scilicet termino Sancti Michaelis ultimo preterito, coram domina regina apud Westmonasterium venit Johannes Shackspere, per Johannem Harborne, attornatum suum, et protulit hic in curia dicte domine regine tunc ibidem quandam billam suam versus Johannem Lambert, filium et heredem Edmundi Lamberte nuper de Barton Henmershe in comitatu predicto yoman, in custodia marescalli &c., de placito transgressionis super casum; et sunt plegii de prosequendo, scilicet Johannes Doo et Ricardus Roo, que quidem billa sequitur in hec verba,—WARR: Johannes Shackespere queritur de Johanne Lamberte, filio et herede Edmundi Lamberte nuper de Barton Henmershe in comitatu predicto yoman, in custodia marescalli marescallie domine regine, coram ipsa regina existente, pro eo, videlicet, quod cum idem Edmundus in vita sua, scilicet decimo quarto die Novembris anno regni domine Elizabethe nunc regine Anglie vicesimo, per quandam indenturam gerentem datum die et anno predictis emisset sibi et heredibus suis de prefato Johanne Shackespere et Maria uxore ejus unum mesuagium sive tenementum, unam virgatam terre et quatuor acras terre arrabilis cum pertinentiis in Wilmecote in dicto comitatu Warwici, habendum et tenendum mesuagium sive tenementum predictum et alia premissa cum pertinentiis prefato Edmundo heredibus et assignatis suis imperpetuum, proviso semper quod si dictus Johannes Shackespere, heredes, executores, administratores vel assignati sui, solverent seu solvi causarent prefato Edmundo quadraginta libras legalis monete Anglie in die festi sancti Michaelis Archangeli, quod tunc esset in anno Domini millesimo quingentesimo et octogesimo, quod tunc deinceps indentura predicta et omnia in eadem contenta vacua forent; virtute cujus idem Edmundus in tenementa predicta cum pertinentiis intravit et fuit inde seisitus in dominico suo ut de feodo, et sic inde seisitus existens postea, scilicet primo die Marcii anno regni dicte domine regine nunc vicesimo nono, apud Barton Henmershe predictam obiit, post cujus mortem mesuagium predictum et cetera premissa cum pertinentiis descendebant prefato Johanni Lamberte ut filio et heredi dicti Edmundi; dictusque Johannes Lamberte, dubitans statum et interesse sua de et in tenementis predictis cum pertinentiis esse vacua, et noticiam habens quod predictus Johannes Shackespere eum implacitare vellet et intendisset pro premissis in consideracione quod predictus Johannes Shackespere adtunc imposterum non implacitaret dictum Johannem Lamberte pro mesuagio predicto et ceteris premissis cum pertinentiis, et quod dictus Johannes Shackespere et Maria uxor ejus, simulcum Willielmo Shackespere filio suo, cum inde requisiti essent assurarent mesuagium predictum et cetera premissa cum pertinentiis prefato Johanni Lamberte, et deliberarent omnia scripta et evidencias premissa predicta concernentia; predictus Johannes Lamberte, vicesimo sexto die Septembris anno regni dicte domine regine vicesimo nono apud Stratford-super-Avon in comitatu predicto, in consideracione inde super se assumpsit et prefato Johanni Shackespere adtunc et ibidem fideliter promisit quod ipse idem Johannes Lambert viginti libras legalis monete Anglie prefato Johanni Shackespere modo et forma sequentibus, videlicet in et super decimum-octavum diem Novembris tunc proximo sequentem viginti solidos, et in et super vicesimum tercium diem ejusdem mensis tres libras, et in et super quartum diem Decembris tunc proximo sequentem sexdecim libras, predictarum viginti librarum residuum, apud domum mancionalem cujusdam Anthonii Ingram generosi scituatam et existentem in Walford Parva in comitatu predicto bene et fideliter solvere et contentare vellet; et predictus Johannes Shackespere in facto dicit quod ipse hucusque non implacitavit dictum Johannem Lambert pro premissis nec aliqua inde parcella, et insuper quod ipse idem Johannes Shackespere et Maria uxor ejus simulcum Willielmo Shackespere filio suo semper hactenus parati fuerunt tam ad assuranda premissa predicta quam ad deliberanda eidem Johanni Lamberte omnia scripta et evidencias eadem premissa concernentia; predictus tamen Johannes Lamberte promissionem et assumpcionem suas predictas minime curans, set machinans et fraudulenter intendens ipsum Johannem Shackspere de predictis viginti libris callide et subdole decipere et defraudare easdem viginti libras prefato Johanni Shackespere juxta promissionem et assumpcionem suas hucusque non solvit nec aliqualiter pro eisdem contentavit licet ad hoc per eundem Johannem Shackespere, postea, scilicet primo die Septembris anno regni dicte domine regine nunc tricesimo apud Barton Henmershe predictam in comitatu predicto sepius requisitus fuit, per quod idem Johannes Shackspere totum lucrum commodum et proficuum que ipse cum predictis viginti libris emendo et barganizando habere et lucrare potuisset totaliter perdidit et amisit, ad dampnum ipsius Johannis Shackspeare triginta librarum, ac inde producit sectam.—Et modo ad hunc diem, scilicet diem Jovis proximum post octabas sancti Michaelis isto eodem termino, usque quem diem predictus Johannes Lamberte habuit licenciam ad billam interloquendam et tunc ad respondendam, etc., coram domina regina apud Westmonasterium venerunt tam predictus Johannes Shackspere per attornatum suum predictum quam predictus Johannes Lamberte per Johannem Boldero attornatum suum, et idem Johannes Lamberte defendit vim et injuriam quando, etc. Et dicit quod ipse non assumpsit super se modo et forma prout predictus Johannes Shakespere superius versus eum narravit, et de hoc ponit se super patriam; et predictus Johannes Shackespere similiter, etc. Ideo veniat inde jurata coram domina regina apud Westmonasterium die veneris proximo post octabas Sancti Hillarii, et qui etc., ad recognoscendum etc. Quia tam etc. Idem dies datus est partibus predictis ibidem etc.

END OF THE FIRST PART.

LIST OF ENGRAVINGS.

		PAGE
1.	The Remains of New Place	iii
2.	Norden's Survey of London, 1593	4
3.	A View of a Portion of the North of the Metropolis and its Suburbs, including the Parish of Shoreditch, taken from an Engraving published in Braun's Civitates Orbis Terrarum, 1574	10
4.	A View of Shoreditch and Finsbury Fields from the ancient Plan of London usually attributed to Aggas	13
5.	Facsimile of the Commencement of the Petition of the Burbages to the Earl of Pembroke and Montgomery, 1635	23
6.	Facsimile of an Entry of Payment to Shakespeare and others for acting in two Plays before the Queen in 1594	31
7.	Greenwich Palace in the Time of Shakespeare	34
8.	View of London and Southwark, 1610	44
9.	Part of the County of Warwick from a Map published in 1603	63
10.	Facsimile of an Account for Mulberry-wood	66
11.	The Guild Chapel and Site of New Place	72
12.	Gargoyles on the Porch of the Guild Chapel	73
13.	Piece of Brick Vaulting discovered at New Place	73
14.	Signature of William Bott, 1565	74
15.	Fine levied when New Place was purchased by Shakespeare in 1597	77
16.	Entry of a Payment to Shakespeare for a Load of Stone, 1598	78

NOTE.—*This work, being electrotyped, although any errors or oversights that may be discovered would be corrected in a re-issue, the latter will be a re-impression rather than a new edition. The present is a copy of the First Impression.*

PRINTED BY
J. E. ADLARD, BARTHOLOMEW CLOSE.

CPSIA information can be obtained at www.ICGtesting.com
Printed in the USA
BVOW07s0205190515

400944BV00006B/35/P